Strategies of Secession and Counter-Secession

Strategies of Secession and Counter-Secession

Edited by
Ryan D. Griffiths and Diego Muro

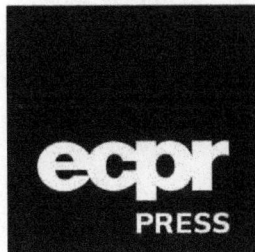

ecpr PRESS

Published by the European Consortium for Political Research, Harbour House, 6–8
Hythe Quay, Colchester, CO2 8JF, United Kingdom

British Library Cataloguing in Publication Data
A catalogue record for this book is available from the British Library

ISBN: HB 978-1-78552-333-5

Library of Congress Cataloging-in-Publication Data
Library of Congress Control Number: 2019955438

ISBN: 978-1-78552-333-5 (cloth)
ISBN: 978-1-5381-5689-6 (pbk)
ISBN: 978-1-78552-334-2 (electronic)
ecpr.eu/shop

Contents

Figures

Tables

Introduction

Ryan D. Griffiths and Diego Muro

How can we understand the strategic interaction between secessionist movements and sovereign states? A casual review of the many secessionist struggles around the world, both violent and peaceful, shows a variety of types. Some, like Catalonia, are pursuing their goals using combinations of electoral capture and civil demonstrations. Meanwhile, the Spanish government is using the courts to stop any unilateral attempts to secede while working to delegitimize the so-called right to decide. Regions like Nagorno Karabakh (Artsakh) lack the same institutional connectivity with the larger state of Azerbaijan and are relegated to a *de facto* (but unrecognized) status where defense, deterrence, and diplomacy are critical. For its part, Azerbaijan invokes its territorial integrity and attempts to deny all forms of recognition to the breakaway region. Other regions from West Papua to Tibet are faced with the hard choice between civil resistance and the use of violence, and their states are keen to suppress their efforts and hide them from the world. What features are common across all of these examples, and how do they differ?

This volume synthesizes a number of theories that purport to explain the strategies of secession and counter-secession. This is an important topic. There are currently over sixty secessionist movements in the world,[1] and many of them are violent.[2] Indeed, Barbara Walter has argued that secessionism is the chief source of violence in the world.[3] Secessionism is destabilizing because, at the least, the attempt to change borders presents a direct challenge to the integrity of existing political systems. Yet surprisingly, the strategic interaction between states and secessionists is an area in which we have incomplete understanding. In this volume we target that gap by bringing together the latest research in both comparative politics and international relations. In this introductory chapter, we provide a basic framework for analysis which outlines the strategic playing field on which secessionists and states interact. We then discuss the organizational structure of the book and provide a preliminary view of the chapters to come.

THE STRATEGIC PLAYING FIELD

We begin with a general definition of secession as "the creation of a new [internationally recognized] state upon existing territory previously forming part of, or being a colonial entity of, an existing sovereign state."[4] This is a broad but commonly used definition that is meant to encompass all attempts by a region to break away from an existing state to create a new, internationally recognized sovereign state. The process of secession involves two key actors. The first is the sovereign state, which we identify as those polities that possess a full seat in the United Nations (UN) General Assembly. This is an uncontroversial move given that full UN membership is the defining feature of contemporary sovereignty; it includes the right to conduct your own affairs and the possession of a legal identity with which you can enjoy a surprisingly large set of benefits, including admittance to major international organizations, access to financial aid, and the ability to use international post and conduct commerce with foreign banks.[5] The second actor is the secessionist movement, which we define as a "self-identified nation inside a sovereign state that seeks to separate and form a new sovereign state."[6] No two cases are the same, but secessionist movements usually originate in some combination of a desire to escape economic or political marginalization, historical grievances, and unhappiness with institutional arrangements. The set of secessionist movements is quite varied. It includes unrecognized but *de facto* states like Abkhazia, independence movements in regions like Quebec, as well as dependencies and other forms of semiautonomy such as Iraqi Kurdistan and the Faroe Islands. Scholars use different definitions for these actors, but they all agree that demands for statehood have increased since the mid-twentieth century.[7]

How then does a secessionist movement become a sovereign state? The hallmark of sovereign statehood in the contemporary international system is full membership in the UN General Assembly. Joining that organization requires that secessionist movement submit an application. The UN membership process requires that the Security Council must approve applications before they are submitted to the General Assembly. Nine of the fifteen members (60%) have to vote in the affirmative without any "no" votes from the Permanent Five (P5) veto-holding members: France, Russia, China, United Kingdom, and the United States. The P5 are the primary gatekeepers to the organization. An application that is approved by the Security Council is then subject to a vote in the General Assembly and has to secure a two-thirds majority. Once that vote is secured, aspiring states can join the UN as a full member.

Importantly, most of the strategic interaction between secessionist movements and states takes place before applications are made to the UN. Indeed, rejections from the Security Council are rare because aspiring nations typically withhold their application until they are confident of success, rather than risk a public rejection.[8] It is in this period prior to the application (should it ever be made) that the strategies of secession and counter-secession are mostly born out, as the key actors maneuver on what can be regarded as a strategic playing field.

This strategic playing field can be broken down into its component parts (see figure I.1). The main objective of a secessionist movement is to become an internationally recognized sovereign state. To gain recognition, a movement must either (1) convince their home state to permit independence or (2) convince the international community to either apply pressure on the central government or circumvent its wishes entirely by recognizing the aspiring nation. To counter these maneuvers, home states need to resist and weaken the pressure from the independence movement and prevent it from gaining support from the international community. As the dashed line in the figure indicates, they literally and figuratively need to defend the perimeter. Figure I.1 also illustrates the central importance of the home state, the single biggest obstacle to obtaining independence.[9] As the case of Kosovo demonstrates, it is difficult for a new polity to gain international recognition as long as the home state resists. In the twenty years since the declaration of independence, Serbia has not rushed to resolve Kosovo's contested statehood, while the P5 remain divided on the issue.

At the most general level, all secessionist cases can be mapped out in this way. Although most movements engage with both the home state and the

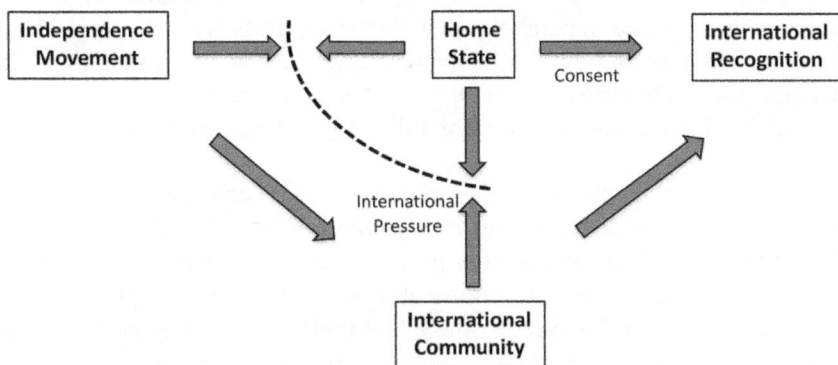

Figure I.1.   The Strategic Playing Field

international community, there is substantial variation. After all, the need to enlist the help of the international community depends on the position of the home state: where the home state is willing to negotiate and, indeed, even permit an independence referendum, securing international support becomes less important; where the home state is uncompromising and potentially willing to suppress the secessionists, the international community rises in importance. For example, Eritrea won independence from Ethiopia after a thirty-year war and peace talks facilitated by the United States.

To win this game, secessionist employs various strategies and tactics to gain attention from the home state and foreign powers. Many strategies are designed to coerce the national government into negotiating. These include the use of outright violence to electoral competition to nonviolent forms of civil resistance. Other approaches focus on persuasion and the appeal to prominent international norms. After all, the bloody conflicts in Kosovo and Bangladesh were instrumental in raising international support that paved the way for independence. This is one of the reasons why secessionists in conflict zones like Eritrea or South Sudan are keen to draw attention to human rights abuse at the hands of the state, and work the language of human rights into their declarations of independence. For secessionist movements in advanced democracies, it is vital that they persuade their domestic and international audiences that not only they have a moral right to choose independence but also that such a choice would be practical in economic terms. Finally, for breakaway regions that are *de facto* independent, like Somaliland, it is important that they demonstrate that they have earned their independence by establishing a functional and viable state.

Secessionist movements use combinations of tactics in their pursuit of independence. For example, Bougainville had a Sydney-based diplomatic wing that was operating at the same time as the Bougainville Revolutionary Army was fighting a guerrilla war against the forces of Papua New Guinea. The Catalan secessionists possessed a powerful diplomatic arm run through *DiploCat* that worked in parallel to the electoral efforts. These actions aimed at putting pressure on both the home state and international community and changing the preferences of key actors. However, great powers and international bodies refused to interfere following intense Spanish diplomatic pressure.

Not unexpectedly, the strategies of counter-secession are in many ways the mirror image of the strategies of secession. States defend domestic and international pressures (the dashed perimeter in figure I.1) by maintaining the veto, resisting pressure to remove it, and weakening attempts by secessionists to compel and persuade others that their cause is righteous. Several general approaches to counter-secession can be identified. One is rhetorical and discursive. Here, counter-secessionists often put forward arguments about legality and stability. States argue that existing constitutional and international norms allow the legal *status quo* to provide peace and prosperity. In their eyes, secessionism is a destabilizing force that causes unnecessary constitutional stress, domestic polarization, and intragroup division. The collapse of the legal order, they argue, can only lead to further state fragmentation and a more anarchical society, and that is why the international right to self-determination needs to be restricted to truly exceptional cases of decolonization, invasion, or gross denial of human rights. Internationally, the principle of noninterference conditions external conduct among sovereign states, requiring that they not meddle in the domestic affairs of their peers. For example, in the European Union (EU) context, an additional legal requirement is contained in article 4 of the Treaty of the European Union, which obliges the EU to respect the territorial integrity of member states and their constitutional systems.[10]

Counter-secessionists also stress stability and the need to preserve the domestic and international order. It is argued that since most states are multinational, the indiscriminate application of the principle of self-determination could destabilize the international system through the breakup of heterogeneous states. Defenders of the *status quo* often reference the dangers of contagion that can follow the spread of secessionism to neighboring polities.[11] Home states argue that the norm of territorial integrity prevents other national governments from supporting secessionist movements or promoting border changes abroad.[12] Finally, counter-secessionists also highlight the dangers of potential violence, transaction costs, and impoverishment as reasons why secession should be avoided.

There are a number of ways in which states counter secessionists with the use and threat of force. In the language of Thomas Schelling, secessionists are trying to compel the state to make a change, and states are trying to deter secessionists from acting.[13] In West Papua it is illegal to fly the nationalist flag (the Morning Star) and gatherings for independence purposes are routinely broken up, sometimes violently. The Iraqi government has threatened to respond militarily if the Kurdish regional government makes a unilateral declaration of independence (UDI). In other cases, attempts at deterrence failed and then gave way to outright civil war. Although home states almost always have a military advantage and quite often win, as Nigeria did with Biafra or Sri Lanka did with Tamil Eelam in 2009, government victory is not a foregone conclusion. Bangladesh was able to win game-changing support from India, altering the course of the secessionist struggle. Bougainville was able to fight Papua New Guinea to a hurting stalemate, paving the way for a peace agreement.

Counter-secessionists who face nonviolent ethno-nationalist efforts through a vote often struggle to prevail. For example, the UK government authorized the Scottish referendum of 2014 believing that a strong "no" vote would take the question of independence off the table for a generation and undercut the electoral strength of Scottish nationalism. However, as the independence supporters lost by a narrow margin, critics accused Prime Minister David Cameron of gambling with nearly a third of the UK's territory and polarizing Scottish society. Another example of counter-secessionist strategy is provided by Catalonia, where secessionists used electoral capture and civil resistance while trying to emulate the Scottish model of holding a binding referendum on independence. However, the steps taken by the Catalan regional government— from holding an illegal referendum on October 1, 2017, to unilaterally declaring independence from Spain on October 27—paved the way for a legal response from the Spanish courts which sanctioned coercive actions by the police. The Constitutional Court warned that the October vote on political independence threatened "national unity," and the Spanish executive quickly sent national police in riot gear to stop the vote, leading to ugly scenes of violence against voters of all ages. The standoff resulted in repression and little reform, suggesting that only compromise could bring a lasting solution to the region.[14]

Ultimately, the response of the home state determines whether a secession will be consensual or contested. Consensual secession requires an agreement with the host state and is a process that is characterized by little or no violence. Commonly cited examples include the dissolution of Czechoslovakia in 1993, also known as the "velvet divorce," or the case of Canada, which authorized Quebec to hold two referendums on independence but also regulated the means by which secession would be negotiated. Consensual secession is largely seen as a matter of domestic law and requires the acknowledgment of the constitutionality of secession. For instance, an agreement between the Scottish government and the UK government made possible the 2014 referendum on whether Scotland would become independent from the rest of the country. If the home state agrees to a negotiated secession, the international community is almost certain to follow suit.

Last, a UDI is the alternative to a negotiated secession. Unilateral secessions are often associated with remedial right theories which posit that independent statehood should be granted in cases of serious violations of human rights, unjust annexation of territories, or systematic violations of agreements on self-government. Examples of UDIs abound, including the American Declaration of Independence, the Confederate States of America, and the 1965 Rhodesian declaration.[15] Typically, UDIs, such as the 2017 Catalan declaration of independence, are unsuccessful because they are perceived as dangerous precedents for secessionist movements worldwide that imperil international order.

Regardless of whether secession is consensual or not, the new polity can only join the international community if other states recognize it as a sovereign state. External recognition constitutes the ticket to membership in the international system, where new entities can enjoy the status and material advantages reserved exclusively for states.[16] Sovereignty of a new state is inevitably constituted through collective recognition. Great powers and regional powers are central to acknowledging the supreme authority of a state over a political body. Given the need for external legitimacy, secessionists will engage in tactics of coercion and persuasion. The purpose of counter-secession strategy is to block and undermine these efforts.

STRUCTURE OF THE BOOK

The rest of the book proceeds as follows. Part I provides a theoretical and conceptual treatment of the topic and Part II provides a series of case studies of secession and counter-secession strategies. All of the chapters are pitched at a fairly general level that cuts across the universe of secessionist cases. In chapter 1, Aleksandar Pavković discusses the origins and utility of declarations of independence and their relationship to both consensual and unilateral secessions. He shows how they typically make use of two distinct rhetorical devices: the appeal to universal norms and the listing of grievances with the home state. He then explores the use of two frequently cited universal norms: the will of the people and right to self-determination. Moreover, he discusses these themes in the context of two cases of unilateral secession: Bangladesh and Kosovo. In doing so, he examines how declarations of independence may be used strategically to garner international support. In chapter 2, Argyro Kartsonaki examines the strategic value and success of appealing to remedial rights when issuing a UDI. She recounts the philosophical and legal underpinnings of remedial right theory, and she provides an empirical analysis of thirty-eight UDIs that were made since 1970. Notably, she finds that while remedial rights are invoked for strategic reasons as elements of UDIs, these invocations do not correlate with successful secession. Thus, the first two chapters by Pavković and Kartsonaki examine both the content and effectiveness of declarations of independence, which are a necessary part of any strategy for gaining international recognition for a newly seceded state.

The next three chapters discuss the counterstrategies of states. In a way, each chapter focuses on a different kind of secessionist setting. In chapter 3, Eiki Berg and Scott Pegg investigate the methods used by parent states to resolve conflicts with internal breakaway regions that have achieved *de facto* statehood. They examine four different strategies that have been pursued: open engagement, tentative engagement, isolation/rejection with limited enforcement, and isolation with active sanctions. Drawing on case studies for each strategy, they show that none of them were successful in resolving the conflict and bringing the breakaway region back under control of the state. In chapter 4, Ahsan Butt focuses his analysis on secessionist conflict, asking why home states choose to escalate tensions following a secessionist bid into violent conflict. His answer stresses the importance of external security concerns. He argues that it is those states that face real security concerns from secession that are likely to respond with force, and that the intensity of their response depends on the level of third-party support for the secessionists. In chapter 5, Rivka Weill takes a different turn to analyze the legal responses of democratic governments to secessionist ambitions. Here, she develops the concept of militant democracy and shows that democracies regularly counter secessionist efforts by making secessionist parties illegal and/or through the use of eternity clauses that constitutionally entrench the territorial integrity of the state. Taken together, these three chapters explore variations in counter-secession strategies.

Part II of the book presents a set of more empirically oriented studies on the strategies of secession and counter-secession. In chapter 6, Faruk Aksoy and Melike Ayşe Kocacık-Şenol examine the relationship between democratic institutions and secessionist tactics. They focus on three components of democracy—constraints on government, civil and political liberties, free and fair elections—and how the relative strength of these components correlates with secessionist tactics such as the use of violence, protests, nonviolent civil resistance, and institutional methods. They conclude with a number of nuanced observations on the effect of democracy on the strategies of self-determination groups as well as future directions for research.

The next three chapters center on secessionist strategy in the context of advanced democracy. In chapter 7, Bart Maddens, Gertjan Muyters, Wouter Wolfs, and Steven Van Hecke study the ways in which secessionist parties in Europe have mobilized themes related to the EU in their rhetorical arguments and party manifestos. In doing so, they show how the discourse of the EU has shaped the strategies of secessionists in member states. In chapter 8, André Lecours zooms in to take a close look at the strategy of the secessionist movement in Quebec around the time of the independence referendums in 1980 and 1995. Lecours carefully maps out the strategic playing field and explains how the Parti Québécois attempted to win support at the local, national, and international levels. In chapter 9, Karlo Basta investigates the role that business elites played in the secessionist efforts in Quebec, Catalonia, and Scotland. He demonstrates the importance that secessionist and counter-secessionist actors assign to the position of big business, and he shows how business-related arguments are used strategically by both sides to persuade the electorate that their position is correct.

The last two chapters provide empirical analyses in different secessionist settings. In chapter 10, Giulia Prelz Oltramonti appraises the so-called viability strategy—that is, the argument that a breakaway region should be recognized as a sovereign state because it has shown that it is viable. This approach is typically discussed in the context of *de facto* states, which provide governmental functions but are denied recognition. Oltramonti focuses on the cases of Abkhazia and Somaliland and shows how these regions use the viability argument to secure their goals. In chapter 11, Livia Rohrback investigates the strategic interaction between the Indonesian government and three internal secessionist movements in Aceh, East Timor, and West Papua. She explains why the central government and each actor chose tactics in accordance with their setting and their ability to harness international support.

It is in the conclusion that we take in the chapters as a whole and draw out broader themes. We discuss the benefits from integrating the research on *de facto* states, secessionist political parties, and secessionist conflict. We then raise a question that cuts across the chapters: How strategic is the behavior of secessionists and states, and why does much of it appear to fail? Moreover, what is the nature and role of the international community, does violence work, and does the appeal to norms have any effect? What changes can be made at both the domestic and the international levels to ameliorate secessionist turbulence? All of these questions constitute directions for further research.

NOTES

1. Griffiths (2016) data updated through 2017.

2. Fearon and Laitin (2003) estimated that 52% of the civil wars between 1945 and 1999 involved secessionism. Similarly, Sorens (2012, 3) claims that "since the 1980s, at least half of all ongoing civil wars in any given year have been secessionist." Andreas Wimmer has further argued that the share of nationalist wars of secession and ethnic civil wars rose from 25% to 75% over the course of the twentieth century (Wimmer 2013, 27). Finally, Griffiths (2015) calculates that there has been an average of fifteen secessionist conflicts per year since 1945.

3. Walter (2009, 3).

4. Radan (2008, 18). See Griffiths (2016, 6), for a discussion of different definitions of secession.

5. Caspersen (2012, 42); Fazal and Griffiths (2014).

6. Griffiths (2016, 205).

7. Walter (2009); Sorens (2012); Coggins (2014); Griffiths (2016); Mendez and Germann (2018).

8. Crawford (2006, 180–181).

9. Osterud (1997).

10. Muro and Vlaskamp (2016).

11. Cunningham and Sawyer (2017).

12. Osterud (1997); Fabry (2010); Atzili (2012); Caspersen (2012); Coggins (2014); Griffiths (2017).
13. Schelling (1966); Art (1980).
14. Muro (2018).
15. Haljan (2014, 9–10).
16. Coggins (2014, 215).

REFERENCES

Art, Robert J. 1980. "To What Ends Military Power?" *International Security* 4(4): 3–35.

Atzilli, Boaz. 2012. *Good Fences, Bad Neighbors: Border Fixity and International Conflict*. Chicago: University of Chicago Press.

Caspersen, Nina. 2012. *Unrecognized States*. Cambridge: Polity.

Coggins, Bridget L. 2014. *Power Politics and State Formation in the Twentieth Century: The Dynamics of Recognition*. Cambridge: Cambridge University Press.

Crawford, James. 2006. *The Creation of States in International Law* (2nd edition). Oxford: Oxford University Press.

Cunningham, Kathleen Gallagher, and Kathleen Sawyer. 2017. "Is Self-Determination Contagious? A Spatial Analysis of the Spread of Self-Determination Claims." *International Organization* 71(3): 585–604.

Fabry, Mikulas. 2010. *Recognizing States: International Society and the Establishment of New States since 1776*. Oxford: Oxford University Press.

Fazal, Tanisha and Ryan D. Griffiths. 2014. "Membership Has Its Privileges: The Changing Benefits of Statehood." *International Studies Review* 16(1): 79–106.

Fearon, James D., and David D. Laitin. 2003. "Ethnicity, Insurgency, and Civil War." *American Political Science Review* 97(1): 75–90.

Griffiths, Ryan D. 2015. "Between Dissolution and Blood: How Administrative Lines and Categories Shape Secessionist Outcomes." *International Organization* 69(3): 731–751.

Griffiths, Ryan D. 2016. *Age of Secession: The International and Domestic Determinants of State Birth*. Cambridge: Cambridge University Press.

Griffiths, Ryan D. 2017. "Admission to the Sovereignty Club: The Past, Present, and Future of the International Recognition Regime." *Territory, Politics, Governance* 5(2): 177–189.

Haljan, David. 2014. *Constitutionalising Secession*. Hart Publishing.

Mendez, Fernando and Micha Germann. 2018. "Contested Sovereignty: Mapping Referendums on Sovereignty over Time and Space." *British Journal of Political Science* 48(1): 141–165.

Muro, Diego. 2018. "The Stillbirth of a Catalan Republic." *Current History* (March): 83–88.

Muro, Diego and Martijn Vlaskamp. 2016. "How Do Prospects of EU Membership Influence Support for Secession? A Survey Experiment in Catalonia and Scotland." *West European Politics* 39(6): 1115–1138.

Osterud, Oyvind. 1997. "The Narrow Gate: Entry to the Club of Sovereign States." *Review of International Studies* 23: 167–184.

Radan, Peter. 2008. "Secession: A Word in Search of a Meaning." In *On the Way to Statehood: Secession and Globalization*, edited by Peter Radan and Aleksandar Pavković. Burlington, VT: Ashgate, 17–32.

Schelling, Thomas C. 1966. *Arms and Influence*. New Haven, CT: Yale University Press.

Sorens, Jason. 2012. *Secessionism: Identity, Interest, and Strategy*. Montreal: McGill-Queen's University Press.

Walter, Barbara F. 2009. *Reputation and Civil War: Why Separatist Conflicts Are So Violent*. Cambridge: Cambridge University Press.

Wimmer, Andreas. 2013. *Waves of War: Nationalism, State Formation, and Ethnic Expulsion in the Modern World*. Cambridge: Cambridge University Press.

Part I

THEORETICAL AND CONCEPTUAL PERSPECTIVES OF THE STRATEGIC PLAYING FIELD

Chapter 1

In Search of International Recognition: Declarations of Independence and Unilateral Secession

Aleksandar Pavković

Declarations of independence are public pronouncements, issued by individuals or collective bodies alleging to represent peoples (populations) of specific territories, which state that a new state, on that territory, has become independent. Apart from making this kind of statement, declarations of independence invite other states to officially recognize the new state as an independent state. No seceded state had, after 1945, gained international recognition as an independent state, without first declaring its independence. In this sense, declarations of independence are obligatory or necessary part of any strategy for gaining international recognition for a newly seceded state. Such declarations are necessary because without them there would be no independence to be recognized: the declarations in effect make *a claim* to independence which other states are then invited to recognize.

It is a separate question whether the argument(s) for independence contained in those declarations in fact contributed (or contribute) to the international recognition of the state declared independent. Most of the time, this would be a very difficult question to answer. In recognizing a new state, other states do not have to (and usually do not) refer, in any way, to its declaration(s) of independence or to its content. In consequence, outside observers may not be able to establish whether (or how) a particular declaration, or its content, affected the other states' decision(s) to grant (or not to grant) recognition. At the end of the chapter, it is tentatively suggested, on the basis of circumstantial evidence, that the appeal to the general principles in the two declarations to be examined here probably had little, if any, impact on the way the two new states were in fact recognized by other states.

Yet, as Derrida (1986, 9) has pointed out, 'One cannot decide . . . whether independence is stated or produced by this utterance [i.e., the declaration]'. This suggests that declaring independence may be viewed as a ritual act through which a state is thought to be created; for this purpose, specific arguments contained in the declaration may in fact be irrelevant, as long the act of declaring independence follows the formula required of that kind of ritual. Even if the state's independence or the state itself is not in any way 'produced' or 'created' through or by a declaration of independence, those who are making such declarations are making public at least their *intention* to create a new sovereign state on a territory by removing the sovereignty of an existing state from that territory. In short, declarations of independence are primarily used as rhetorical instruments for legitimizing the rejection or overthrow of the sovereignty of an existing state (host state) and replacing it with the sovereignty of a new state (Nardin 2015, 100). This chapter will analyse several rhetorical devices used in the declarations of independence of Bangladesh and of Kosovo to legitimize the rejection of the sovereignty of the respective host states.

In their attempts to legitimize the creation of new state, declarations of independence most frequently use two distinct rhetorical devices: first, they appeal to universal norms or principles which are thought to justify the creation of new states in general and, second, they list the grievances of the population concerned which led to their break with the former host state and to the overthrow of its sovereignty. Both rhetorical devices are justificatory but they function in a different way. By appealing to general norms and principles, the declaration is making an inference from general to particular: since these very norms in general justify the creation of states, they also justify this particular instance of the state creation. The grievances listed in the declaration are specific harms and injustices committed by the host state; the declarations which list them in effect argue that these grievances are grievous enough to justify the withdrawal from the state which committed them. The argument is often left implicit: the grievances or rather their description in the declaration should make it obvious that remaining in the state would be excessively harmful for the population concerned or unbearably unjust (or both). As we shall see, the declaration of the independence of Kosovo, in 2008, departs from this template by failing to list, in any detail, grievances of this kind; instead, it welcomes various international organizations which are set to support the administration of the state and to protect its independence.

While the grievances listed in declarations naturally vary, depending on the context of the declaration, the principles or norms are often the same. In this chapter we shall explore the use of the two most frequent principles: the will of the people and the right of self-determination. Thus, each of the two declarations examined in this chapter – that of Bangladesh in April 1971 and of Kosovo in February 2008 – appeal to one but not both of these principles. And, as we shall see, this is not the only difference between these two declarations.

The two declarations we shall examine here are those of unilateral secession: in both cases, the host state opposed the secession by the force of arms. Moreover, in the context in which these declarations were issued, the secessionists did not expect that by issuing their declaration they will gain the consent of the host state to the secession; hence, these declarations were not primarily addressed to their (former) host state. Unilaterally seceded states need to appeal to other states and international organizations directly, knowing that the lack of consent from the host state may be the greatest hurdle to their international recognition and admission to the membership of the United Nations (UN). In the context of unilateral secession, general principles justifying the creation of an independent state may appear to override the absence of the host state consent. These principles are formulated and adopted by international organizations as principles which justify the creation of new states *in general* without any reference to the consent of the host state: in that sense, these principles appear to justify the creation of new states *independently* of whether the host state has given consent to it or not. Therefore, by appealing to one of the two principles in their declarations of independence, the secessionists are providing other states with general grounds, independent of the consent of their host states, for recognizing their unilateral secession as well. Any strategy of gaining recognition from other states in the absence of the consent or recognition from the host state would thus need to include an appeal to such general principles justifying creation of new states. An appeal to general principles appears then to be an essential part of a strategy for gaining recognition for unilateral secessions which does not rely on the consent of the host state.

THE WILL OF THE PEOPLE AND THE RIGHT TO SELF-DETERMINATION: A BRIEF HISTORY

As rhetorical devices, the concepts of 'the will of the people' and of 'the right to self-determination' (or 'principle of self-determination') originate in different intellectual traditions and differ in their conceptual connotations. The concept of the will of the people originates in the idea of the general will found in the works of Jean Jacque Rousseau, in particular in his *Social Contract* (1762); one of its first legislative expressions is found in article 6 of the Declaration of the Rights of Man and the Citizen passed by the National Assembly in Paris in August 1789. The concept is closely linked with the concept of popular sovereignty – the rule of the people – and thus with democracy either in its direct, plebiscitary form or its indirect, representative forms (assemblies, parliaments): plebiscites or representative assemblies are believed to express the will of the people who are voting in the plebiscite or represented in an assembly. But as seen in the 1908 manifesto of Ferdinand I of Bulgaria, even in the absence of the expression of either kind, monarchs or political leaders may also respond to or follow the will of the people by issuing declarations of independence. This suggests that the concept of the will of the people does not require or presuppose any specific overt action on behalf of the people whose will that is. The phrase is already found in the 1811 Venezuelan (Armitage 2007, 211) and the 1821 Mexican declarations of independence (Fisch 2015, 75). By proclaiming that 'the general will is decided in favor of the Independence of Peru from Spanish domination'[1] (Anna 1975, 221), the Peruvian declaration of 15 July 1821 was probably the first to legitimize state independence by a direct appeal to the will of the people (here 'the general will'). The phrase 'the will of the people' is not, of course, restricted to the declarations of independence; any regime or rule which is not considered democratic may be proclaimed to be against the will of the people.

While the concept of the will of the people is not a juridical concept, codified in international or municipal law, it is sometimes used in legal or quasi-legal opinions. The Arbitration Commission of the EU Conference on Yugoslavia (called, after its chairman, 'The Badinter Commission') in its opinion no. 4 mentions the 'will of the peoples' of Bosnia and Herzegovina and suggests that a referendum of all its citizens would 'constitute' or express this will. Elsewhere in its opinions, the Commission uses the expression 'the desire for independence': in its opinion no. 1, the Commission notes that several Republics of the SFR Yugoslavia expressed their 'desire for independence' 'by a referendum'. This suggests that the 'desire for independence' and 'the will of the people(s)' in the Arbitration Commission opinions are used interchangeably in the context of the justification for secession/independence.

The phrases 'self-determination' and 'the right of self-determination' are first found in the writings of German historians in the 1860s (Fisch 2015, 118) and were used in the debates within social democratic and Marxist parties, in particular in the multinational empires of the Habsburgs and Romanovs. Already in 1916, Lenin, as the leader of the Bolsheviks in Russia, linked the right of self-determination to the creation of an independent state and claimed that all peoples, including the colonial ones, have that right (Fisch 2015, 121). On 15 November 1917, the Soviet government, under his chairmanship, proclaimed 'the right of the peoples of Russia to free self-determination, even to the point of separation and the formation of an independent state'[2] (Declaration of the Rights of the Peoples of Russia, 1917; Fisch 2015, 130). On 4 December 1917, the Senate of Finland declared the independence of Finland referring to the Finnish people's 'right to determine its fate' (To the Finnish People, 1917); and on 18 December, Lenin, on behalf of the Soviet government, recognized Finnish independence 'in accordance with the principle of national self-determination'. Soon after, on 16 February 1918, the Council of Lithuania, proclaimed the independence of Lithuania 'on the ground of the recognized right of self-determination' (Resolution 1918). But this *right* found its first codification in international law only in 1960, in the UN General Assembly Declaration on Granting Independence to Colonial Countries and Peoples which assigns this right, in its second article, to 'all peoples' but provides no clue as to who these peoples are. Yet article 5 in effect restricts the use of this right to the legitimization of the independence of the European overseas colonies (past and present). Finally, article 6 rules out its use to legitimize secession from UN member states, since 'any attempt at the partial or total disruption of the national unity and the territorial integrity of a country is incompatible with the purposes and principles of the Charter of the United Nations' (GA 1514, 1960: #6). In spite of these limitations, the right of self-determination is here – and in later UN declarations – explicitly constructed so as to legitimize the creation of independent states out of the territories which were not independent before: article 5 of the above declaration, demands an 'immediate transfer of [state or sovereign] powers' to the populations of the territories which have not attained independence in order to make them independent. As a universal human right, possessed of all peoples, this instrument of legitimization of independence itself appears (in spite of the restrictions of article 6) to be independent of the contingencies of history, ethnicity, or geography. In view of its universality, it is understandable that from the end of World War II onwards declarations of independence, as Armitage (2007, 110) notes, increasingly refer to such universal human rights.

In his historical survey of the concept of self-determination, Fisch (2015, 115) notes that in the second half of the nineteenth century, the European Great Powers acted as arbiters of independence: these Powers were granting independence to various segments of the Ottoman Empire whose populations were not at the time 'determining' themselves in any particular way nor were they expected or asked to perform any acts of 'self-determination'. These were, in Fisch's view cases of 'alien-determined self-determination'. An example of 'alien-determined self-determination' is found in the history of Bulgaria's path to independence. In the Russo-Turkish war of 1878, the Russian military conquered a large territory in the Eastern Balkans, populated by the Bulgarians and, as a result, the peace agreement between the Russian and Ottoman governments, in San Stefano, envisaged a large and independent state of Bulgaria. In June 1878, at the Congress of Berlin, following Austria-Hungary's and Great Britain's objections, the Great Powers divided the so-envisaged large state and recognized only a smaller segment as the principality of Bulgaria, to be placed under the rule of a Christian prince from a European dynasty but still paying tribute to the Ottoman state (Crampton 2005, 86). Only in 1908 did the then Prince Ferdinand (of the House of Saxe-Coburg and Gotha-Kohary) declare independence of the (by then significantly enlarged) Kingdom (or Empire) of Bulgaria. His 'Manifesto' starts with the expression of gratitude to the Russian Tsar and his Romanian allies for liberating his country from slavery (i.e. the Ottoman rule) and ends with the proclamation of independence of the Kingdom of Bulgaria made 'in order . . . to respond to the will of the people' (Manifesto 1908). This declaration implies that a non-native monarch can, without any help from a referendum, express the will of the people through a declaration of independence.

This chapter explores the declarations of independence of two post-1945 cases of 'alien-determined self-determination' in which independence from the former host state was also a result of military intervention by outside state(s): the cases of Bangladesh and Kosovo. One notable difference between these two cases of unilateral secession is found in the responses of their former host states: Pakistan, the former host state of Bangladesh, recognized the independence of Bangladesh in February 1974, two- and- a- half years since Bangladesh's declaration of independence in April 1971; at the time of writing in 2018, Serbia, the former host state of Kosovo still refuses to recognize the independence of Kosovo which was last declared in February 2008. This chapter is not concerned with this and other differences in the responses of these two former host states.

BANGLADESH

Bangladesh's first declaration of independence was contained in the pre-recorded radio message by Sheik Mujibur Rahman, broadcast on 25 March 1971 from a makeshift radio transmitter in Dacca, following the military takeover of East Pakistan (Bangladesh's appellation within Pakistan) by Pakistani armed forces. Sheik Rahman was the leader of the Awami League, a Bengali party in East Pakistan, which in January 1971 won a majority of seats in the Parliament of the whole of Pakistan; unlike most of the leaders and deputies from his party who fled to India before 25 March, he remained in East Pakistan, was arrested by the Pakistan Army, and transferred to West Pakistan (Sisson and Rose 1990, 159). His brief declaration began with 'Today Bangla Desh is a sovereign and independent country' and continued to describe the attack of the Pakistani Army in various places in the former East Pakistan, now Bangladesh. It ended with a statement and a prayer: 'The Bengalis are fighting the enemy with great courage for an independent Bangladesh. May Allah aid in our fight for freedom. *Joy Bangla* [Victory to Bangladesh]' (Guhathakurta and van Schendel 2013, 225).

On 27 March, Major Zauir Rahman (no relation to Sheik Rahman), as the head of the Bangladesh armed forces and on behalf of Sheik Rahman, proclaimed the independence of Bangladesh over makeshift radio transmitter in Kalurghat, Chittagong, without mentioning the first declaration by Sheikh Rahman. Having proclaimed independence, he went on to declare, 'We have already framed a sovereign, legal Government under Sheikh Mujibur Rahman. . . . The new democratic Government is committed to a policy of non-alignment in international relations. It will seek friendships with all nations and strive for international peace. I appeal to all Governments to mobilize public opinion in their respective countries against the brutal genocide in Bangladesh'. The declaration ended with the claim that this government is 'entitled to recognition from all democratic nations in the world' (Guhathakurta and van Schendel 2013, 226).

Both declarations were short; neither mentioned self-determination, the right to self-determination, or the will of the people. The first primarily dealt with the Pakistan Army attack and the fighting that ensued, while the second emphasized the legality of the newly formed government, its peace-seeking international policy, and appealed for international support and recognition.

Three weeks after these two declarations, on 17 April 1971, a number of Bengali politicians who had fled to India crossed over the border to the village of Baidyanathala in Bangladesh, and under Indian military protection, proclaimed themselves a Constituent Assembly. This Assembly went on to 'declare and constitute Bangladesh to be a sovereign People's Republic and thereby confirm the declaration of independence already made by . . . Sheikh Mujibar Rahman' and in the same paragraph appointed him the President of the Republic, giving him the power to appoint the government and to 'do all other things that may be necessary to give to the people of Bangladesh an orderly and just Government' (Guhathakurta and van Schendel 2013, 227–229).

The preamble of this declaration makes it clear that the initial declaration of independence was a response to the war against the Bengali people: 'While still conferring with the elected representatives of the Bengali people', the Pakistani authorities 'declared an unjust and treacherous war' and

in the facts and circumstances of such treacherous conduct Bangabandhu Sheikh Mujibur Rahman, the undisputed leader of the 75 million people of Bangladesh, in due fulfillment of the legitimate right of self-determination of the people of Bangladesh, duly made a declaration of independence at Dacca on March 26, 1971, and urged the people of Bangladesh to defend the honour and integrity of Bangladesh.

In spite of the treacherous and unjust war levied against them, the declaration stated that the 'people of Bangladesh by their heroism, bravery and revolutionary fervour have established effective control over the territories of Bangladesh' (Guhathakurta and van Schendel 2013, 228).

In the preamble of this declaration, 'war' – variously described as 'treacherous', 'unjust', 'savage', and 'ruthless' – is mentioned three times, while 'genocide' is mentioned twice (including 'numerous acts of genocide'). There is no mention of the will of the people, and the right of self-determination is mentioned only once as 'being duly fulfilled' by the initial declaration by Sheikh Rahman.

How this right is 'duly fulfilled' through a declaration that did not mention it is, of course, not entirely clear.[3] One possible interpretation is that Sheikh Rahman, without mentioning the right, has in fact exercised this right by declaring independence on behalf of the seventy-five million inhabitants of Bangladesh whose leader he is believed to be. In other words, the people of Bangladesh, prior to the war, had already had the right of self-determination, which was then exercised through his initial declaration of independence.

While this is not the only possible interpretation of the above phrase 'in due fulfilment', this interpretation divorces the exercise of this right from the achievement of independence of Bangladesh. In early December 1971, the Indian army entered East Pakistan/Bangladesh and on 16 December 1971, after heavy fighting, the Pakistani Army surrendered to the Indian Army which, together with the Bengali Freedom Fighters, took full control over the territory of Bangladesh. During the fighting, on 6 December 1971, the Indian government recognized the independence of Bangladesh, without any reference to its earlier declarations of independence. According to the earlier interpretation, the Indian Army's takeover of Bangladesh had nothing to do with self-determination – let alone with the right of self-determination. The right of self-determination had already been exercised by Sheikh Rahman on 25 March 1971 by or through his declaration of independence, and this exercise has nothing do with the later military takeover of Bangladesh by the Indian Army.

According to this interpretation, a people's right of self-determination can be exercised by or through a declaration of independence (made by a purported leader of that people) which makes no mention of the right. In this way, independence from the host state may result from a military intervention and the subsequent takeover of territory by another state – and yet, prior to the military intervention, the people's right of self-determination had already been exercised through the declaration of independence. In this way, a declaration of independence establishes the grounds for international recognition of the independence of the new state, *regardless of* how this independence was achieved. The key element of this strategy for seeking international recognition is the claim that the people of the given territory, East Pakistan, through its representatives (whether self-proclaimed or elected) declared the independence of their state/territory; it is of no consequence of whether or how the people had in fact achieved this independence or not.

KOSOVO[4]

The first declaration of Kosovo independence was passed on 2 July 1990 by the majority Kosovo Albanian deputies of the Assembly of the Socialist Autonomous Province of Kosovo. As its clause 4 suggests, this was a response to the amendments to the constitution of the Socialist Republic of Serbia of March 1989 (later incorporated in the Constitution of Serbia of 1990), which restricted the legislative and political autonomy of the province of Kosovo. Entitled the 'Constitutional Declaration', it declared Kosovo (using its Albanian name) to be an 'independent and equal unit within the framework of the Yugoslav federation (confederation) and an equal subject with its counterparts in Yugoslavia'. The first clause states:

1. This declaration expresses and proclaims the view of the inhabitants of Kosovo and of this Assembly towards the original constitutional stand of the people of Kosovo and of this Assembly as an act of political self-determination within the framework of Yugoslavia. (Auerswarld and Auerswald 2000, 44)

The Assembly also confirmed, in clause 3, Kosovo's new political and constitutional position within which 'all citizens and equal nationalities in Kosovo where Albanians, as the majority of the population . . . as well as the Serbs and others living in Kosovo, are considered as a people-nation and not a nationality (national minority)' (Auerswald and Auerswald 2000, 44).[5]

This, first, declaration aimed to change both the status of Kosovo from an autonomous province of Serbia to a federal unit (republic) of the Yugoslav federation (or confederation) and the status of the Albanian population of Kosovo from a nationality (minority) to a nation (people) within Yugoslavia. From this it is clear that its primary – and possibly only intended – audience appears to be confined to the SFR Yugoslavia, including the target population, the Kosovo Albanians, as well as the governments of the Yugoslav federation and its republics.

According to its opening sentence, the Declaration itself is proceeding 'from the expressed will of the majority of people of Kosovo' and, the Declaration itself, in its first clause, is regarded as 'an act of political self-determination within the framework of Yugoslavia'. There is, however, no mention of the *right* of self-determination.

Following the initial declarations of independence, in June 1991, of the federal units of Croatia and Slovenia from SFR Yugoslavia, on 22 September, the same Assembly of the Republic of Kosovo, constituted by the majority Kosovo Albanian deputies, passed the Resolution proclaiming the 'Republic of Kosovo as a sovereign and independent state, with the right to participate as a constituent republic in Yugoslavia on the basis of freedom and equality' (Auerswald and Auerswald 2000, 55). Clause 1 of the Resolution confirms that it is made in accordance to the 'will of the people' and with the previous Constitutional Declaration of 1990, as well as in line with the Constitution of Kosovo of 7 September 1990.

This, second declaration of September 1991, is the first to proclaim Kosovo a sovereign and independent republic and to refer to the 'will of the people' (as opposed to the 'majority of the people' in the first declaration). It contains *no* reference to self-determination or the right to self-determination. On 28 September 1991, the Government of Albania 'hailed and supported' this resolution, proclaiming it 'a free and direct expression of the will [of] our brothers in Kosovo' (Auerswald and Auerswald 2000, 56). This is regarded as the first – and, until 2008, the only – recognition of Kosovo's independence by a UN member state. From this it may be inferred that this time the audience of this declaration included other states outside the confines of the SFR Yugoslavia.

Following the reiterated declarations of independence of Croatia and Slovenia, on 19 October 1991, the same Assembly of Kosovo issued a statement concerning the results of the referendum, carried out on 29–30 September 1991, which confirmed that 99.87% of those voting voted 'in favour of Kosovo's sovereignty and independence'. This statement ends with another declaration: 'Therefore, the Assembly officially declares Kosovo to be a sovereign and independent republic' (Auerswald and Auerswald 2000, 59). This statement makes no mention of self-determination, the right to self-determination, nor of the 'will of the people'.[6] In spite of the absence of any of those general principles, the third declaration appears to be addressing an international audience, in particular the European Community bodies. It is on the basis of this, third, declaration and the results of the referendum that the chairman of the Assembly and the prime minister of Kosovo requested international recognition from the European Community – which proved not to be forthcoming. In their letter requesting recognition, the Kosovo officials stated that independence is both a right and the will of people (Trifunovska 1999, 767–769).

In March 1999, the North Atlantic Treaty Organization (NATO) started an aerial bombing campaign against the Federal Republic of Yugoslavia, thus in effect providing air support to the secessionist Kosovo Liberation Army (KLA); in 1998, the KLA had led a mass armed uprising against the Yugoslav/Serbian forces in Kosovo. In June 1999, following the agreement between the European Union (EU) and Russian negotiators and the Yugo-slav government, the Yugoslav army and officials left Kosovo and NATO-commanded armed forces took control of the province. UN Security Council (UNSC) resolution 1244 authorized the establishment of the UN mission in Kosovo as well as the deployment of a NATO-led military force (Kaufman 2002, 200–201); both still operate in Kosovo at the time of writing. Follow-ing the failure of the protracted negotiations with Serbia over Kosovo's 'final status', on 17 February 2008, the Kosovo Albanian deputies (the Serb depu-ties were absent) of the Provisional Assembly of Kosovo, elected under the UN auspices, adopted a Declaration of Independence, the last declaration in the series of the Kosovo declarations.

The 2008 Kosovo Declaration, in its first clause affirms that the Declara-tion 'reflects' 'the will of our people' (Albanian and English versions) or 'the will of the people' (French version) (Kosovo Declaration 2008). But apart from the appeal to this general principle, most of the clauses of the Kosovo declaration concern the international obligations, regulations, and norms, which Kosovo is adopting; the international organizations, which are welcomed in Kosovo; and the plans for its future interstate relations. The first clause, for example, states that Kosovo, through this Declaration, fully accepts the plan of Martti Ahtisaari,[7] the UN special envoy, which envisages a conditional and supervised independence of Kosovo. In its further clauses the Declaration accepts and welcomes the presence of the NATO forces and of the UN and EU administration in Kosovo. Further, the declaration expresses the intention of Kosovo to join the EU and to develop and improve relations with the Republic of Serbia (its former host state)[8] and to bring about the reconciliation of the two peoples.

Unlike the last Bangladesh's declaration which reiterates the initial decla-ration and condemns the war and atrocities against Bengali people, the last Kosovo Declaration makes no reference to war and to any of the previous Kosovo declarations/resolutions of independence.[9] Nonetheless, it does pay homage to the men and women who sacrificed their lives 'for the building of a better future of Kosovo'. While the declaration makes no reference to the war, atrocities, discrimination, or genocide, it refers in its preamble, to the 'years of the conflict and violence which had troubled the conscience of all civilized peoples'.[10] In short, the account of the grievances – or rather the grievance – that led to the declaration of independence is here very brief and vague. More importantly, the grievance – violence and conflict – is viewed from a perspective of its impact not on the Kosovo Albanians (or not only on the Kosovo Albanians) but on 'all civilized peoples'. In addition, this declara-tion (similar to the Bulgarian manifesto of 1908) expresses gratitude to 'the world' (the Albanian and English versions) or the 'international community' (the French version)[11] for intervening in 1999 and 'removing the governance of Belgrade over Kosovo and placing Kosovo under United Nations interim administration'. The military aspect of this intervention and its primary agent – NATO – are not mentioned (Kosovo Declaration 2008).

In spite of its extensive references to international law, this declaration makes no mention of the right of self-determination or of self-determination: unlike Bangladesh's, Kosovo's independence in its latest declaration is not regarded as a result of an act of self-determination. And, unlike the Bangladesh declaration, the Kosovo Declaration appeals to the will of the people as the general principle which legitimizes the independence of the new state. There is no reference to the expression of the will in a referendum; the referendum of Kosovo Albanians held, without international supervision or approval, in 1991 is not mentioned.

DECLARATIONS OF INDEPENDENCE AND INTERNATIONAL RECOGNITION

The last declaration of independence of Bangladesh and Kosovo refers, briefly, to one of the two general principles discussed in this chapter but neither attempts to explain how their preferred general principles justify the independence of the two states. Their mention in the declaration appears more as a symbolic gesture to the existing principles of legitimization rather than an attempt to provide a systematic argument for independence based on these principles. The principal arguments for their independence are found elsewhere in the two declarations.

Both the initial declaration and the last, April, declaration of independence of Bangladesh list the attack of the Pakistani Army on the Bengali people and the ensuing war and crimes against Bengali people as the principal – in fact – and the only grievance that led to the declaration of independence. This grievance – including the crime of genocide – is outlined in some detail. It provides, within the declaration, an obvious justification for the separation from the previous host state and the establishment of an independent state: independence, within this discourse of the declaration, is the only remedy available from these crimes committed by the Pakistani state against the Bengali people.

The Kosovo Declaration makes no reference to the war waged in 1998–1999 and avoids any mention of the NATO military intervention that led to Kosovo's independence. In this sense, this declaration does not list the war and suffering caused by war as a grievance which needs redress in the form of independence. The main focus of the declaration is Kosovo's acceptance of the international political and legal framework for its independence and of the international institutions – including the UN and NATO – which are to administer this framework on Kosovo's territory. In effect, the declaration argues that the international political/legal framework – the Ahtisaari plan – and the UN agencies and NATO military forces, in effect bring about the independence of Kosovo. In short, the Kosovo Declaration appears to argue both that these international organizations brought independence to Kosovo and that they are there to enable and protect it.

After it declared its independence in April 1971, no state recognized Bangladesh until 6 December 1971. The first state to recognize Bangladesh, on 6 December 1971, was Bhutan, followed by India, whose troops were at the time advancing through Bangladesh. Within two months of the first recognitions, around twenty states, including the USSR and the UK, had recognized its independence. In the case of Bangladesh, the trigger for its wider international recognition was not its declaration of independence in April 1971 but its initial recognition by India, its sponsor state.

In contrast, within a day of the Kosovo declaration on 17 February 2008, ten states, including the United States and the UK, recognized Kosovo's independence; within ten days of its proclamation, yet another ten, mainly NATO member states, did so. At the time of writing, more than 110 UN member states have recognized its independence (Kosovo Thanks You 2018). These do not include China and Russia, two permanent members of the UNSC; India and Bangladesh have not recognized Kosovo's independence either. In spite of this, as a strategy of gaining swift international recognition, the Kosovo Declaration appears, at first sight, to have been more effective than the Bangladesh one. But unlike the Bangladesh's declaration, the timing and proclamation of the Kosovo declaration was 'closely choreographed and coordinated' (Visoka 2017, 48) with Kosovo's main sponsor, the United States, and its principal NATO allies; it was prepared and publicized well in advance, enabling the United States and its allies to recognize Kosovo a day after its declaration of independence. Therefore, it was the international coordination of its proclamation, not the rhetoric of declaration, that most likely led to the swift recognition of Kosovo's independence by a large number of states. While such coordination appears to have been lacking in the case of Bangladesh and its last declaration of independence in April 1971, the first states to recognize Bangladesh, in January 1972, were also allies or supporters of its sponsor state, India.

Moreover, the history of Kosovo's declarations of independence, prior to the 2008 one, suggests that the use of 'the right of self-determination' or of 'the will of the people' or both in their declarations of independence fail to serve as a trigger for international recognition. An elaborate argument using both of these principles in the letter to the European Community of October 1991, by the officials of the self-declared Republic of Kosovo requesting its recognition, which contained a detailed and elaborate argument using both principles, did not even solicit a reply (Trifunovska 1999, 767–769). As we have seen, in the last declaration of 2008, only one principle, that of the will of the people, is briefly mentioned, and the declaration focuses on the policies of the acceptance of and welcome to international organizations and institutions. The previous failures of the two principles to elicit international recognition or response did not lead to their complete abandonment; however, the main focus of the arguments put forward in the last declaration shifted to the articulation of the specific policies to be enacted by the newly independent state. Since the sponsor states which were prepared to recognize the new state expected and welcomed such policies, it is quite understandable that the declaration focused on those policies at the expense of general principles and specific grievances. Perhaps this focus on the expected policies in the declaration was also a result of the coordination (and 'choreography') of the declaration with the sponsor states. In spite of the emphasis, in the last Kosovo Declaration, on to the future/expected policies of the new state, its brief appeal to a general principle, the will of the people, suggests that appeals to general principles still remain a part of the standard repertoire or strategy for seeking international recognition.

NOTES

1. The phrase "volonté générale" (general will) was apparently first used in theological treatises of Arnaud and Pascal to refer to God's will.

2. According to Fisch (2015, 134) the U.S. president Woodrow Wilson took the same phrase from Lenin's vocabulary but restricted its meaning to self-government or the 'consent of the governed'. Unlike Lenin, Wilson, according to Fisch, never meant to give colonial peoples or any ethnic groups the right to establish independent states.

3. It has been suggested that this declaration (unlike the first two declarations) was 'drafted by an Indian well schooled in the art of legal writing' (Sisson and Rose 1990, 143).

4. This English spelling, used in various international documents, is followed throughout; an alternative is 'Kosova', reflecting the English pronunciation of the original Albanian 'Kosovë'. The Serbian appellation of the province is 'Kosovo i Metohija'.

5. The English translation was published in Tirana in 1993 (Truth on Kosovo 1993). The original Albanian is available at http://archive.koha.net/?id=&l=64698 (accessed on 23 November 2017).

6. The constitution of Kosovo, which this Assembly enacted on 7 September 1990, makes several references to the right of self-determination as well as to the 'sovereign will' of the people. It seems that the drafters of the Kosovo Albanian Assembly's declarations and resolutions thought that declarations and resolutions proclaiming independence and sovereignty need not appeal or refer to this right, whereas the constitutional documents need to be grounded both on the right of self-determination and on the 'will of the people' or the 'sovereign will'.

7. The only personal name found in this declaration is that of Martti Ahtisaari: it is mentioned seven times in the declaration, starting with its preamble. The last Bangladesh declaration, which appoints Sheikh Rahman as the president of Bangladesh and proclaims him the leader of the 75 million people of Bangladesh, mentions his name three times.

8. The Republic of Serbia was the successor state of the State Union of Serbia and Montenegro from which Montenegro (peacefully) seceded in 2006. The Federal Republic of Yugoslavia, created in 1992 out of Serbia and Montenegro, was transformed, under EU auspices, into the State Union of Serbia and Montenegro in 2003.

9. Although no previous declaration is mentioned in the most recent, 2008 declaration, the first declaration, the Constitution Declaration of 1990, was, at its official anniversary celebration in 2010, proclaimed a historical document comparable to the Declaration of the Independence of the United States of America of 1776, and all the deputies who voted for it were awarded the Medal of Independence (Sejdiu 2010).

10. Michael Walzer (1977 [2006], 107) justifies humanitarian intervention in support of a secession (in particular, Bangladesh) provided that the acts committed against the people (about to secede) are such that they 'shock the moral conscience of mankind' (quotes in the original). John Stuart Mill (1859), in his short article on nonintervention, distinguishes between 'civilized peoples' (like those of Christian Europe) and 'barbarians' (in Asia and elsewhere) and argues that since the former have superior moral rules, the 'civilized people' or their governments are (morally) entitled to intervene in civil wars in other states.

11. The French translation of the declaration departs from the original in Albanian in several respects, suggesting a more nuanced diplomatic terminology. See Kosovo Declaration (2008).

REFERENCES

Anna, Timothy E. 1975. 'The Peruvian Declaration of Independence: Freedom by Coercion'. *Journal of Latin American Studies* 7(2): 221–248.

Armitage, David. 2007. *Declaration of Independence: A Global History*. Cambridge, MA: Harvard University Press.

Auserwald, Philip E., and David P. Auserwald, eds. 2000. *The Kosovo Conflict: A Diplomatic History through Documents*. Cambridge: Kluwer International.

Crampton, Robert J. 2005. *A Concise History of Bulgaria*. Cambridge: Cambridge University Press.

Declaration Rights of the Peoples of Russia 1917. 'Declaration of the Rights of the People of Russia'. Accessed 20 November 2017. https://www.marxists.org/history/ussr/government/1917/11/02.htm.

Derrida, Jacques. 1986. 'Declarations of Independence'. *New Political Science* 7(1): 7–15. doi: 10.1080/07393148608429608.

Fisch, Jörg. 2015. *The Right of Self-Determination of Peoples: The Domestication of an Illusion*. Translated from the German by Anita Mage. Cambridge: Cambridge University Press.

GA 1514. 1960. 'Declaration on the Granting of Independence to Colonial Countries and Peoples'. Adopted by General Assembly, Resolution 1514 (XV) of 14 December 1960. http://www.un.org/en/decolonization/declaration.shtml.

Guhathakurta, Meghna, and Willem van Schendel, eds. 2013. *The Bangaladesh Reader: History, Culture, Politics*. London: Duke University Press.

Kaufman, Joyce P. 2002. *NATO and the Former Yugoslavia: Crisis, Conflict and the Atlantic Alliance*. Lanham, MD: Rowman & Littlefield.

Kosovo Declaration 2008. 'Kosovo Declaration of Independence'.

Albanian: http://www.assembly-Kosovo.org/?cid=1,128,1635.

English: http://www.assembly-Kosovo.org/?cid=2,128,1635.

French: https://www.kuvendikosoves.org/common/docs/declaration_d_indepen dance_fr.pdf Accessed on 6 February 2019.

Kosovo Thanks You. 2018. Accessed 20 September 2018. http://www.kosovo thanksyou.com/organizations/.

Manifesto 1908. 'Manifest' by Ferdinand I. Declaration of Bulgarian Independence 22 September 1908. Accessed 18 August 2018. https://en.wikisource.org/wiki/ Bulgarian_Declaration_of_Independence.

Mill, John Stuart. 1859 [2006]. 'A Few Words on Non-Intervention' in *Frazer's Magazine*, reprinted in *New England Review*, 27(6): 252–264.

Nardin, Terry. 2015. 'The Diffusion of Sovereignty'. *Journal of European Thought* 41(1): 89–102.

Sejdiu. 2010. 'Sejdiu: 2 Juli 1990 je bio vrh artikulisanja osećaja slobode'. (Sejdiu [the Former President of Kosovo]: 2 July 1990 was the Peak of the Articulation of the Feeling of Freedom). Accessed 1 December 2017. http://www.president-ksgov. net/?page=3,6,1198.

Sisson, Richard, and Leo E. Rose.1990. *War and Secession: Pakistan, India and the Creation of Bangladesh*. Berkley: University of California Press.

To the Finnish People. 1917. 'To the Finnish People'. Finnish Declaration of Independence of 4 December 1917. Accessed on 18 August 2018. https://en.wikipedia. org/wiki/Finnish_Declaration_of_Independence.

Trifunovska, Snezana, ed. 1999. *Former Yugoslavia through Documents: From Its Dissolution to the Peace Settlement*. The Hague: Nijhoff.

Truth on Kosovo. 1993. *Truth on Kosova*. Tirana: Academy of Sciences of the Republic of Albanian, Institute of History, Encyclopedia Publishing House.

Visoka, Gëzim. 2017. *Shaping Peace in Kosovo: The Politics of Peacebuilding and Statehood*. Cham: Palgrave Macmillan.

Walzer, Michael. 1977 [2006]. *Just and Unjust Wars: A Moral Argument with Historical Illustrations*. New York: Basic Books.

Chapter 2

The False Hope of Remedial Secession: Theory, Law, and Reality

Argyro Kartsonaki

Remedial secession theories, also known as just cause theories, critically challenge the traditional thinking on territorial integrity and sovereignty, maintaining that a group should and/or might have the right to secede if the host state has repeatedly and manifestly failed to respect and protect its fundamental human rights. This approach has gained in dynamics after the World Summit of 2005 and the United Nations' (UN's) announcement that sovereignty no longer exclusively protects states from foreign interference, but there is a charge of responsibility that holds states accountable for the welfare of their people (UN 2005). This public questioning of the absolute supremacy of the principle of state sovereignty has also been sometimes translated as an endorsement to a remedial right to secession. This reached new heights with Kosovo's unilateral declaration of independence from Serbia in 2008 and its rapid recognition by the United States and the majority of the EU states.[1]

This chapter appraises the strategic value of invoking remedial reasons in Unilateral Declarations of Independence (UDIs) as a tactic separatists might use to gain international recognition. International recognition is of outmost importance for a secessionist entity, as it is what turns this new aspiring polity from an illegal and officially nonexistent entity into a legitimate and sovereign state, determining the success or failure of the separatist attempt (Shelef and Zeira 2017). In cases of UDIs, the importance of international recognition rises even further, since by definition the host state opposes independence and hence the unilateral nature of the attempt.

The strategic goal of a UDI is to convince existing states to recognize the aspiring state, or invoke international support that would put pressure on the host state to permit independence. Griffiths and Muro in the introduction of this volume suggest two ways in which this strategy would work: coercion or normative appeal or a combination of the two. A UDI falls into the latter category. It is a form of coercion as it is usually preceded by disorder, and it is characterized by political tension, social conflict, and often violent conflict (Lemke and Carter 2016). It is, however, also a normative appeal to both the target population and the international community. The UDI is the tool with which separatist leaders communicate to existing states their demands and the reasons why they seek independence. A UDI is a declaration of intent, a declaration of normative rights, and a strategic move to incite domestic and international support (Armitage 2007; Jenne, Saideman, and Lowe 2007).

This study complements and furthers existing research in the field of strategy of secession and international recognition (Ker-Lindsay 2012; Coggins 2014; Cunningham 2014; Walter 2006) by shedding light to the usefulness of remedial secession as a tactic to gain international recognition. This chapter analyses thirty-eight UDIs investigating whether separatists invoked remedial justifications in order to attract international recognition, what kind of justifications, and how states reacted to this, that is, whether they recognized the new polity or not. The analysis has as starting point, 1970, when the right to statehood as a form to exercise the right of self-determination was first included in the UN Declaration on Friendly Relations. It examines unilateral secessionist attempts that took place between 1970 and 2017 analysing the content of their UDIs.

The findings show no correlation between the invocation of remedial reasons and the achievement of international recognition. The vast majority of unilateral secessions failed to achieve uncontested statehood, regardless of whether they presented remedial reasons or not. Appeals to remedial justifications may raise the sympathy of existing states, prompting them to issue public statements condemning violence and abuses. However, for this sympathy to translate into international recognition, geopolitical factors have to converge, which would prompt the international community to put enough pressure on the host state coercing it to allow secession, turning thus the secession from unilateral to consensual. The strategy, therefore, of appealing to remedial reasons can be successful up to a certain point, that of applying pressure on the host state or inciting public outcry for atrocities. However, it is not enough to convince the UN member states, and especially all five permanent Security Council members, to bypass the will of the host state and recognize the aspiring polity.

This chapter is structured as follows: it begins with the theoretical foundations of the research, presenting a review of normative arguments around remedial secession. Then it examines three widely cited legal documents often employed in order to explain, defend, or condemn secession, the UN Declaration on Friendly Relations, the Supreme Court of Canada Reference *re* the Secession of Quebec, and the International Court of Justice (ICJ) Advisory Opinion on the legality of Kosovo's UDI. The chapter continues with an analysis of UDIs examining whether, and, if so, what kind of, remedial reasons were put forward by separatists. Finally, the research explores the outcome of these separatist attempts, whether they achieved UN membership or not, concluding with a summary of the main findings.

REMEDIAL SECESSION THEORIES

Common to remedial secession theories is the position that a people may have the right to secede if they (have) suffered some form of major injustices by their host state. This is a critical point that distinguishes remedial theories from other approaches to secession, such as choice theories that focus on the will of the people as main justification for secession (Wellman 2005; Beran 1984; Copp 1998) or nation-orientated theories (Moore 1998; Miller 1997; Margalit and Raz 1990).

Nevertheless, what constitutes injustices that would entitle a group the right of remedial secession remains a matter of ambiguity. For example, Buchanan argues that if the physical survival of the group is in danger, then they should have the right to secede (Buchanan 1991; 1997). Another reason that would justify the right to secession would be the previous annexation or occupation of the demanded territory by the host state, a view shared by other scholars especially when referring to the secession of the three Baltic States from the former Soviet Union (USSR) before it disintegrated (Catala 2013; Mancini 2008; Simon 2011). Brilmayer (1991, 2015) also connects a group's demands for secession with the group's attachment to a specific territory stressing that mistreatment alone without a convincing bond to this territory does not give the right to secession.

Coppieters (2003) suggests that due to structural affinities between the moral analysis of the use of force and that of unilateral forms of secession, it is possible to apply the criteria of just war to cases of secession. Thus, he claims that the *jus ad bellum* criteria of just cause, legitimate authority, right intentions, last resort, proportionality, and chance of success can be used in order to assess the justification for independence.

Bolton and Visoka (2010) propose the following conditions that could facilitate – or block – remedial secession: (1) violations of autonomy agreements by the host state; (2) unjust annexation of territory; (3) human rights abuses perpetrated by the host state; (4) international intervention to mediate a status outcome; (5) support of powerful countries; (6) exhaustion of negotiations; (7) a commitment from the seceding entity to uphold minority rights. Related to point (1) Buchanan has also posited that previous violations of status agreements between host state and separatist entity would constitute a reason for secession (Buchanan 2004).

Birch (1984) set four conditions, of which at least one must be present for secession to be justified: (1) unjust annexation of the seceding territory to the host state; (2) failure of the central government to protect the basic human rights of the seceding group; (3) failure of the government to protect the political and economic interests of the separatist region; (4) the government having ignored or rejected a settlement proposed by the seceding region that aimed to preserve essential interests of this region. Birch maintained that these four prior conditions must exist for the claim to secede to be justifiable.

Another condition that has been mentioned as justifying secession is the failure of the host state to meet 'meaningful multinational arrangements' (Costa 2003, 64), referring to the official recognition of the state as multinational and the adoption of necessary measures that guarantee the equality between the different national groups, such as through extensive territorial self-government and/or meaningful equality through other power-sharing arrangements (Costa 2003).

Thus, it seems that the normative literature agrees that if at least one, or a combination of more than one, of the following criteria is present then a people may seek remedial secession: threats to physical safety of the members of the group that demands secession or long-standing discrimination against this group; attachment to a specific territory and/or unjust annexation of this territory by the host state; violations of agreements or of status within the borders of the state, such as a unilateral revocation of autonomous status of the region in question; and, remedial secession as a last resort when all other means of cooperation and attempts to resolve the conflict have failed.

Nonetheless, these criteria emerge from the normative literature around secession and are not legally binding. As a matter of fact, there is no international law explicitly regulating secession (Mancini 2008; Arp 2010; Crawford 2006). This leads to significantly diverse interpretations of legal documents referring to issues of or around secession. The following section examines the UN General Assembly (UNGA) Declaration on Friendly Relations, the Supreme Court of Canada Reference *re* the Secession of Quebec, and the ICJ Advisory Opinion on the legality of Kosovo's UDI.

LEGAL DOCUMENTS

Perhaps the most widely cited document of both supporters and opponents of the existence of a remedial right to secession is the UN Declaration on Friendly Relations.[2] The Declaration states that 'the establishment of a sovereign and independent State, the free association or integration with an independent State or the emergence into any other political status freely determined by a people constitute modes of implementing the right of self-determination by that people'. However, the Declaration continues by reaffirming respect to 'the territorial integrity or political unity of sovereign and independent States conducting themselves in compliance with the principle of equal rights and self-determination of peoples as described above and thus possessed of a government representing the whole people belonging to the territory without distinction as to race, creed or color principles' (Principle 5, UNGA 1970b).

This clause of the Declaration on Friendly Relations affirms that the creation of an independent state constitutes an acceptable way of exercising the right to self-determination. Nevertheless, this is only possible against the will of the affected state, if the latter does not behave in accordance with the UN principles, that is, when it fails to provide to its citizens the opportunity to exercise the right of self-determination internally within its borders.

Despite the explicit reference to the possibility of creating an independent state, it is uncertain whether a Declaration has any binding power or whether it can be used as international law on how states should respond to separatist attempts. One point of contention is that 'the text of the Declaration on Friendly Relations is incomplete if viewed as a blueprint for world order. Too many issues are not covered; too many of those that are covered are dealt with in a vague manner' (Rosenstock 1971, 735). For example, who are the people that have this right, how is it going to be implemented, by whom and under what conditions. The legal value of the Declaration is undermined by this vagueness; the issue of the ambiguity of the 'people', for instance, is particularly problematic as a 'people' has been a judicially nonexistent entity, and as such they cannot be the possessor of a legal right (Fitzmaurice 1975, 761).

Second, the resolutions of the UNGA constitute recommendations that are not legally binding for states. The UN Charter states that 'the General Assembly shall initiate studies and make recommendations for the purpose of promoting international co-operation in the political field and encouraging the progressive development of international law and its codification' (UN Charter 1945). Thus, the General Assembly may influence the development and content of international law, but the decisions themselves do not constitute peremptory law (Sinclair 1994; Fitzmaurice 1975). Also, in meetings shortly before the signing of the Declaration, representatives of member states pointed out that the resolution provided 'guidelines' for the conduct of states, being 'recommendatory in nature' and not legally binding (UNGA 1970a).

Another document that has been widely used in secession studies is the decision of the Supreme Court of Canada (1998) on Reference *re* Secession of Quebec (among other, Van den Driest 2015; Yee 2010; Radan 2012). This ruling acknowledges the above UN Declaration on Friendly Relations and its clause on self-determination. In reference to this, it states that 'A right to external self-determination (which in this case potentially takes the form of the assertion of a right to unilateral secession) arises in only the most extreme of cases and, even then, under carefully defined circumstances' (article 126). Articles 132 and 133 define these extreme circumstances that would allow secession. Article 132 refers to the undisputed right of independence in the context of decolonization and article 133 mentions the right to external self-determination in cases of alien subjugation, domination, or exploitation outside the colonial context. However, the Court remained sceptical on other applications of the right to external self-determination outside the earlier-mentioned conditions. Article 134 recognizes that a number of commentators have further asserted that the right to self-determination may ground a right to unilateral secession as last resort in a third circumstance, that is, when people are blocked from the meaningful exercise of their right to self-determination internally. The Court, though, ruled that 'it remains unclear whether this third proposition actually reflects an established international law standard' (Supreme Court of Canada 1998, article 135). The court did not elaborate further on this specific provision, as it ruled that even if it existed it was not applicable in the case of Quebec. Thus, the Court neither rejected nor sanctioned the right to external self-determination as last resort maintaining the vagueness around it.

The Reference *re* Secession of Quebec has often been examined in combination with the ICJ's advisory opinion on the legality of Kosovo's UDI (Burri 2010; Summers 2014; Christakis 2011; Yee 2010). In the same vein with the Supreme Court of Canada, the ICJ resolved:

> Whether, outside the context of non-self-governing territories and peoples subject to alien subjugation, domination and exploitation, the international law of self-determination confers upon part of the population of an existing State a right to separate from that State is, however, a subject on which *radically different views* (emphasis added) were expressed by those taking part in the proceedings and expressing a position on the question. Similar differences existed regarding whether international law provides for a right of 'remedial secession' and, if so, in what circumstances. (ICJ 2010, §82)

The fact that radically different views were expressed on this question during the proceedings demonstrates the lack of any uniform legal opinion on remedial secession (Yee 2010). Furthermore, the opinion clarified that, although a number of participants in the proceedings regarded Kosovo's secession as a manifestation of the right of remedial secession, in almost every instance this was presented *only* (emphasis added) as a secondary argument (ICJ 2010, §82). In any case, the ICJ decided that 'issues relating to the extent of the right of self-determination and the existence of any right of "remedial secession" are beyond the scope of the question posed by the General Assembly' (ICJ 2010, §83) avoiding any further reference to this matter. Hence, the Court refrained from providing any justification that would endorse the existence of a general right to remedial secession.

The absence of a specific law or court decision that explicitly regulates secession led to diverse opinions regarding the existence and/or the applicability of remedial secession. These interpretations range from a complete denial of the existence of a right to remedial secession (Van den Driest 2015; Del Mar 2013; Vidmar 2010; Yee 2010) to its outright acceptance as an established right both in codified and in customary international law derived by state practice (Seymour 2007; Anderson 2013; Raič 2002). In the middle ground, Cassese (1995) claims that since it is not explicitly prohibited then secession may be implicitly authorized in the most exceptional circumstances, even if this has yet to become customary law, while Fisher (2015) argues that state practice has become more favorable to a right to remedial secession in selected cases. Sterio (2010) maintains that in theory there is a right for a group to secede if it had suffered major injustices. However, its application and the admittance of an entity in the international system depend on political considerations and the support of powerful states.

This chapter contributes to this debate from an international relations point of view focusing on state practice. The following section examines unilateral secessions, whether they employed remedial justifications in their declarations of independence and what was the outcome of their attempts. This will also inform the international law debate examining whether state practice towards secessionist attempts verifies the existence of a remedial right to secession as customary law.

UDIS AND THEIR OUTCOME

This section analyses the content and outcome of thirty-eight UDIs, proclaimed after 1970. This research focuses on declarations of independence because they constitute formal statements issued by separatists to announce to world states their intention to create their own independent state. They often constitute tactical moves making official appeals to world states to recognize the seceding entity (Armitage 2007). Therefore, they usually promote the reasons why they pursue independent statehood and why they are worthy for, and entitled to, it.

For case selection, this study used Florea's dataset (2014), expanded to 2017 with the use of Sambanis, Germann, and Schädel's (2018) and Griffiths and Wasser's (2019) datasets. Cases were selected according to secessionist type, including only unilateral secessions that proceeded to a declaration of independence. Based on the review of the relevant literature presented in the first section, this research coded for the following remedial secession elements: historical attachment to territory and previous annexation of that territory by the host state; past atrocities mounting at the level of ethnic cleansing or genocide and/or current threats to the physical safety of the group; discrimination; societal, economic, and political exclusion of the secession-seeking group; violations of status or agreement between host state and separatist entity; and secession as last resort when all other means have failed to resolve the conflict. All criteria carry an equal weight.

Findings

Table 2.1 presents a summary of the findings, showing whether separatists put forward remedial reasons as a strategy to promote their cause and what the outcome of the separatist attempt was (UN membership or not).

Table 2.1 shows that seventeen out of thirty-eight separatist movements, that is, 45% of the cases, claimed a historical attachment to territory that was unjustly annexed by the host state. Secession in such cases was demanded as restoration of statehood. The Supreme Council of the Republic of Latvia, for example, declared:

> The independent state of Latvia, proclaimed on November 18, 1918, was granted international recognition in 1920 and became a full member of the League of Nations in 1921. . . . Accordingly, the Republic of Latvia continues to exist *de jure* as a subject of international law and is recognized as such by more than 50 countries of the world. . . . Being determined to restore the free, democratic and independent Republic of Latvia *de facto*, the Supreme Council of the Latvian SSR resolves
>
> 1. To recognize the supremacy of the fundamental principles of international law over national law and to consider illegal the Treaty of August 23, 1939, between the USSR and Germany, and the subsequent termination of the sovereignty of the Republic of Latvia on June 17, 1940, which was the result of Soviet military aggression. . . .
> 2. To re-establish the authority of the Constitution of the Republic of Latvia, adopted by the Constitutional Assembly on February 15, 1922, in the entire territory of Latvia (Restoration of Independence 1990, 1–2).

In the same vein, Azawad proclaimed that 'in 1960, on the occasion of the granting of independence to West African peoples, France attached AZAWAD without its consent to the Malian state that France had just created'

Table 2.1. Unilateral Declarations of Independence and Their Outcome

Separatist region	Host state	Year of UDI	Occupation/ restoration of statehood	Past abuses	Threats to physical safety/acts of genocide	Discrimination/ exclusion	Violation of agreements	Last resort	UN membership
						Remedial secession in UDIs			
Bangladesh	Pakistan	1971		X	X	X	X		X
West Papua (Irian Jaya)	Indonesia	1971							
Bangsamoro Republik	Philippines	1974	X	X	X			X	
Cabinda	Angola	1975	X	X	X				
Aceh	Indonesia	1976	X	X	X	X		X	
Tamil Eelam	Sri Lanka	1976	X		X	X		X	
Western Sahara	Morocco	1976	X						
TRNC	Republic of Cyprus	1983		X	X	X	X	X	
Khalistan	India	1986			X				
Bougainville	Papua New Guinea	1990	X		X				
Abkhazia	USSR/ Georgia	1990							
Chechnya	USSR/Russia	1990	X	X					
Rehoboth Basters	Namibia	1990					X		
Croatia[i]	Yugoslavia	1991							X
Slovenia[ii]	Yugoslavia	1991							X

(Continued)

Table 2.1. (Continued)

	Case Studies			Remedial secession in UDIs					
Separatist region	Host state	Year of UDI	Occupation/ restoration of statehood	Past abuses	Threats to physical safety/acts of genocide	Discrimination/ exclusion	Violation of agreements	Last resort	UN membership
Kosovo	Yugoslavia	1991				X	X		
Latvia[iii]	USSR	1990	X						X
Lithuania[iv]	USSR	1990	X						X
Estonia[v]	USSR	1991	X		X				X
Nagorno Karabakh	Azerbaijan	1991		X	X				
Serbian Krajina	Croatia	1991							
Somaliland[vi]	Somalia	1991	X	X					
South Ossetia	Georgia	1991			X			X	
Transnistria	Moldova	1991	X					X	
Republika Srpska	Bosnia and Herzegovina	1992		X				X	
Awdal	Somalia	1995		X	X	X			
Anjouan	Comoros	1996							
Padania	Italy	1996				X	X		
Caprivi Strip	Namibia	1997	X		X	X		X	
Abkhazia	Georgia	1999	X		X				
East Turkistan	China	2004	X		X				
Kosovo	Serbia	2008		X					
Azawad	Mali	2012	X	X	X			X	

Donetsk	Ukraine	2014			X		
Lugansk	Ukraine	2014			X		
Ambazonia (Southern Cameroons)	Cameroun	2017	X	X		X	
Catalonia	Spain	2017			X		X
South Yemen	Yemen	2017		X	X		

[i] Croatia is included in the analysis, because it declared independence before Yugoslavia started to dissolve.
[ii] Slovenia declared independence before the dissolution of Yugoslavia.
[iii] Latvia declared independence and was admitted in the UN before the dissolution of USSR.
[iv] Lithuania declared independence and was admitted in the UN before the dissolution of USSR.
[v] Estonia declared independence and was admitted in the UN before the dissolution of USSR.
[vi] Data extracted from the Constitution of the Republic of Somaliland, incorporating the Declaration of Independence in its preamble.

(Declaration of Independence 2012, 1). Bougainville also condemned colonial and postcolonial practices of unjust annexation stating that

> Bougainville Island was politically separated from the Solomon Group of Islands and seeded [*sic*] to the German colony of New Guinea by an agreement made in 1886 between England and Germany, and was subsequently included in the Australian Trust Territory of Papua [and] New Guinea in 1918; Bougainville was then included in the Independent State of Papua New Guinea despite the objections of the people of Bougainville, on the 16th September 1975. (Declaration of Independence 1990, 1)

The next justification for remedial secession concerned gross human rights violations the separatist groups suffered in the past; thirteen movements (34%) claimed that secession would be a justified remedy to the scale of atrocities the host state committed. The Turkish Republic of Northern Cyprus (TRNC), for instance, claimed that

> the Greek Cypriot leadership has in the past tried to force a choice on the Turkish Cypriots between 'death or exile'. In order to eradicate totally the Turkish-Islamic presence in the island, numerous plans of aggression and massacre . . . against the Turkish Cypriot People were prepared. Ever since 1955, when the EOKA terrorist organization first launched its campaign of terror and violence, intimidation and extermination plans have been put into operation on many occasions in hundreds of Turkish Cypriot villages and in the Turkish Cypriot quarters of the towns. (Declaration of Independence 1983, 4)

Furthermore, eighteen cases (47%) referred to threats to physical safety at the time of the declaration of independence. For example, South Ossetia stated:

> On November 23, 1989, the Georgian government launched an undeclared war against the people of South Ossetia. The Ossetian people were subjected to political, economic, energy and information blockade. The media started a frenzied anti-Ossetian campaign with calls to abolish the autonomy of South Ossetia and drive them out of Georgia. All this was accompanied by terror against the Ossetian people, the burning of houses, the destruction of roads and railways. Since 1991, the Supreme Council and the Government of the Republic of Georgia have declared an open war against civilians, placing a stake on the physical destruction of the Ossetian people. The Georgian President, the Ministry of the Ministry of Internal Affairs and other representatives of the republic's leadership in all mass media, the population of Georgia was openly called for the physical elimination of Ossetians. (Declaration of Independence 1991, 1)

Similarly, Bangladesh accused the Pakistani government for 'levying an unjust war and committing genocide' (Proclamation of Independence 1971, 2) and South Cameroons said that 'the life of our people has been a life of tragedy, a life of injustice, a life of continuing oppression, a life of suffering, a life of sorrow, a life of rape, a life of tribulation and a life of death' (Proclamation Restoring Independence 2017, 1).

In twelve cases (32%), separatist groups mentioned discrimination in the form of economic, social, and political exclusion. Tamils accused Sri Lanka, among others, that

> successive Sinhalese governments since independence have always encouraged and fostered the aggressive nationalism of the Sinhalese people and have used their political power to the detriment of the Tamils by
>
> (a) Depriving one half of the Tamil people of their citizenship and franchise rights thereby reducing Tamil representation in Parliament,
> (b) Making Sinhala the only official language throughout Ceylon thereby placing the stamp of inferiority on the Tamils and the Tamil Language,
> (c) Giving the foremost place to Buddhism under the Republican constitution thereby reducing the Hindus, Christians, and Muslims to second class status in this Country,
> (d) Denying to the Tamils equality of opportunity in the spheres of employment, education, land alienation and economic life in general and starving Tamil areas of large scale industries and development schemes thereby seriously endangering their very existence in Ceylon (Tamils Declaration of Independence 1976).

More recently Catalonia claimed 'a profoundly unjust economic treatment, and linguistic and cultural discrimination' from the central government of Spain (Declaration of the Representatives of Catalonia 2017).

Furthermore, six cases (16%) declared that the host state violated previous agreements with the seceding entity. For example, Padania claimed that 'the Italian State has systematically annulled all forms of autonomy and self-government of Municipalities, Provinces and Regions' (Declaration of Independence 1996, 1), while the TRNC maintained that

> the establishment of the Republic of Cyprus as an independent State was based on the partnership of the Turkish Cypriot People and the Greek Cypriot People. This joint Republic, which was established through the agreement of the two national communities, has been deliberately undermined and destroyed by the Greek Cypriot Administration since 1963. (Declaration of Independence 1983, 1)

Finally, eleven cases (29%) referred to independence as being the last resort after all means to reach a mutual agreement with the host state had been tried and failed. Kosovo, for instance, declared independence after 'recalling the years of internationally-sponsored negotiations between Belgrade and

Pristina over the question of our future political status' and 'regretting that no mutually-acceptable status outcome was possible, in spite of the good-faith engagement of our leaders' (Declaration of Independence 2008, 1).

Overall, thirty-two out of thirty-eight UDIs (84%) made reference to a justified right to statehood according to at least one criterion of remedial secession. This finding shows, therefore, that the majority of separatist leaders used remedial justifications as a strategy to convince the international community to recognize the new polity. However, this tactic did not bring about the desired outcome: only six out of thirty-eight separatist cases achieved UN membership. Interestingly enough, two cases that achieved UN membership, Slovenia and Croatia, did not follow this tactic and made no appeal to remedial reasons in their declarations.

Slovenia and Croatia unilaterally declared independence from the former Yugoslavia in 1991, before Yugoslavia had begun to disintegrate. Slovenia declared independence on the basis of 'the fundamental principles of natural law, i.e., the right of the Slovene nation to self-determination' and the will of the people as expressed by the 'absolute majority in the plebiscite held' on the issue of independence (Slovenian Declaration of Independence 1991, 1). The Croatian Proclamation of Independence stressed the historical right of Croatia to independent statehood on this particular territory and the determination of the Croatian people 'to defend their independence and territorial integrity against any aggressor' (Croatian Proclamation of Independence 1991, §II). Croatia pre-emptively declared independence as a 'defense to repression and terrorism organized outside the borders of the Republic of Croatia' (Croatian Proclamation of Independence 1991, §II), expressing also the commitment to respect the rights of Serbs and other minorities living on its territory.

The European Community (EC) decided the recognition of the new states emerging from Yugoslavia at the extraordinary European Political Cooperation meeting of 16 December 1991, provided that they committed to respect the rule of law, democracy and human rights, protection of minorities, respect for inviolability of all frontiers, and peaceful resolution of conflicts (S/23293 1991). Being recognized by all the member states of the EC and by numerous other states, they were admitted to the UN on 22 May 1992. This was in accordance with the Badinter Commission and its opinions that Yugoslavia was in a process of dissolution and that its successor states would be its six republics, respecting the existing frontiers at the time of independence (Conference on Yugoslavia 1992). A remedial right to independence was mentioned neither by the EC nor by the Badinter Commission as a reason to justify international recognition.

Continuing to the Baltic States, Lithuania was the first to declare independence from the Soviet Union in March 1990 with the Act on the Re-Establishment of the State of Lithuania, nearly two years before the disintegration of the USSR. Despite being a case of occupation and subjugation and despite having a constitutional right to secession,[3] Lithuania's attempts to independence were fiercely opposed by the Soviet Union (Olcott 1990; Keller 1991) and were ignored by world states; more than a year after its declaration of independence, Lithuania had failed to attract international recognition (Kamm 1991).

Latvia announced the Restoration of Independence of the Republic of Latvia in March 1990 annulling Latvia's annexation to the Soviet Union in 1940 (Restoration of Independence 1990, 1). This act foresaw a transition period, so that a mutual agreement can be reached between Latvia and the USSR. After the coup of August 1991, Latvia officially proclaimed independence passing the Law on Statehood of the Republic of Latvia (Law on Statehood 1991, 1). In August 1991, Estonia also proclaimed independence, stating that 'the USSR coup posed a serious threat to Estonia and also made it impossible for Estonia to restore independence in bilateral negotiations' (Estonian National Independence 1991, 1).

All three Baltic States presented remedial reasons in their UDIs, that is, restoration of statehood after unjust annexation. This raised some international sympathy with world states expressing their support for the Republics' drive for independence; however, they refrained from granting official recognition. It was only after the failed coup of August 1991 and the certainty that the USSR would disintegrate that a domino of international recognitions began (Kamm 1991). Even then, however, their application for membership to the UN was only considered after the USSR consented in September 1991. The UN Security Council in its resolution proposing the acceptance of the three Baltic States affirmed that 'the independence of the Republic of Estonia, the Republic of Latvia and the Republic of Lithuania was restored peacefully, by means of dialogue, with the consent of the parties concerned' (UNSC 1991), stressing, therefore, the agreed nature of their secession, rather than any remedial reasons.

Similarly, Bangladesh entered the UN only after it obtained Pakistan's approval. Despite the well-reported atrocities that were committed in Bangladesh (Bass 2014), no state other than India had recognized Bangladesh before the Pakistani forces surrendered in December 1971 (Crawford 1999, 96). After its secession, China vetoed its application for membership into the UN accusing the Soviet Union and India for launching a war of aggression against Pakistan, misinterpreting, distorting, and violating the principles of the UN Charter (S/PV.1660 1972). Eventually, Bangladesh was accepted in the UN, but only after Pakistan recognized it first in 1974, allowing China to lift the veto.

Thus, the findings show that the separatists' strategy of putting forward justifications of remedial secession was insufficient to convince the UN

member states, and especially all five permanent Security Council members, to bypass the host state and recognize the new polity. Even for cases
that had achieved a significant number of recognitions, such as Bangladesh,
UN membership was withheld until its host state recognized it first. On the
contrary, Slovenia and Croatia were accepted in the UN even without following the strategy of appealing to remedial reasons. Slovenia and Croatia
mainly appealed to the principle of self-determination and their commitment
to democratic values, and the EC recognized both of them with the condition
that they adhered to these principles. Finally, even though the Soviet Union
was in a course of disintegration and Lithuania, Latvia, and Estonia provided
remedial secession justifications, the UN did not consider their application
until the USSR consented.

CONCLUSION

This chapter showed that separatist leaders invoke remedial justifications as
a strategy to convince the international community to grant them international recognition. However, this tactic is not correlated with UN admission.
Furthermore, recognition resolutions issued by the UN Security Council do
not refer to remedial justifications. The vast majority of the examined UDIs
appealed to at least one element of remedial secession in order to convince
world states to recognize them. The remedial reasons included unjust annexation or occupation, past abuses against the seceding population, threats to
physical safety, discrimination or exclusion, violations of previous agreements between the host state and the separatist region, and secession as last
resort when other attempts to resolve the conflict had either been ignored by
the host state or failed. Six out of thirty-eight unilateral secessions resulted in
UN membership; however, none of them because of remedial justifications
they provided. The approval of the host state was necessary for the attainment of UN membership for the cases of Lithuania, Latvia, Estonia, and
Bangladesh, while Slovenia and Croatia were admitted in the UN after the
Badinter Commission resolved that Yugoslavia was in a state of dissolution
and therefore there was no state to provide consent.

This leads to the conclusion that there are no normative or moral considerations that lead to international recognition. It is rather considerations of
stability in the affected regions, as the cases of Croatia and Slovenia show,
and the geopolitical timing of the secession as evident by the case of the three
Baltic States. The case of Bangladesh demonstrated the effect of global power
rivalry on withholding recognition and the importance of host state's consent for its attainment. Therefore, the strategy of appealing to human rights
violations can be effective up to a certain point – that of raising sympathy.

However, for international recognition to happen, the seceding entity has either to gain support of all five permanent UN member states or to achieve the consent of the host state.

These findings contribute also to the legal debate around remedial secession, as they show that remedial secession has not turned into customary law. State practice remains unaltered: borders do not change without the consent of the host state, and the only way to recognition is still through decolonization, dissolution of states, or consent of the host state (Griffiths 2017). Remedial reasons and human rights violations may produce the vocal sympathy of world states, publicly condemning violence and atrocities committed by the host state. This, however, does not extend to official state recognition and the direct undermining of the principles of territorial integrity and sovereignty.

NOTES

1. Except for Greece, Cyprus, Spain, Romania, and Slovakia.
2. The full name of the declaration is United Nations Declaration on Principles of International Law concerning Friendly Relations and Co-operation among States in accordance with the Charter of the United Nations.
3. Article 72/1977 of the USSR Constitution stated that 'each Union Republic shall retain the right freely to secede from the USSR' (Constitution USSR 1977).

REFERENCES

Act on Re-establishment. 1990. *Act on the Re-Establishment of the State of Lithuania.* Vilnius: The Supreme Council of the Republic of Lithuania.

Anderson, Glen. 2013. 'Unilateral Non-Colonial Secession in International Law and Declaratory General Assembly Resolutions: Textual Content and Legal Effects'. *Denver Journal of International Law and Policy* 41(1): 345–395.

Armitage, David. 2007. *The Declaration of Independence.* Cambridge, MA: Harvard University Press.

Arp, Bjorn. 2010. 'ICJ Advisory Opinion on the Accordance with International Law of the Unilateral Declaration of Independence in Respect of Kosovo and the International Protection of Minorities'. *German Law Journal* 11(8): 847–866.

Bass, Gary. 2014. *The Blood Telegram: Nixon, Kissinger and a Forgotten Genocide.* London: C. Hurst and Co.

Beran, Harry. 1984. 'A Liberal Theory of Secession'. *Political Studies* 32(1): 21–31.

Birch, Anthony H. 1984. 'Another Liberal Theory of Secession'. *Political Studies* 32(4): 596–602.

Bolton, Grace, and Gezim Visoka. 2010. 'Remedial Secession or Earned Sovereignty?' *South East European Studies at Oxford Occasional Paper* 11(10): 1–23.

Brilmayer, Lea. 1991. 'Secession and Self-Determination: A Territorial Interpretation'. *Yale Journal of International Law* 16(1): 177–202.

Brilmayer, Lea. 2015. 'Secession and the Two Types of Territorial Claims'. *ILSA Journal of International and Comparative Law* 21: 325–331.

Buchanan, A. 1997. 'Theories of Secession'. *Philosophy and Public Affairs* 26(1): 31–61.

Buchanan, Allen. 1991. *Secession, the Morality of Political Divorce from Fort Sumter to Lithuania and Quebec*. Boulder, London: Westview Press.

Buchanan, Allen. 2004. *Justice, Legitimacy and Self-Determination*. Oxford: Oxford University Press.

Burri, Thomas. 2010. 'The Kosovo Opinion and Secession: The Sounds of Silence and Missing Links'. *German Law Journal* 11(08): 881–889.

Cassese, Antonio. 1995. *Self-Determination of Peoples, a Legal Reappraisal*. Cambridge: Cambridge University Press.

Catala, Amandine. 2013. 'Remedial Theories of Secession and Territorial Justification'. *Journal of Social Philosophy* 44(1): 74–94. doi: 10.1111/josp.12011.

Christakis, Theodore. 2011. 'The ICJ Advisory Opinion on Kosovo: Has International Law Something to Say about Secession?' *Leiden Journal of International Law* 24: 73–86. doi: doi:10.1017/S0922156510000609.

Coggins, Bridget. 2014. *Power Politics and State Formation in the Twentieth Century: The Dynamics of Recognition*. New York: Cambridge University Press.

Conference on Yugoslavia. 1992. 'Conference on Yugoslavia Arbitration Committee' *International Legal Materials* 31: 1494–1526.

Copp, David. 1998. 'International Law and Morality in the Theory of Secession'. *The Journal of Ethics* 2: 219–245.

Coppieters, B. 2003. 'War and Secession: A Moral Analysis of the Georgian – Abkhaz Conflict'. In *Contextualing Secession*, edited by B. Coppieters and R. Sakwa. Oxford: Oxford University Press, 187–212.

Costa, Josep. 2003. 'On Theories of Secession: Minorities, Majorities and the Multinational State'. *Critical Review of International Social and Political Philosophy* 6(2): 63–90. doi: 10.1080/1369823051000170276.3.

Crawford, James. 1999. 'State Practice and International Law in Relation to Secession'. *British Yearbook of International Law* 69(1): 85–117.

Crawford, James. 2006. *The Creation of States in International Law*. New York: Oxford University Press.

Croatian Proclamation of Independence. 1991. *Deklaracija o proglašenju suverene i samostalne Republike Hrvatske*. Zagreb: Sabor Republike Hrvatske.

Cunningham, Kathleen Gallagher. 2014. *Inside the Politics of Self-Determination*. Oxford: Oxford University Press.

Declaration of Independence. 1983. *Declaration of Independence of the Turkish Republic of Northern Cyprus*. Lefkoşa: Turkish Cypriot Parliament.

Declaration of Independence. 1990. *Declaration of Independence Republic of Bougainville*. Bougainville: Francis Ona.

Declaration of Independence. 1991. *Декларация о независимости Республики Южная Осетия* (*Declaration of Independence of the Republic of South Ossetia*). Tskhinvali: Supreme Council of the Republic of South Ossetia.

Declaration of Independence. 1996. *Dichiarazione di Indipendenza e Sovranità' della Padania* (*Declaration of Independence and Sovereignty of Padania*). Venice: Lega Nord per l'Indipendenza della Padania.

Declaration of Independence. 2008. *Kosovo Declaration of Independence*. Pristina: Assembly of Kosovo.

Declaration of Independence. 2012. *Declaration of Independence of Azawad*. Gao: National Movement for the Liberation of Azawad.

Declaration of the Representatives of Catalonia. 2017. *Declaració dels Representants de Catalunya* (*Declaration of the Representatives of Catalonia*). Barcelona: The Catalan Parliament.

Del Mar, Katherine. 2013. 'The Myth of Remedial Secession'. In *Statehood and Self-Determination: Reconciling Tradition and Modernity in International Law*, edited by Duncan French. Cambridge: Cambridge University Press, 79–108.

Estonian National Independence. 1991. *Estonian Supreme Council Decision on the Estonian National Independence*. Tallinn: Supreme Council of the Republic of Estonia.

Fisher, Steven R. 2015. 'Towards "Never Again": Searching for a Right to Remedial Secession under Extant International Law'. *Buffalo Human Rights Law Review* 22: 261–296.

Fitzmaurice, Gerald. 1975. 'The Future of Public International Law and of the International Legal System in the Circumstances of Today'. *International Relations* 5(1): 743–775. doi: 10.1177/004711787500500101.

Florea, Adrian. 2014. 'De Facto States in International Politics (1945–2011): A New Data Set'. *International Interactions* 40(5): 788–811.

Griffiths, Ryan D. 2017. 'Admission to the Sovereignty Club: The Past, Present, and Future of the International Recognition Regime'. *Territory, Politics, Governance* 5(2): 177–189.

Griffiths, Ryan D., and Louis M. Wasser. 2019. 'Does Violent Secessionism Work?' *Journal of Conflict Resolution*, 63(5): 1310–1336.

ICJ. 2010. *Accordance with International Law of the Unilateral Declaration of Independence in Respect of Kosovo*. The Hague: International Court of Justice.

Jenne, Erin K., Stephen M. Saideman, and Will Lowe. 2007. 'Separatism as a Bargaining Posture: The Role of Leverage in Minority Radicalization'. *Journal of Peace Research* 44(5): 539–558. doi: 10.1177/0022343307080853.

Kamm, Henry. 1991. *Soviet Turmoil; Yeltsin, Repaying a Favor, Formally Recognizes Estonian and Latvian Independence*, Tallinn: New York Times, p. 17.

Keller, Bill. 1991. 'Soviet Tanks Roll in Lithuania; 11 Dead'. *The New York Times* [cited 27 March 2017. http://www.nytimes.com/1991/01/13/world/soviet-tanks-roll-in-lithuania-11-dead.html?pagewanted=all.

Ker-Lindsay, James. 2012. *The Foreign Policy of Counter Secession*. Oxford: Oxford University Press.

Law on Statehood. 1991. *Law on the Statehood of the Republic of Latvia*. Riga: Supreme Council of the Latvian SSR.

Lemke, Douglas, and Jeff Carter. 2016. 'Birth Legacies, State Making, and War'. *Journal of Politics* 78(2): 497–512. doi: 10.1086/684631.

Mancini, Susanna. 2008. 'Rethinking the Boundaries of Democratic Secession: Liberalism, Nationalism, and the Right of Minorities to Self-Determination'. *International Journal of Constitutional Law* 6 (3–4): 553–584.

Margalit, A., and J. Raz. 1990. 'National Self-Determination'. *Journal of Philosophy* LXXXVII: 439–461.

Miller, David. 1997. 'Secession and the Principle of Nationality'. *Canadian Journal of Philosophy* 26 (sup1): 261–282.

Moore, Margaret, ed. 1998. *National Self-Determination and Secession*. New York: Oxford University Press.

Olcott, Martha Brill. 1990. 'The Lithuanian Crisis'. *Foreign Affairs* 69(3): 30–46.

Proclamation of Independence. 1971. *The Proclamation of Independence of Bangladesh*. Mujibnagar: Constituent Assembly of Bangladesh.

Proclamation Restoring Independence. 2017. *Proclamation Restoring the Independence of the Former British Trust Territory of the Southern Cameroons and Asserting Its Sovereign Statehood*. Buea: The Governing Council of the Southern Cameroons/Ambazonia Consortium United Front.

Radan, Peter. 2012. 'Secessionist Referenda in International and Domestic Law'. *Nationalism and Ethnic Politics* 18(1): 8–21. doi: 10.1080/13537113.2012.654083.

Raič, David. 2002. *Statehood and the Law of Self-Determination*. Vol. 43. The Hague: Martinus Nijhoff Publishers.

Restoration of Independence. 1990. *Declaration of the Supreme Council of the Latvian SSR of the Restoration of Independence of the Republic of Latvia*. Riga: Supreme Council of the Latvian SSR.

Rosenstock, Robert. 1971. 'Declaration of Principles of International Law Concerning Friendly Relations: A Survey'. *American Journal of International Law* 65: 713–735.

S/23293. 1991. *Declaration on Yugoslavia*. Brussels: Extraordinary EPC Ministerial Meeting.

S/PV.1660. 1972. *Security Council Official Records*. New York: United Nations.

Sambanis, Nicholas, Micha Germann, and Andreas Schädel. 2018. 'SDM: A New Data Set on Self-Determination Movements with an Application to the Reputational Theory of Conflict'. *Journal of Conflict Resolution* 62(3): 656–686. doi: 10.1177/0022002717735364.

Seymour, Michel. 2007. 'Secession as a Remedial Right'. *Inquiry: An Interdisciplinary Journal of Philosophy* 50(4): 395–423. doi: 10.1080/00201740701491191.

Shelef, Nadav G., and Yael Zeira. 2017. 'Recognition Matters! UN State Status and Attitudes toward Territorial Compromise'. *Journal of Conflict Resolution* 61(3): 537–563. doi: 10.1177/0022002715595865.

Simon, Thomas W. 2011. 'Remedial Secession: What the Law Should Have Done, from Katanga to Kosovo'. *Georgia Journal of International and Comparative Law* 40(1): 105–174.

Sinclair, Ian. 1994. 'The Significance of the Friendly Relations Declaration'. In *The United Nations and the Principles of International Law*, edited by Vaughan Lowe and Colin Warbrick. London: Routledge, 1–32.

Slovenian Declaration of Independence. 1991. *Declaration of Independence*. Ljubljana: Government of the Republic of Slovenia.

Sterio, Milena. 2010. 'On the Right to External Self-Determination: Selfistans, Secession, and the Great Powers' Rule'. *Minnesota Journal of International Law* 19(1): 137–176.

Summers, James. 2014. 'Kosovo'. In *Self-Determination and Secession in International Law*, edited by Christian Walter, Antje Von Ungern-Sternberg, and Kavus Abushov. Oxford: Oxford University Press, 235–254.

Supreme Court of Canada. 1998. *Reference re Secession of Quebec.*

Tamils Declaration of Independence. 1976. *Tamils Declaration of Independence (Vaddukoddai Resolution).* Vaddukoddai: Tamil United Liberation Front.

UN. 2005. 'The Responsibility to Protect Office of the Special Adviser on the Prevention of Genocide 2005'. http://www.un.org/en/preventgenocide/adviser/responsibility.shtml.

UN Charter. 1945. *Charter of the United Nations.* http://www.un.org/en/documents/charter/index.shtml.

UNGA. 1970a. *A/C .6/SR.1178. 25th Session United Nations General Assembly.*

UNGA. 1970b. *A/RES/25/2625 Declaration on Principles of International Law concerning Friendly Relations and Co-operation among States in accordance with the Charter of the United Nations.* http://www.un-documents.net/a25r2625.htm.

UNSC. 1991. *Resolution 711.* United Nations Security Council.

USSR. 1977. *Constitution of the Union of Soviet Socialist Republics. Adopted at the Seventh (Special) Session of the Supreme Soviet of the USSR, Ninth Convocation.* http://www.departments.bucknell.edu/russian/const/77cons03.html.

Van den Driest, Simone F. 2015. 'Crimea's Separation from Ukraine: An Analysis of the Right to Self-Determination and (Remedial) Secession in International Law'. *Netherlands International Law Review* 62(3): 329–363.

Vidmar, Jure. 2010. 'Remedial Secession in International Law: Theory and (Lack of) Practice'. *St Antony's International Review* 6(1): 37–56.

Walter, Barbara F. 2006. 'Building Reputation: Why Governments Fight Some Separatists but Not Others'. *American Journal of Political Science* 50(2): 313–331. doi: 10.1111/j.1540–5907.2006.00186.x.

Wellman, Ch. H. 2005. *A Theory of Secession.* New York: Cambridge University Press.

Yee, Sienho. 2010. 'Notes on the International Court of Justice (Part 4): The Kosovo Advisory Opinion'. *Chinese Journal of International Law* 9(4): 763–782. doi: 10.1093/chinesejil/jmq033.

Chapter 3

Do Parent State Strategies Matter in Resolving Secessionist Conflicts with *De Facto* States?

Eiki Berg and Scott Pegg

INTRODUCTION

De facto states are secessionist entities that control territory, provide governance, secure popular support, and persist over extended periods of time, but whose self-proclaimed sovereignty is not recognized by the international community of sovereign states (Pegg 1998). They are a small subset of the much larger category of secessionist movements, distinguished mainly by their higher degrees of territorial control, state capacity, and persistence. Although 'the demand for independence remains a common feature of international life' (Griffiths 2015, 734), *de facto* states are much rarer entities. Caspersen (2012, 12), for example, identifies fifteen *de facto* states in existence since 1991, plus the two borderline cases of Kosovo and Taiwan. Seven of her cases (nine, if including Kosovo and Taiwan) are still operational today.

In studying *de facto* states, scholars can focus on their internal dynamics or direct their attention towards their relations with patron states (their supporters or backers, like Russia for Abkhazia) or with parent states (the widely recognized sovereign states they are trying to secede from, like Azerbaijan for Nagorno-Karabakh). The viability of *de facto* states in the context of significant dependence on patron state diplomatic, economic, and military support has been extensively explored (Broers 2013; Pegg 2017). Ker-Lindsay's (2012) seminal work usefully directed scholarly attention away from secessionist movements and towards the counter-secessionist strategies of the sovereign parent states they want to separate from.

This study contributes to the small but growing literature on parent states by addressing the question, 'Do parent state strategies matter in resolving secessionist conflicts with de facto states?' At first glance, this might seem like an unnecessary question to address because parent states can decisively resolve conflicts with *de facto* states in two main ways. First, parent states can resolve secessionist conflicts through forcible eradication. In the realm of *de facto* states, this strategy has been pursued successfully by Croatia (Serbian Krajina, 1995), Russia (Chechnya, 1999), and Sri Lanka (Tamil Eelam, 2009). The humanitarian costs of such a strategy can be catastrophic, as seen most recently in Tamil Eelam (Human Rights Watch 2009). Yet the diplomatic and economic costs for Sri Lanka were quite minimal since the international community's prioritization of respect for sovereignty and territorial integrity typically means that 'successful efforts to retake secessionist territory have produced relatively little by way of criticism' (Ker-Lindsay 2012, 57).

Second, parent states can also resolve secessionist conflicts decisively by allowing secessionists to leave. In terms of *de facto* states, this strategy has been pursued by Ethiopia (Eritrea, 1993) and Sudan (South Sudan, 2011). International practice has been consistent in demonstrating that if the parent state recognizes the *de facto* state, widespread sovereign recognition from other states follows. While there is sustained pessimism within the *de facto* state literature about the prospects for parent states willingly recognizing *de facto* states (Pegg 1998; Geldenhuys 2009; Caspersen 2012), parent states can accommodate secessionist demands if they choose to do so. Yet most parent states avoid both these options. They are unwilling to permit secession and unable to forcibly eradicate well-ensconced secessionist movements. Instead, they place themselves somewhere in the middle of this continuum. This is the territory we investigate. Leaving aside forcible eradication and allowing secessionists to leave, we examine a variety of different strategies that parent states have pursued in dealing with *de facto* states.

Specifically, we investigate four different parent state strategies that have all been pursued in recent years: (1) open engagement (Moldova), (2) tentative engagement (Georgia), (3) isolation/rejection with limited capacity to enforce it (Somalia), and (4) isolation/active sanctions (Cyprus). These four strategies are archetypes or models and not precise representations. They are also not cast in stone. Parent states can shift their emphasis over time and some of them, like Georgia, seem torn between isolationist and integrative impulses.

The central argument advanced in this study is that despite wide variation in parent state strategies, none of these conflicts have been resolved and all the respective *de facto* states have now been in existence for twenty-five years or more. Continued existence as a *de facto* state – neither advancing to widely recognized sovereignty nor being enticed or forced to reintegrate into the parent state – seems the safest prediction. As the explanation for this cannot be found in the diversity of parent state strategies pursued, it must lie elsewhere in internal *de facto* state dynamics, external support from patron states, or the larger international normative environment. We turn first to detailed discussions of each of our four cases of parent state strategies.

MOLDOVA: OPEN ENGAGEMENT

In contrast to many other parent states' approaches, Moldova is more receptive to allowing links between the Transnistrian Moldovan Republic (TMR) and the outside world. The conflict between the two sides of the River Dniester has never 'frozen' intercommunal ties. Family and social connections between the two communities have been carved into ethnic hybridity and multilingualism. There have been no restrictions set on the movement of people from the parent state to the secessionist territories or vice versa. Entry into the TMR from either Moldova proper or Ukraine is visa-free and subject to relatively mild border regulations in designated checkpoints. Transnistrians are equally served by the international airports of Chisinau or Odessa, given that they travel with 'recognized' documents. With some reservations, the *Dniester Valley Security Zone* has not prevented Chisinau residents from registering their cars in Tiraspol nor banned the Moldovan national football team from playing some of their international home matches at Transnistria's Sheriff Stadium.

Harnessing these bonds and networks has been a primary objective for most external actors in Moldova (Roubanis, Hatay, and Baltag 2013, 113), including contacts established with *de facto* state authorities. When the U.S. ambassador asked whether Chisinau would welcome a U.S. initiative to meet with the TMR's President Igor Smirnov, he received a reply from Foreign Minister Andrei Stratan demonstrating full confidence that any such initiative undertaken by the U.S. ambassador would be to the benefit of Moldova (WikiLeaks cable, Chisinau 2008–04–09). This reflects the Moldovan approach to the TMR which seems to be driven by a cost-benefit analysis rather than the invocation of sacrosanct norms and principles of international law on sovereignty and territorial integrity as pursued by other parent states. All political parties agree on negotiations as the only method available to reach a settlement while excluding the use of force or economic sanctions (Strǎuțiu, Munteanu, and Șpechea 2017).

The alternatives to a clear-cut engagement policy, such as setting up a hard boundary with the TMR and/or denying their enterprises access to external markets are rejected because they would entrench the separation between the parent state and the *de facto* state and leave little room for manoeuver (Cristescu and Matveev 2011). What is more, the Moldovan government does not depict Transnistria as being under Russian occupation, even though it demands a full military withdrawal of Russian troops from this contested territory (Coppieters 2018). In 2011, Chisinau authorities announced a 'small steps policy' in relations with Tiraspol with the aim to 'raise the level of confidence between Chisinau and Tiraspol, in this way creating the space required for a final political settlement of the Transnistrian conflict' (Berbeca 2013, 57). The flipside of this coin, critics would say, is that the TMR has been able to exit from international isolation, develop relationships with Moldova based on parity, and thus strengthen the secessionist cause.

For example, in the economic sector, Transnistrians have been able to export goods with stamps bearing the inscription 'Republic of Moldova, Tiraspol Customs' since 1996, as part of a package deal in the conflict resolution process. Moreover, based on provisions of the so-called Primakov Memorandum from May 1997, Chisinau recognized Transnistria's right to 'establish and maintain their own international contacts in the economic, scientific-technical and cultural domains' (Berbeca 2013, 60). Since 2006, new stamps have been granted only to those TMR companies registered as legal entities in Chisinau (Berg and Toomla 2009).

Transnistria, being legally part of Moldova, has recently benefited from a European Union (EU) autonomous trade preferences regime that offers favourable access to the EU market. About 30% to 50% of TMR exports go to the EU (mainly textiles, metal products, energy, and footwear) with low tariffs, while Transnistria can maintain its own higher import tariffs on certain products (Ivan 2014). Yet future trade relations between the EU and the TMR will be covered under the Deep and Comprehensive Free Trade Agreement (DCFTA), which would imply, inter alia, adopting significant pieces of EU/Moldovan legislation (Plăcintă 2017, 65). The full implementation of DCFTA would require a higher level of control and enforcement of rules by Moldovan authorities, which will not sit well with *de facto* state authorities (Ivan 2014).

Moldova has also demonstrated unusual tolerance towards secessionists in civil matters. The parent state authorities have allowed Transnistrians to apply for national identification documents (Gvidiani 2017). They have used EU visa liberalization as an incentive to make Moldovan citizenship more attractive to Transnistrians. Clear steps have been taken in reconnecting telecommunication networks, recognizing Transnistrian university diplomas and car number plates, while reaffirming a special status for Transnistria within Moldova (OSCE 2016). It has even not been a problem to provide a 'safe third country' for the TMR's ex-president Yevgeniy Shevchuk and his wife, ex-foreign minister Nina Shtanski, in June 2017, after they faced criminal charges for corruption (Racheva 2017). In November 2017, the parties reopened the bridge over the River Dniester, which had been blown up twenty-five years earlier during the war. However, by all accounts, this open engagement practised by the parent state has not brought the two sides of the conflict any closer and Moldova remains divided. Clear majorities of Moldovans want the reintegration of Transnistria into their state, while clear majorities of Transnistrians prefer integration into Russia.

GEORGIA: TENTATIVE ENGAGEMENT

Georgia initially did not have a specific strategy for dealing with its breakaway regions other than simply enabling or restricting interactions on an *ad hoc* basis. The Shevardnadze government adopted a relatively tolerant attitude. The more the Russian government began to impose sanctions on Abkhazia, effectively closing Abkhazia's northern border, shutting down 'lifelines' with local northern Caucasus sympathizers, and interrupting electricity flows throughout 1995 and 1996 (Hopf 2005, 229–230), the less Georgia seemed to be concerned about its own isolationist measures. After 1996, peacekeeping checkpoints were scaled back and trade between Abkhazia/South Ossetia and Georgia took off. The fact that the Ergneti market in South Ossetia provided a survival strategy for locals in the conflict zone and the Enguri power station in Abkhazia supplied Georgia with energy justified not pushing too hard against *de facto* state authorities.

Things started to change when Mikheil Saakashvili came to power in 2003. His election signified a shift towards a proactive reintegration agenda. On the one hand, Saakashvili aimed to rebuild Georgia's military strength, so it could provide leverage vis-à-vis the *de facto* state authorities; on the other hand, he sought to attract ordinary people in the breakaway regions with economic opportunities (Toal 2017, 144). There was also a third approach of creating parallel structures which gave 'localized political form to Georgia's aspiration for "regime change"' in areas under the control of the *de facto* state authorities (Toal 2017, 152), first relocating the Tbilisi-based Abkhazian government-in-exile to Upper Kodori Gorge in Abkhazia in 2006, and then one year later establishing a 'Provisional Administration of South Ossetia' in the region with the capital in Kurta village, a few kilometres northeast of Tskhinvali (Toal 2008, 680).

Although Saakashvili's government assisted the breakaway regions economically and provided them with humanitarian aid (International Crises Group 2004), the military logic of 'restoring law and order' in the lost territories gained more prominence. Inspired by Croatia's Operation Storm (1995) that eradicated Serbian Krajina and driven by a miscalculation that a forceful reintegration of the secessionist entities had been blessed by the West, Saakashvili swallowed a provocative hook on 7 August 2008, just to find out five days later that Tbilisi had lost not only the August 2008 war but also full control over the breakaway regions.

After the August 2008 war, Georgia elaborated its own policy towards Abkhazia and South Ossetia which was torn between elements of isolation and engagement. This policy rested on the 'Law on Occupied Territories' (2008), the 'Strategy on Occupied Territories: Engagement through Cooperation' (2010), the 'Action Plan for Engagement on the Implementation of the Strategy' (2010), and the 'Modalities for Conducting Activities in the Occupied Territories' (2010). It acknowledged that Russia had occupied Abkhazia and South Ossetia, and that ongoing annexation complicated the reconciliation and peaceful reintegration of the occupied territories into Georgia's constitutional ambit. Then it enforced a special legal regime which included limitations on free migration and restricted all possible economic activities and real estate transactions with the secessionists.

It did not take long before the previous isolationist approach became more nuanced. The Georgian government introduced a new strategy on engagement through cooperation which explored legal avenues for interactions with its breakaway regions while ensuring that these activities promoted eventual deoccupation. The proposed strategy relied on a status-neutral liaison mechanism to facilitate communication among the Georgian government, *de facto* state authorities, and the voluntary associations operating there. The idea was to create incentives for the populations currently residing in Abkhazia and South Ossetia, given that they applied for a 'neutral identification card' which would allow the holder to claim all the social benefits available to Georgian citizens, conduct business in Georgia, and seek employment. This card enabled the holder to acquire a 'neutral travel document', allowing travelling abroad.

Somewhat surprisingly, the Georgian government has encouraged the United States to get more actively involved in Abkhazia. For example, in a letter to the U.S. ambassador, Minister for Reintegration Temur Yakobashvili explained, 'Our policy towards the population on the occupied territories will be proactive with the special emphasis to establish and to reinforce ties between returning and receiving communities' (WikiLeaks cable, Tbilisi 2009–09–08). Although essentially permissive, the promoted engagement remained very restrictive regarding the activities of international organizations and nongovernmental organizations. This reflected a fundamental dilemma between isolation and engagement where, on the one hand, Georgia feared that a more open and accommodative approach towards these two entities could devolve into 'creeping recognition' and, on the other hand, it worried that stigmatization (wording such as 'occupied territories') resulted in Abkhazia's even greater dependence on Russia.

Today, bilateral Georgian-Abkhazian confidence-building projects that include meetings, seminars, trainings, and study visits of various professional groups take place only on neutral territories. This obviously creates serious obstacles to the institutionalization of cross-border activities and arguably pushes Abkhazia and South Ossetia deeper into Russia's embrace. People from the breakaway regions can cross the administrative boundary line only with Georgian passports or status-neutral passports. From November 2011 until February 2016, Georgian authorities issued 43 status-neutral travel documents and 298 status-neutral IDs (personal interview, Tbilisi 12 October 2016), which is too little to support any kind of sustained or serious engagement discourse. Although Russian-Georgian tensions have eased somewhat, the prospects for a negotiated settlement in Abkhazia and South Ossetia appear bleak. To date, Georgia has neither been able to offer sufficient incentives nor been able to apply enough pressure to unfreeze this conflict.

SOMALIA: SOLATION/REJECTION WITH LIMITED CAPACITY TO ENFORCE IT

Somaliland is unique among *de facto* states in that, for much of its existence, it has not had a viable parent state to contend with. In the immediate post-Siad Barre era, rival clan-based militias fought for control of Mogadishu, while the Somaliland government sought to establish itself and gradually extend its control over key assets like Berbera's port and Hargeisa's airport in a series of civil wars which ended in 1997 in central Somaliland. Somalia, however, remained without a formal government until 2000 when the Transitional National Government (TNG) was formed. It soon proved entirely ineffective at establishing control in Somalia. Bradbury (2008, 199) observes that it 'failed to establish meaningful authority further than a few kilometers around Mogadishu', and Bryden (2004, 178) notes that 'by mid-2002 it had become clear that the TNG existed in name only'.

Its inability to provide governance did not, however, prevent the TNG from quickly being accepted as the legitimate sovereign government of all pre-1991 Somalia. A few days after taking office, Somali president Abdiqasim Salad Hassan travelled to New York to attend the United Nations (UN) Millennium Summit. In the view of one senior UN official, 'Abdiqasim's uncontested attendance of the summit was a "negative readmission procedure" – nobody objected, and the silence was taken for consent' (Anonymous 2002, 254). Although Abdiqasim had not appointed a government and did not control any territory, he attended summits of the Arab League, the Intergovernmental Authority on Development (IGAD), the Organization of African Unity, and the Organization of Islamic Conference (OIC). Somalia, thus, 'could justifiably claim universal acceptance' (ibid., 254).

The TNG was replaced by the Transitional Federal Government (TFG) which took seven months to relocate from Kenya to Somalia and did not enter

Mogadishu until after Ethiopia invaded Somalia in 2006 (Bradbury 2008, 200). Menkhaus (2014, 159) concludes that 'After seven years in existence, the TFG was still unable to exercise control over most of the capital Mogadishu, . . . and had almost no functional civil service'. Yet the TFG was again quickly embraced by the international community as Somalia's legitimate government and admitted into all relevant regional and international organizations (Bradbury 2008, 200).

Somalia's 'transitional' governments seemingly came to an end with the 2012 London Conference, out of which emerged the Somali Federal Government (SFG). In addition to continuing the diplomatic successes of its transitional predecessors with membership in all relevant international organizations, the SFG was also formally recognized by the United States in January 2013, the first time the United States had recognized a Somali national government since 1991. Still, the SFG 'has yet to develop even a modest capacity to exercise its authority over territory or deliver basic security and social services', and it 'has been able to remain in Mogadishu mainly because of the protection it receives from African Union peacekeepers' (Menkhaus 2014, 163).

Somaliland has certainly benefitted from the manifest dysfunctionality in Mogadishu since 1991. As Kolstø (2006, 732–733) explains, 'As long as the parent state is mired in political chaos and economic misery, it is not only prevented from launching a new war to recapture the lost territory but also fails to attract the population of the breakaway region'. The quality of Somaliland's democracy, its relative peace and stability, its lower rates of multidimensional poverty, lower average levels of deprivation, and dramatically lower levels of violence experienced, all compare favourably to south-central Somalia (Pegg and Kolstø 2015, 199). Still, Somalia's manifest failure to establish a viable state has not hindered its ability to act internationally. As Geldenhuys (2009, 146) observes, 'Somalia has retained its juridical statehood – a feature that has allowed it to effectively veto Somaliland's progress to confirmed statehood'.

Somalia has used its juridical statehood to deny Somaliland observer status at the African Union and IGAD. Various UN agencies work in Somaliland but only under the guise that it is part of their country programming for Somalia. One can, for example, calculate a UN population estimate for Somaliland (3,508,150) by adding its six regions together, but it is only reported as part of 'the 18 pre-war regions of Somalia' (United Nations Population Fund 2014). Across different clan configurations, Somali politicians unanimously 'remain wedded to the "indivisibility" of Somalia, and repeatedly state their antipathy to a sovereign Somaliland' (Walls and Kibble 2010, 51).

One important vehicle used by Somalia to undermine Somaliland is the ostensibly non-secessionist state of Puntland (proclaimed in 1998).

Somaliland bases its claim for sovereign recognition on its former status as a British protectorate (south-central Somalia was an Italian colony) and its separate colonial borders. It makes a 'state' claim to represent all the people living inside its former colonial borders. Puntland, in contrast, makes a 'national' claim to represent all members of the extended Harti clan family – some of whom reside in the eastern Sool, Sanaag, and Togdheer regions of Somaliland. Puntland is not seeking independence from Somalia. Rather, its aim is to deny Somaliland international recognition by rendering its eastern regions conflictual and unstable (Hoehne 2009, 274).

Somaliland's strengths and Somalia's weaknesses have afforded Somaliland a high degree of latitude to pursue various forms of 'engagement without recognition' (Berg and Pegg 2018). There are daily flights to Hargeisa from Addis Ababa, Djibouti, and Dubai. Leading businesses such as Daallo Airlines, Dahabshiil, and Telesom operate across the Somali-speaking space. The United Arab Emirates recently signed an agreement to establish a military base in Berbera and the Dubai-based DP World entered into an agreement with Somaliland and Ethiopia to renovate and develop Berbera's port to handle increased trade volumes to and from Ethiopia. Yet Somalia increasingly tries to undermine these initiatives or use them to secure its own claim over Somaliland. Somalia's recent draft telecommunications law, for example, has sparked fears in Somaliland over their shared use of the +252 international dialling code with some Somaliland diplomats calling for their *de facto* state to purchase another code to ensure Somaliland's ability to control telecommunications within its territory (*The National* 2017). Somalia's Ministry of Ports and Marine Transport recently declared the DP World Berbera port deal as 'non-existent, null and void', prompting a sharp response from Somaliland (*Somaliland Sun* 2018).

Somalia and Somaliland engaged in a series of direct talks from 2012 to 2014, but these talks broke down in acrimony. Somalia has largely tried to pursue a strategy of isolation and rejection of Somaliland's claim to sovereignty. Despite its frequent designation as a 'failed state', it has been successful in using its juridical statehood to deny sovereign recognition to Somaliland and to prevent it from engaging with various regional and international organizations. Somaliland's contrasting success in building an increasingly viable and democratic state has allowed it to engage widely and win various forms of tacit support but has not enabled it to transcend its *de facto* statehood. Somalia is currently far too weak to reassert its control over Somaliland, and it remains implacably opposed to countenancing its independence. Most Somaliland citizens see little economic, political, or security incentive to rejoin Somalia. The safest prediction is a continuation of the *status quo*.

CYPRUS: ISOLATION/ACTIVE SANCTIONS

The Republic of Cyprus has chosen to pursue the most comprehensive strategy of isolation and sanctions against Northern Cyprus. It has utilized its international recognition from 1960 as the sole legitimate authority on the island to isolate, embargo, and sanction the Turkish Cypriot community since 1963 and, after 1983, the Turkish Republic of Northern Cyprus (TRNC). Perhaps its most important victories in this regard were the UN Security Council (UNSC) Resolution 186 (1964) establishing the UN Peacekeeping Force in Cyprus and referencing the 'Cyprus Government' in a manner which implied recognition of the now entirely Greek Cypriot administration as the government of Cyprus. Then came UNSC Resolutions 353 and 360 (1974) confirming the territorial integrity of the Republic of Cyprus, and finally the passage of UNSC Resolutions 541 (1983) and 550 (1984), which declared the attempt to create a state for Turkish Cypriots as invalid and called on all other states not to recognize 'any Cypriot state other than the Republic of Cyprus'.

Nicosia's campaign to isolate the Turkish Cypriots, however, extends far beyond these UNSC Resolutions. In 1979, the Republic of Cyprus succeeded in obtaining a resolution at the Universal Postal Union Congress declaring postage stamps issued by the Turkish Cypriot Postal Administration as 'illegal and of no validity' (Necatigil 1989, 152). Any mail destined for Northern Cyprus must be routed through the postal code 'Mersin 10, Turkey'. Nicosia also declared the ports of Famagusta, Karavostasi, and Kyrenia as closed for all vessels with captains of ships who dock in them subject to imprisonment and fines. Leveraging its status as the sole recognized government of Cyprus, Nicosia also did not ask the International Civil Aviation Organization (ICAO) to include Northern Cyprus's Ercan Airport in the ICAO Regional Air Navigation Plan. Thus, Ercan is not recognized by the ICAO and passengers using it are considered to have made an illegal entry into and exit from the Republic of Cyprus (Cyprus Ministry of Foreign Affairs 2016). Accordingly, there are no direct flights to or from Northern Cyprus other than those from Turkey. Travellers wishing to visit Northern Cyprus must 'stop over' in Istanbul or Ankara, and this adds significantly to the costs and inconvenience of flying there. The Greek Cypriot embargo against the TRNC was strengthened significantly in 1994 when the European Court of Justice (ECJ) ruled in the '*Anastasiou* Case' that British authorities could no longer accept movement certificates (which prove a good's origins) and phytosanitary certificates (which guarantee plant health) from Turkish Cypriot authorities. This ruling 'was disastrous for the Turkish Cypriots . . . as it effectively ruled out any direct trade with the European Union' (Ker-Lindsay 2012, 166).

Cyprus insists that all mentions of *de facto* state authorities or institutions are put in quotation marks and preceded by qualifiers like 'so-called'. Thus, one sees references to the 'prime minister' or 'central bank' in all official documents. Nicosia has succeeded in lobbying other states and organizations to adopt this language. Thus, all U.S. diplomatic cables follow this practice, which they almost never do for Somaliland and only occasionally do for Abkhazia and Transnistria (Pegg and Berg 2016, 273–274). Feeling secure in its success at preventing sovereign recognition of the TRNC, Nicosia has increasingly turned its attention towards preventing the gradual legitimization or 'Taiwanization' of Northern Cyprus. It goes to great lengths to challenge even trivial forms of acknowledgement of its 'northern counterpart'. In pursuit of this policy, Nicosia has 'prevented the Turkish Cypriots from joining any sporting or cultural bodies or participating in international events – regardless of whether participation somehow indicates statehood. Tourism adverts for Northern Cyprus and weather maps showing a border on the island have been the subject of official complaints' (Ker-Lindsay 2012, 183).

The greatest potential disruption to this strategy might have occurred in the early 2000s when pro-settlement forces started gaining momentum in the north, culminating in support for the Annan Plan by nearly 65% of Turkish Cypriot voters on an 87% turnout. Greek Cypriots, however, having been guaranteed that their admission to the EU was not contingent on a final settlement to the Cyprus conflict, turned against the Annan Plan, ultimately rejecting it by nearly 76% on an 89% turnout. This split result was both a blessing and a curse for the Turkish Cypriots. Having routinely been blamed for their intransigence in previous negotiation rounds, the Turkish Cypriots enjoyed a brief honeymoon where they were perceived as the cooperative party, while Greek Cypriots adjusted to a new reality that they were viewed as obstructionists. Preventing legitimization turned out to be a far greater challenge than preventing formal recognition (Ker-Lindsay 2012, 175).

An analysis of WikiLeaks U.S. diplomatic cables reveals considerable sympathy for Northern Cyprus and several attempts to ease its economic isolation (Pegg and Berg 2016). The OIC upgraded Northern Cyprus's observer status from 'The Turkish Cypriot Community' to 'The Turkish Cypriot State' after the Annan Plan vote (Ker-Lindsay 2012, 140–141). One tangible benefit of this new mood was the passage of the EU's 'Green Line Regulation' which facilitated intra-island trade across the UN-administered buffer zone. In implementing something like the Green Line Regulation, the EU would normally liaise with ministry officials from both states. The reluctance to engage *de facto* state authorities, though, led to this task being delegated (with Nicosia's approval) to the Turkish Cypriot Chamber of Commerce (*Kibris Türk Ticaret Odasi* or KTTO) which 'became an unexpected but important partner for the Commission and a vital part of the Green Line Regulation' (Kyris 2015, 109).

Yet the Republic of Cyprus is now a full member of the EU which means that it enjoys 'veto rights over all matters (even symbolic ones) that may come close to implying recognition of the TRNC' (Berg 2013, 480). Thus, any EU attempt, for example, to allow direct flights to Ercan Airport would be subject to a Republic of Cyprus veto. Indeed, the Green Line Regulation was the only one of three proposed EU measures after the Annan Plan vote allowed to proceed. The other two, involving foreign assistance to Northern Cyprus and allowing direct exports from it to the EU, were vetoed by Nicosia (Berg and Pegg 2018).

Public opinion on both sides of the Green Line continues to oscillate back and forth between more pro-settlement and more pro-*status quo* forces. The isolate and embargo strategy has arguably both advanced a pro-settlement agenda in Northern Cyprus and contributed to the re-emergence of hardliners when the anticipated benefits of voting for the Annan Plan failed to materialize. The guarantee of EU membership with or without a settlement allowed Greek Cypriot voters to seemingly have their cake and eat it too. Yet the island remains divided and Nicosia's strategy of using its veto power to pressure Turkey over its aspirations to EU membership has largely run aground as most Turks have now given up on EU membership. The economic costs of supporting Northern Cyprus have been manageable for Turkey for decades and the political costs of abandoning it would arguably be much greater for its elected leaders. Nicosia may have won the war against sovereign recognition, but its struggle to deny the TRNC legitimacy or prevent other countries from engaging it without recognition is on much shakier ground.

CONCLUSION

This study asked, 'Do parent state strategies matter in resolving secessionist conflicts with de facto states?' If we rule out both forced reintegration attempts and permissive exits as the choices leading to decisive endgames, then the short answer is 'no'. Indeed, it does not seem to matter much which strategy parent states opt for in the range from open engagement (most accommodative) to isolation/active sanctions (least accommodative). Whatever strategy parent states choose to pursue, the contours of the bigger picture do not seem to change. Peaceful reintegration as an aspired conflict resolution outcome remains a difficult goal to achieve. This is particularly true because parent state strategies rank much lower in the list of conditioning factors than the larger international normative environment, external support from patron states, or internal *de facto* state dynamics.

The international normative environment continues to prioritize respect for sovereignty and territorial integrity in particular. There is a broad consensus that post–Cold War state practice has strengthened and not weakened the normative consensus against unilateral secession and in favour of the territorial integrity of existing states (Crawford 2007, 415; Fabry 2012; Ker-Lindsay 2013). This means that widespread sovereign recognition of *de facto* states in the absence of consent from their parent states is extremely unlikely. Pegg's (1998, 5) argument that 'the de facto state is illegitimate no matter how effective it is' remains true today.

Yet parent states also operate in an anarchical system where their ability to transform regional balances of power is often quite limited. Somalia's manifest dysfunctionality prevents it from forcibly reincorporating Somaliland. Patron states like Russia and Turkey provide *de facto* states with even greater security. However unjust their creation was in the eyes of the parent state, Northern Cyprus and Abkhazia now feature defined frontiers which are easy for organized military forces to defend at relatively low cost. Patron states have demonstrated long-term support for *de facto* states, and this greatly limits the ability of parent states to influence events.

Finally, *de facto* states have shown at least some ability to develop institutions that respond to the needs of their societies tolerably well. All four of our cases have seen peaceful transfers of power from governments to oppositions. Abkhazia, Somaliland, and Transnistria, all have had at least some success incorporating multiple different ethnic or clan groups into their respective *de facto* states and only one of our cases, Northern Cyprus, is based on ethnic homogenization. None of this is to deny that tens of thousands of ethnic Georgians and Greek Cypriots have been forcibly displaced from their homes and have suffered in myriad other ways from the creation of these *de facto* states. It is only to suggest that *de facto* states with institutions that are reasonably responsive to their societies make it harder for parent states to entice their residents to abandon them and seek reintegration.

Thus, the international normative environment, external support from patron states, and internal dynamics within *de facto* states all serve to limit potentially decisive resolutions to these conflicts. Facing these constraints, parent states have chosen to respond in several ways. Although Moldova has chosen to pursue an open engagement strategy with Transnistria, this has not proven to be more successful than the Cypriot strategy of isolation/active sanctions against Northern Cyprus – both secessionist entities seem to be relatively sustainable and prefer the continuation of the *status quo* to reintegration on the terms offered so far. Whereas Georgia has tentatively embarked down an accommodative road with Abkhazia, thus being both restrictive and accommodative at the same time, neither its strategy nor Somalia's strategy of isolation/rejection with almost no capacity to enforce it has made any substantive progress in resolving the underlying conflicts.

What explains this kind of variation? Is it because parent states have different capacities to react? Indeed, Somalia's position looks meagre compared to that of Cyprus: no concessions needed since the UNSC resolutions back up the deoccupation claim, and the Greek Cypriot community has veto power in the EU decision-making process. Still, if the dominant mood reflects opposition to the act of secession, why are some parent states more accommodative than others? In the view of Ker-Lindsay (2014, 28), there are several reasons that vary across cases: emotional attachment to the territory. internally displaced persons, economic factors, historical and cultural issues, fear of further secession, and national pride.

Take, for instance, a specific example where the policy differences between two parent states' positions could not be starker. Moldova has decided to accept and recognize degrees awarded by universities in Transnistria. In contrast, the Republic of Cyprus asserts that, 'The "universities" in the occupied areas operate under the "laws" and "institutions" of the illegal "TRNC". . . . As such, they cannot be accepted or recognized by internationally recognized educational organizations' (Cyprus Ministry of Foreign Affairs n.d.). To explain that difference, one should look back to the early 1990s Moldova where the military conflict was less violent and did not bring about ethnic cleansing in Transnistria, with the result that ethnic diversity and multilingualism continues to characterize both sides of the Dniester River. Whereas the partition of Cyprus destroyed the Greek Cypriot dream of *enosis*, then the strategy of isolation/active sanctions against TRNC may be viewed as 'an act of empowerment in the face of defeat' and as a method of restoring a sense of honour and self-esteem (Ker-Lindsay 2014, 43).

This seemingly brings us to the depressing conclusion that only the brutal use of force against secessionists or amicable negotiated divorce from the parent state can resolve these conflicts. Still, while locating themselves in the middle of this continuum, parent states avoid the costs of renewed warfare and provide that the issue of 'lost territories' can be used politically to serve their domestic interests. The recent Law on Occupied Territories in Donbas, adopted by the Ukrainian parliament on 18 January 2018, does not affect the prospects for ending the conflict, but instead seeks a *modus vivendi* with Russia-backed secessionists acceptable both to the Ukrainian public and the international community (Szeligowski 2018). True, it may bring some relief to the open wounds but most likely fails to do more than similar initiatives launched long before in Cyprus and Georgia. We are back to square one.

REFERENCES

Anonymous. 2002. 'Government Recognition in Somalia and Regional Political Stability in the Horn of Africa'. *Journal of Modern African Studies* 40(2): 247–272.

Berbeca, Veaceslav. 2013. 'Nesting Stakes: From the Consolidation of Political Cleavages to Institutional Resistance in Moldova'. In *Managing Intractable Conflicts: Lessons from Moldova and Cyprus*, edited by M. Akgun. Istanbul: Istanbul Kultur University Publisher, pp. 53–62.

Berg, Eiki. 2013. 'Merging Together or Drifting Apart? Revisiting Political Legitimacy Issues in Cyprus, Moldova, and Bosnia and Herzegovina'. *Geopolitics* 18(2): 467–492.

Berg, Eiki, and Raul Toomla. 2009. 'Forms of Normalization in the Quest for De Facto Statehood'. *The International Spectator* 44(4): 27–45.

Berg, Eiki, and Scott Pegg. 2018. 'Scrutinizing a Policy of "Engagement without Recognition": US Requests for Diplomatic Actions with De Facto States'. *Foreign Policy Analysis* 14(3): 388–407.

Bradbury, Mark. 2008. *Becoming Somaliland*. Bloomington: Indiana University Press.

Broers, Laurence. 2013. 'Recognizing Politics in Unrecognized States: 20 Years of Enquiry into the De Facto States of the South Caucasus'. *Caucasus Survey* 1(1): 59–74.

Bryden, Matt. 2004. 'State-within-a-Failed State: Somaliland and the Challenge of International Recognition'. In *States within States: Incipient Political Entities in the Post-Cold War Era*, edited by Paul Kingston and Ian S. Spears. New York: Palgrave Macmillan, 167–188.

Caspersen, Nina. 2012. *Unrecognized States: The Struggle for Sovereignty in the Modern International System*. Cambridge: Polity Press.

Coppieters, Bruno. 2018. ' "Statehood", "De Facto Authorities" and "Occupation": Contested Concepts and the EU's Engagement in its European Neighbourhood'. *Ethnopolitics* 17:4, 343–361. DOI: 10.1080/17449057.2018.1495361

Crawford, James. 2007. *The Creation of States in International Law* (2nd edition). Oxford: Oxford University Press.

Cristescu, R., and D. Matveev. 2011. 'Peacebuilding and Conflict Prevention in Moldova: The Role of the EU'. Paper prepared in the framework of the Civil Society Dialogue Network. Brussels: European Peacebuilding Liaison Office.

Cyprus Ministry of Foreign Affairs. 2016. 'Closed Ports and Airports'. Accessed 11 March 2018. http://www.mfa.gov.cy/mfa/mfa2016.nsf/mfa13_en/mfa13_en? OpenDocument&print.

Cyprus Ministry of Foreign Affairs. n.d. 'The Illegally Operating "Universities" in the Occupied Areas of the Republic of Cyprus. Position of the Government of the Republic of Cyprus'. Accessed 15 March 2018. http://www.mfa.gov. cy/mfa/embassies/embassy_thehague.nsf/64136C6EE9414C40C2257F54002E92 A3/$file/The%20illegally%20operating%20-universities-%20in%20the%20occu pied%20areas%20of%20Cyprus.pdf.

Fabry, Mikulas. 2012. 'The Contemporary Practice of State Recognition: Kosovo, South Ossetia, Abkhazia, and Their Aftermath'. *Nationalities Papers* 40(5): 661–676.

Geldenhuys, Deon. 2009. *Contested States in World Politics*. New York: Palgrave Macmillan.

Griffiths, Ryan D. 2015. 'Between Dissolution and Blood: How Administrative Lines and Categories Shape Secessionist Outcomes'. *International Organization* 69(3): 731–751.

Gvidiani, Alin. 2017. 'Modalități de stabilire și de documentare: A faptelor juridice ce au loc în regiunea transnistreană – Realizări și dificultăți'. *Yearbook of the Laboratory for the Transnistrian Conflict Analysis* I(1): 140–147.

Hoehne, Markus V. 2009. 'Mimesis and Mimicry in Dynamics of State and Identity Formation in Northern Somalia'. *Africa* 79(2): 252–281.

Hopf, Ted. 2005. 'Identity, Legitimacy, and the Use of Military Force: Russia's Great Power Identities and Military Intervention in Abkhazia'. *Review of International Studies* 31: 225–243.

Human Rights Watch. 2009. *War on the Displaced: Sri Lankan Army and LTTE Abuses against Civilians in the Vanni.* New York: Human Rights Watch.

International Crises Group. 2004. *Georgia: Avoiding War in South Ossetia.* Europe Report No. 159. Tbilisi/Brussels: International Crisis Group.

Ivan, Paul. 2014. 'Transnistria – Where to?' *European Policy Centre Policy Brief*, 13 March.

Ker-Lindsay, James. 2012. *The Foreign Policy of Counter Secession: Preventing the Recognition of Contested States.* Oxford: Oxford University Press.

Ker-Lindsay, James. 2013. 'Preventing the Emergence of Self-Determination as a Norm of Secession: An Assessment of the Kosovo "Unique Case" Argument'. *Europe-Asia Studies* 65(5): 837–856.

Ker-Lindsay, James. 2014. 'Understanding State Responses to Secession'. *Peacebuilding* 2(1): 28–44.

Kolstø, Pål. 2006. 'The Sustainability and Future of Unrecognized Quasi-States'. *Journal of Peace Research* 43(6): 723–740.

Kyris, George. 2015. *The Europeanisation of Contested Statehood: The EU in Northern Cyprus.* Farnham, UK: Ashgate.

Menkhaus, Ken. 2014. 'State Failure, State Building, and Prospects for a "Functional Failed State" in Somalia'. *The Annals of the American Academy of Political and Social Science* 656(1): 154–172.

The National. 2017. 'Somaliland Diplomat: It's Time to Establish Our Own Country Calling Code'. Accessed 9 March 2018. http://www.thenational-somaliland. com/2017/07/03/somaliland-diplomat-time-establish-country-calling-code/.

Necatigil, Zaim M. 1989. *The Cyprus Question and the Turkish Position in International Law.* Oxford: Oxford University Press.

OSCE Chairperson-in-Office Steinmeier, in Moldova, calls for swift and full implementation of confidence-building measures. Chisinau/Tiraspol, 26 July 2016, available at http://www.osce.org/cio/256406

Pegg, Scott. 1998. *International Society and the De Facto State.* Aldershot, UK: Ashgate.

Pegg, Scott. 2017. 'Twenty Years of De Facto State Studies: Progress, Problems, and Prospects'. In *Oxford Research Encyclopedia of Politics*, edited by William R. Thompson. http://politics.oxfordre.com/view/10.1093/acrefore/97801 90228637.001.0001/acrefore-9780190228637-e-516.

Pegg, Scott, and Eiki Berg. 2016. 'Lost and Found: The WikiLeaks of De Facto State – Great Power Relations'. *International Studies Perspectives* 17(3): 267–286.

Pegg, Scott, and Pål Kolstø. 2015. 'Somaliland: Dynamics of Internal Legitimacy and (Lack of) External Sovereignty'. *Geoforum* 66: 193–202.

Plăcintă, Daniela. 2017. 'EU-MD DCFTA Agreement – Impact and Implications on Transnistria's Relations with Moldova and Moldova-EU Relations'. *Yearbook of the Laboratory for the Transnistrian Conflict Analysis* I(1): 54–72.

Racheva, Yelena. 2017. 'Utechka prezidenta: O skandal'nom begstve eks-glavy Pridnestrov'ya spetskoru "Novoy" rasskazali pobedivshiye opponenty i sam Yevgeniy Shevchuk. Novaya Gazeta, 3 Iyulya'. https://www.novayagazeta.ru/articles/2017/07/03/72989-utechka-prezidenta.

Roubanis, Ilia, Mete Hatay, and Alexandru Baltag. 2013. 'Challenges to Keeping the Negotiation Process on Track'. In *Managing Intractable Conflicts: Lessons from Moldova and Cyprus*, edited by M. Akgun. Istanbul: Istanbul Kultur University Publisher, pp. 109–119.

Somaliland Sun. 2018. 'Somaliland: State Cautions Somalia on Issues DP World and Berbera Port'. Accessed 9 March 2018. http://www.somalilandsun.com/2018/03/03/somaliland-keep-away-from-our-sacrosanct-internal-affairs-state-tells-somali/.

Strǎuţiu, Eugen, Nicoleta Munteanu, and Marius Şpechea. 2017. *Opţiunile partidelor politice din Republica Moldova în problema transnistreanǎ*. Cluj-Napoca: Editura Mega.

Szeligowski, Daniel. 2018. 'Ukraine's Law on the Occupied Territories in Donbas'. *PISM Bulletin* 12(1083) (24 January). Accessed 12 March 2018. https://www.pism.pl/publications/bulletin/no-12-1083.

Toal, Gerard. 2008. 'Russia's Kosovo: A Critical Geopolitics of the August 2008 War over South Ossetia'. *Eurasian Geography and Economics* 49(6): 670–705.

Toal, Gerard. 2017. *Near Abroad: Putin, the West and the Contest over Ukraine and the Caucasus*. Oxford: Oxford University Press.

United Nations Population Fund. 2014. *Population Estimation Survey 2014 for the 18 Pre-War Regions of Somalia*. Nairobi: United Nations Population Fund.

Walls, Michael, and Steve Kibble. 2010. 'Beyond Polarity: Negotiating a Hybrid State in Somaliland'. *Africa Spectrum* 45(1): 31–56.

Chapter 4

State Strategies against Secessionists

Ahsan I. Butt

INTRODUCTION

In the aftermath of decolonization in the middle of the twentieth century, it has not been uncommon for nation-states to face separatist movements. Indeed, modern states have faced over 160 such groups demanding autonomy or independence. Sometimes, such demands lead to war. After all, a group making claims on the territory of a sovereign state is almost by definition contentious; perhaps that state is unwilling to give up control of its land. In other cases, states may see things differently. If a nationalist movement wants autonomy or independence from us, governments reason, then that is what we will give them. The chasm between these positions is the subject of this chapter: namely, the counterstrategy of the state facing demands from separatists. Specifically, why are some secessionist movements given negotiated concessions, while others are subject to violence, sometimes harshly so?

The fundamental premise behind this question is that it is not secessionism *per se* which causes secessionist war. Rather, there is a substantial escalatory step between, on the one hand, an ethno-nationalist group making a demand of secessionism and, on the other, a state violently rejecting it. The group is responsible for separatism, the state for separatist war. To be sure, secessionist movements may deploy violence, but in a strategic interaction with states; they would be unlikely to escalate to this step if they could receive their demands—independence or autonomy—completely peacefully. It is usually the state, not the secessionist group, that compels war in such interactions. For example, one of the most brutal separatist conflicts worldwide took place in Indian Kashmir in the early 1990s, but this horrific war only arose because New Delhi denied Kashmiri separatist claims made through the ballot box in the late 1980s.

Analyzing why states choose war when faced with movements for independence, then, is synonymous with asking why separatist conflict takes place. Conceivably, there would be no such wars in international politics if all states peacefully acquiesced to all secessionist demands. In turn, given the widely acknowledged importance of secessionist conflict as a share of all political violence worldwide (Walter 2009, 1), it can be said that delineating states' decision-making during secessionist crises is key to understanding war and peace in the contemporary world more generally.

When dealing with secessionism, central governments must address two basic questions: (1) should we fight for this territory, and (2) if yes, how hard do we fight? Below, I develop a model that explains both decisions—whether to coerce and how intensely to do so—as a function of the state's external security. Since secession implies a large and rapid shift in the balance of power, it leads to a commitment problem. Only a state confident that it will not face future threats can afford peaceful concessions to separatists, since those very concessions could form the basis of stronger claims in the future. By contrast, if the state fears war after secession, either against the new neighbor due to deep identity divisions with the nationalist movement or an existing regional or global rival due to the war-proneness of its neighborhood, it will coerce. If a state chooses to coerce, the intensity of its violence depends on the level of third-party support for the separatists. For both materialist and emotional reasons, as I detail later, more outside backing is met with more violence. A state's counterstrategy against secessionists, in other words, is driven by the security implications of the movement.

BUILDING A MODEL OF STATE STRATEGY AGAINST SEPARATISTS

I explain a state's decision-making at what I term "secessionist moments": those times when a movement's demand for autonomy or independence is made abundantly clear to its central government. This secessionist moment may take the form of an electoral victory by a secessionist party, a massive rally or riot, an important assassination or kidnapping, or something similar. Essentially, a secessionist moment is a focal point event that proves to all observers, including the separatists themselves, that the movement cannot be brushed under the carpet and clarifies that a state must confront the separatist movement one way or the other. The state must answer the question, "How do we respond to this?"

The main structural factor that impinges on states' decision-making during secessionist crises is the large and rapid power shift that accompanies a change in borders. Such reversals in the balance of power are acceptable only for those states that do not fear future war. Only these confident states can afford peaceful, conciliatory measures against separatists; others must do whatever they can to oppose changes in the territorial *status quo*. Whether a state chooses to stand in the way of secessionists' demands thus turns a great deal on whether it is a fearful or sanguine state. This distinction between states confident in their security and those which are not depends, in turn, on (1) the identity distance between the seceding ethnic group and the central state, and (2) the geopolitical currents in the state's regional neighborhood.

Secession as a Shift in the Balance of Power

To understand why the threat of future war looms large at such times, it is important to first appreciate that, geopolitically, potential secession represents a drastic and adverse power shift. States experiencing secession lose power to two (sets of) actors: the newly created neighbor as well as existing regional and global rivals.

With respect to the seceded ethnic group, the state loses power on four dimensions: military, economic, demographic, and institutional. First, gaining control of a modern state's apparatus invariably means the control of what Tilly (1985, 181) calls the "concentrated means of coercion," or more colloquially, a military or police force. Economically, the group transitions from being a victim of racism or exploitation in the *status quo ex-ante* to raising taxes (Olson 1993), industrializing appropriate sectors of the economy, and building infrastructure in its territory, such as bridges or dams. It can also trade strategically with other countries (Hirschman 1969, 13–14), creating and solidifying alliances in the process (Gowa and Mansfield 1993). Third, the new state can serve as a magnet for the diaspora. Big changes in population, driven by immigration or otherwise, can be dangerous for one's rivals. As Ottoman leader Enver Pasha said during World War I, "If today in the Caucasus a small Armenia possessing a population of five to six hundred thousand and sufficient territory is formed, in the future this government, together with the Armenians that will come mainly from America and from elsewhere, will have a population of millions. And in the east we will have another Bulgaria and it will be a worse enemy than Russia" (Reynolds 2009). Fourth, once an ethnic group gains admission to the very exclusive club of recognized nation-states, its social and institutional power increases (Coggins 2014), not least because it can enter formal intergovernmental organizations (Abbott and Snidal 1998).

After secession, a state would not just lose power relative to its new neighbor but also to existing rivals, mainly because of losses in population and territory. Scholars of power politics (Mearsheimer 2001; Waltz 1979) and datasets in international relations both attest to the importance of population

(Correlates of War National Material Capabilities Dataset). Larger populations usually translate into bigger economies and militaries, which explains
the importance of pure demographics in considerations of power. For
instance, the ratio of India's material capabilities to Pakistan's increased by
almost 50%, from 4.6:1 to 6.7:1, when the latter lost its eastern wing in 1971
(National Material Capabilities Dataset). Meanwhile, suddenly losing vast
swathes of territory leaves states open to predation by opportunistic rivals
(Huth 1996, 114). For example, when the Ottoman Empire lost huge chunks
of land in the Balkan wars of 1908, it only whet the appetite of states such as
France, Britain, and especially Russia, each of which interpreted the division
of Ottoman lands as weakness to be taken advantage of.

Concessions and the Commitment Problem

Secession, then, axiomatically means a large and rapid loss in relative power.
But such a shift may not necessarily be an apocalyptic development. If a state
is confident that it will not face war after secession, then there is no reason
to fear the border changes that inhere in the process. Losses in the balance of
power do not have meaningful implications for states unlikely to face war. On
the other hand, for states that are fearful of future war, the prospect of such
territorial changes is more alarming.

The conundrum for such insecure states is that concessions to the secessionist movement increase the likelihood of the border changes that they are
so fearful of. Even if the state grants merely autonomy, and not complete
independence, the movement may use the organizational and institutional
fruits of that autonomy to make more vociferous demands from a stronger
position in the future (Grigoryan 2015). Moreover, autonomy would yield
more coherent subnational identities (Elkins and Sides 2007) and regionalist
parties (Brancati 2006), which cyclically generate more congealed demands
for secession. If a state really wishes to avoid border changes, accommodation is the last thing it should offer: such policies allow groups to aggregate
administrative, political, economic, and social capital.[1]

This logic should sound familiar to students of international relations, a
field in which it is taken as a truism that when faced with such adverse shifts
in the balance power, rational actors are better off fighting than negotiating.
After all, the trends in relative power imply that the declining actor will likely
achieve a worse deal in the future (Gilpin 1981; Fearon 1995; Powell 2006).
Put simply, it is better to nip the threat in the bud today rather than risk war
against a stronger adversary tomorrow.

If a state is fearful of future war, it cannot afford concessions to the secessionists; it must fight. But how does one distinguish between fearful and
sanguine states?

Insecure States: The Fear of Future War

After secession, the rump state may face war. Such a conflict could be fought against its new neighbor, as Ethiopia and Eritrea did in the 1990s, or against existing state rivals, as the Ottoman Empire did after each stage of the Balkan wars. The state must make a separate assessment for each possibility.

War against the Seceded State: Identity Division

The state's consideration of the probability of war against the seceded state rests on the form and content of the nationalisms of both the state and the movement. The central issue is whether the ethnic group's nationalism directly confronts that of the state. The relational dialectic between the nationalisms of the two actors, the central state and the seceding group, can help estimate the probability of war and peace in the future (Hale 2008, 48 and 75). If the state deems the ethnic group's nationalism intrinsically opposed to its own, it will assess the group to have vengeful motives. If, however, the national identity of the group has more of an indifferent than oppositional relationship with that of the state, then the latter can be more reassured.

Two main factors can trigger the state's judgment that the group's nationalism is directly oppositional. First, is the identity cleavage that the group is mobilizing on the same one that defines the state? The secessionist group, almost by definition, would have mobilized around some identity marker, be it language, religion, race, or ethnicity. Doubtless, political actors have multiple and overlapping identities, but during times of crisis and polarization, which secessionism usually signifies, it is reasonable to assert that one identity dominates others (Posner 2005). For our purposes, there is a greater chance of oppositional nationalisms if both actors define their nation on the same dimension, for example, religion. By contrast, when the group's mobilization occurs along different lines than the state's centralizing nationalism, then there is the possibility that the two identities are mutually compatible.

Second, how recent and intense was violence (if any) between the two nations? Some rivalries go back decades if not centuries, while others are fresher. Some have seen severe violence regularly, others rarely or not at all. For example, during World War II, there was considerably less violence between Czechs and Slovaks than between, say, Croats and Serbs (Kramer 1992, 4), paving the way for a peaceful divorce fifty years later. Recent and/ or intense violence allows ethnic entrepreneurs to rhetorically whip up hysteria and sharp emotions, raising the risk of revenge in the future.

The identity division variable is not set in stone and, in fact, adjusts to changes in nationalisms and rhetoric; it acknowledges that identity is fungible and context-specific. In one important case, for example, the Ottoman Empire shifted its emphasis away from a relatively pluralistic "Ottomanism" to a nationalistic "Turkism" in the run-up to World War I, a transition that directly led to the Armenian genocide (Melson 1992, 153–62; Mann 2005, 129; Bloxham 2005, 59; Butt 2017). But the bottom line is that if the national identities of the two actors in question are opposed, then the state will be forced to consider the seceding group as vengeful or expansionist, and thus problematic for its future security. As U.S. secretary of state William Seward said about the Confederacy: it "must, like any other new state, seek to expand itself northward, westward, and southward. What part of this continent or of the adjacent islands would be expected to remain in peace?" Conversely, where the identity distance is muted, the state can be confident that were the ethnic group to eventually win statehood, it would not turn its guns toward its erstwhile host state.

War against Existing Rivals: Regional War-Proneness

Perhaps no structural factor impacts a state's likelihood of surviving as its geographical location.[2] War does not occur equally in all parts of the world. For example, the rate at which South Asian countries threaten or carry out militaristic action against each other is twice that of states in South America, while Western Europe's figure is half that of the Middle East (Butt 2013, 591). For our purposes, the state's assessment of facing war against existing states turns on the degree of militarization in the region. Like human beings in residential neighborhoods, states "feel" more or less secure depending on the level of violence in their immediate vicinity.

This level of confidence in the future is crucial to consider when states are deciding about the possibility of border changes. Israel and Canada have many differences, to be sure, but both are reasonably wealthy constitutional democracies, with one crucial difference: the level of warfare and conflict in each of their regions. That North America is so much more peaceful than the Middle East means that, even before considering any factor about the movements themselves, the prospect of a Quebecois state is less alarming for Canada than a Palestinian one is for Israel.

Indeed, it is quite telling that in regions where interstate war is difficult to rule out, such as the Middle East, South Asia, South East Asia, the Balkans and Caucuses, and sub-Saharan Africa, there is a strong association between the outbreak of secessionism and hostilities. Conversely, in optimistic "post-security" environments such as Western Europe and the Pacific, the demand for autonomy or statehood does not necessarily translate into war. Correlation is assuredly not causation, but it stands to reason that geopolitical conditions will influence how comfortable states are with the prospect of being scythed up. That secessionist demands result in violence, less in low-threat areas and more in high-threat areas, underlines the weight external factors place on state decision-making during secessionist crises.

Overall, the state can face future war against either the newly created state or existing states. It considers future war against the seceded state likely if the identity division between the center and the ethnic group is deep, while a militarized neighborhood will generate a fear of war at the hands of regional or global rivals. If either of these conditions is met, the state is a fearful state that must tread carefully when contemplating concessions to the separatists (figure 4.1). If, on the other hand, the state considers neither type of war likely, then the state qualifies as secure, one whose sanguinity opens up the possibility of peaceful measures when dealing with the movement. In a nutshell, fear of future war is sufficient for state coercion of separatists, while confidence in a peaceful future is necessary for a strategy of negotiated concessions.

Extent of Coercion: Third-Party Support

Once a state assesses that it may face war in the future, it is compelled to clamp down on the secessionists. After all, concessions could pave the way to a change in borders that could prove disastrous for the state. To avoid the prospect of a fight against a relatively strengthened rival down the road, the state uses coercion to stop the secessionists in their tracks. The question then becomes: How coercive will the state be? States maintain a terrifying variety of lethal and nonlethal coercive tools at their disposal—from beatings and imprisonment to mass killings and genocide—and the relative balance of these will be determined by the level of third-party support for the separatists.

Foreign rivals can get involved in a state's secessionist conflict for any number of reasons. They may want to swallow the territory for themselves, a dynamic known as irredentism (Horowitz 2000, 281–285). In other cases,

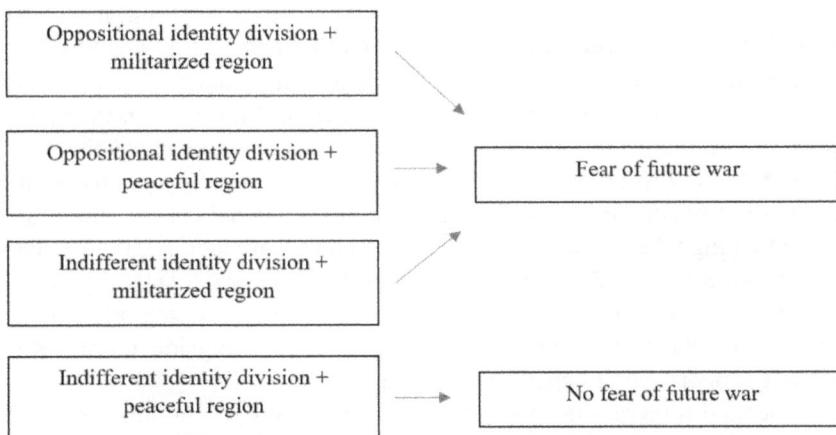

Figure 4.1.   Confident, Secure States versus Insecure, Fearful States

an intervening state may not care for the territory in question but, spurred by standard geopolitical aims such as the destabilization or weakening of a rival, backs the secessionist group in its aims. In yet other cases, the third party may not have geopolitical motives *per se* but rather be pushed by an ethnic affinity with the separatists (Moore and Davis 1998) or domestic pressure (Saideman 1997).

Regardless of why such states intervene, the recipient of their support tends to face greater hostility and violence from the central government as a result. Two factors explain why increasing third-party support is met by increasing coercion. First, outside help strengthens the ethnic movement (Kalyvas and Balcells 2010) and, consequently, there is more force required to defeat it (Downes 2007).

Second, getting into bed with a foreign state generates emotional reactions from the state and its security forces. As scholars have pointed out, emotion-driven violence is a central element of ethnic conflicts (Kaufman 2001, 3, 27–28; Petersen 2002, 37). One important emotion that makes itself known during secessionist wars is betrayal. Betrayal is arguably the most relevant emotion insofar as third-party backing for domestic rebels is concerned. Such alliances conjure dark feelings of "fifth columns" (Mylonas 2012, 41–42), and both leaders and security forces generally respond with great ruthlessness when they genuinely perceive (as opposed to opportunistically allege) such a marriage of convenience.

The more third-party support there is, the greater its effects. Verbal, financial, or sanctuary support to the secessionist group qualifies as "limited" support. It is true that rhetoric can sometimes be alarming because it signals greater involvement down the line. For example, Union leaders consistently worried what guarded statements by the British government might mean for its support for the Confederacy (Butt 2017). But by itself, mere verbal support does not accomplish much. Financial support is more meaningful than just words, but the help money promises is limited. Distributing financial support on the ground to actors for whom it was intended is a challenging task. Even when delivered in reasonably large doses, cash does not change the type of resources the ethnic movement can draw upon; it just changes the extent to which those resources can be deployed. Finally, sanctuary may seem a strange form of support to categorize as "limited," given borders' importance in demarcating where states can practice counterinsurgency while respecting rules of sovereignty (Salehyan 2009). Nevertheless, sanctuaries are purely defensive in nature unless combined with other forms of support, which is why, despite their importance, they are classified alongside more limited forms of support such as rhetoric or money.

The second rung on the spectrum of third-party support is "moderate." To qualify for this category, foreign backing must include military aid, usually in the form of equipment, supplies, and/or training. As scholars (Kalyvas and Balcells 2010) have explained, such "technologies of rebellion" can significantly enhance the military capabilities of insurgents. The best source for modern arms and equipment are states, though some nonstate actors assuredly run highly capable smuggling networks of arms. Sometimes outside help will tip the balance in balance of power on the ground by, say, providing a crucial technology, such as Stinger missiles or AK-47s. States, especially those which share a border with the region experiencing secession, can also help train rebel forces which, depending on the context, can be badly versed in the grammar of organized battle.

At "high" levels of support, the third-party support becomes directly involved and its forces fight alongside the rebels. It is no longer just that the secessionist group and the outside power want the same things; now they are doing the same things too. From the perspective of the central government, the conflict can no longer be regarded as a civil war with outside involvement. Rather, it treats the crisis as a full-blown interstate war waged by the third-party state.

Dependent Variable: State Strategy

To briefly recap, any state facing a secessionist movement faces two questions. First, does it anticipate future war, either against the seceded state or an existing rival? Second, if the state does consider future war likely, how heavily are any third parties intervening on behalf of the secessionists? There are therefore four possibilities. The state can face an (1) externally unthreatening movement or an externally threatening one that is tied to (2) limited, (3) moderate, and (4) high levels of third-party support. Respectively, these four possibilities correspond to the four strategies at a state's disposal when dealing with separatism: "negotiations and concessions," "policing," "militarization," and "collective repression" (figure 4.2).

The state has the space to try "negotiations and concessions" only when it does not fear a change in borders. By the terms of this strategy, it negotiates the need for, and possible modalities of, autonomy or independence, while foreclosing the possibility of any significant violence. Essentially it sends a message to the movement: we would like you to stay, but if you still choose to leave, we will not stop you. The government may, thus, offer territorial or political autonomy, lower taxes or higher aid, or more space for the ethnic group's culture regionally (e.g., language at schools) or nationally (e.g., celebratory festivals or museums). Regardless of the precise details, the main implication of this strategy is that because it takes place in optimistic, "post-security" environments, political bargaining is done over the table, not in tanks and trenches. This strategy sees two possible outcomes in equilibrium:

Independent variable I

```
┌─────────────────────────┐
│      LIKELIHOOD OF       │
│       FUTURE WAR         │
└─────────────────────────┘
```

Low   High

```
┌─────────────────────┐          ┌─────────────────────┐
│   Border changes    │          │   Border changes    │
│    acceptable       │          │    unacceptable     │
└─────────────────────┘          └─────────────────────┘
```

Independent variable II

```
┌─────────────────────┐
│    THIRD-PARTY      │
│      SUPPORT        │
└─────────────────────┘
```

Limited   Moderate   High

Dependent variable

| NEGOTIATIONS AND CONCESSIONS | POLICING | MILITARIZATION | COLLECTIVE REPRESSION |

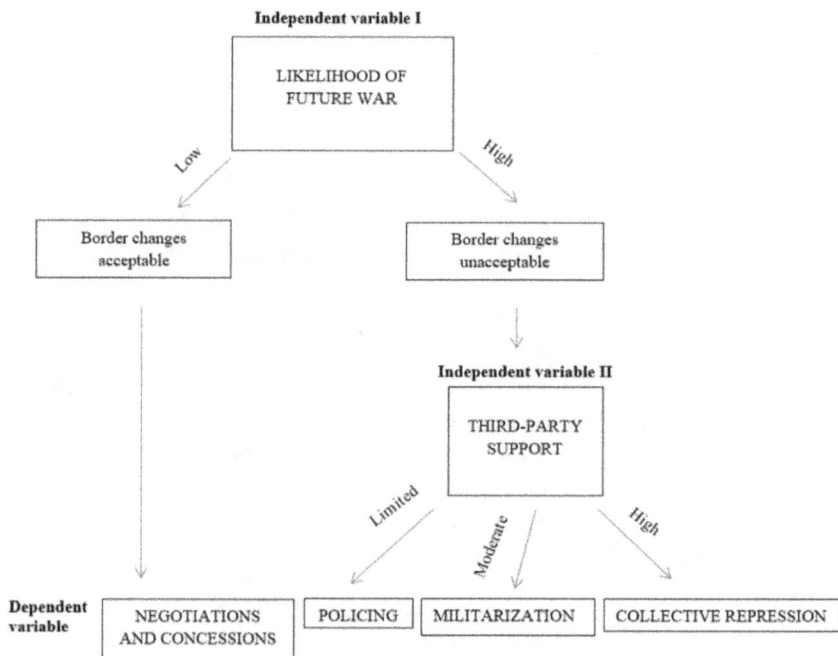

Figure 4.2.   Modeling State Strategy of Counter-Secession

the ethnic group may accept the concessions, resulting in autonomy, as it took place in Quebec or Scotland, or it may reject them as not going far enough, which will pave the way for the creation of a new state, as in the Velvet Divorce or the separation of Norway and Sweden.

If the state fears future war, then it must coerce because it cannot afford border changes. The lightest form of coercion is "policing," a strategy that the state favors when separatists have only "limited" third-party support. Policing may include the imprisonment and intimidation of leaders and activists, bans on large gatherings or rallies, or widespread censorship of secessionist media. If violence is used, it is mostly nonlethal violence. That said, low numbers of casualties—say in the dozens annually—are consistent with policing. Given that third-parties are not deeply involved, the state still has the space to use concessions, but these are more of a tactical nature, designed mainly to separate (no pun intended) moderate secessionists from radicals (Cunningham 2011). There is certainly no offer of an independent state or anything close. One example of policing is Rajiv Gandhi's initial strategy in Punjab in 1984–1985; another example is Israel's policies between the first intifada and the Oslo agreements.

Moderate support from external rivals means that the ethnic group now poses a fairly serious military threat. Consequently, the state chooses "militarization." This strategy is a telltale sign that the state is mired in a full-blown civil war. Militarization translates into significant coercion, but this violence is aimed mostly against insurgents or those perceived to be helping them. Militarization strategies can be quite nasty, featuring torture and disappearances, but importantly, the domain for such a sharply clawed tactic is relatively circumscribed, not pursued as a matter of official or quasi-official state policy. Odds are, if one is witnessing a separatist war, it is a consequence of a militarization strategy. India's behavior in Punjab between 1987 and 1993 qualifies as militarization, as does Pakistan's strategy in Baluchistan in the 1970s.

Finally, the most violent strategy the state can use is "collective repression," which comes into play when the ethnic group enjoys "high" external support. Indiscriminate violence, resulting in casualties in the tens or hundreds of thousands of deaths, as well as the wholesale destruction of villages, neighborhoods, and even some entire towns, is part and parcel of such a strategy. The severity of the external threat drives states to collective repression. Materially, the ethnic group is, for all intents and purposes, as powerful as the external patron, given the fact that it is fighting alongside it. The state can afford no half measures in such a conflict. Second, when third-party support has escalated to such extreme levels, the emotional implications of betrayal begin to make themselves felt, both among ruthless leaders as well as angry (and racist) security forces. At the extreme, such strategies can result in genocide, as in the Ottoman Empire's treatment of Armenians, who allied with Russia during World War I to seek independence, or in West Pakistan's destruction in what became Bangladesh. Even if the damage is not quite on a genocidal scale, it is still highly indiscriminate and pays little heed to laws or norms of war, as with India's behavior in Kashmir.

CONCLUSION

Outlining a model of separatist conflict based on a state's external security concerns has two main benefits. Theoretically, it helps balance a literature focused primarily on factors internal to the state, such as its ethnic heterogeneity (Toft 2003; Walter 2009) or domestic institutions (Cunningham 2014; Griffiths 2015). By bringing a state's security fears into focus, we can better understand decisions such as Israel's in the aftermath of the first intifada, where despite being the type of state domestic arguments would consider likely to make major concessions, Tel Aviv did not come close to granting a Palestinian state. More generally, it stands to reason that if geopolitics is central to questions closely associated with secessionist war—such as ethnic conflict (Mylonas 2012), the intensity of intrastate violence (Kalyvas and Balcells 2010; Balch-Lindsay, Enterline, and Joyce 2008; Kuperman 2008; Jenne 2007), or the recognition of sovereign states (Coggins 2014)—then separatist conflict too must be affected by international politics.

Empirically, this model's typology, expanding beyond the standard coercion-concessions dichotomy to include levels of repression, provides more analytical purchase on separatist violence, both in history and today. India was much tougher in Kashmir than it was in Assam in the 1990s, and much tougher in Punjab after 1987 than before, while Pakistan was harsher in East Pakistan than Baluchistan in the 1970s. Domestic arguments cannot explain such variation because variables such as demography and institutional structure are relatively constant across such contexts. Because most (136/163 or 83%) of secessionist movements took place in a state experiencing multiple movements, and most (58%) of these "multiple-movement" states sometimes used violence and other times did not, internal variation is a huge slice of the separatist conflict pie. By considering a state's external security concerns of the moment, it becomes possible to explain variation in separatist violence (1) across space and time within states as well as (2) across states.

If the theory holds, it offers lessons to actors involved in separatist conflicts as well as to those hopeful to curtail the violence generated by them. First, the lesson to leaders of separatist movements is to be careful in soliciting outside support. The costs of repression at the hands of the state when a movement ties itself to outside actors is probably not worth it in most conditions, unless a movement is expressly banking on a "provocation" strategy (Kydd and Walter 2006). Second, the international community should endeavor to ameliorate the state's concerns with shift in the balance of power attendant with secessionism by, say, providing defensive guarantees or significant military aid—contingent on "good" behavior with the independence movement. Furthermore, the international community must impress upon rivals of the state in question to refrain from helping the secessionists.

That said, in the real world, the typical intervener in such conflicts is not a humanitarian state interested in mitigating violence but rather an opportunistic or irredentist rival of the state. Even if a state intervention is motivated by humanitarian, not selfish geopolitical, concerns, it would be challenging to convince it that promising military benefits for the host state is the key to dampening the crisis. Such a move is likely to be interpreted as being held for ransom, and powerful states are unlikely to want to reward a government holding a gun to the collective head of its secessionist minority. Regardless, the point remains that the roots of governments' counterstrategies against internal secessionism, whether peaceful, mildly coercive, or genocidal, lie in the external security implications of the movement.

NOTES

1. For a nuanced position on whether federalism and accommodation spurs or stops future secessionism, see Bakke (2015).
2. Tanisha Fazal's (2007) *State Death* has a chapter titled "Location, location, and timing."

BIBLIOGRAPHY

Abbott, Kenneth, and Duncan Snidal. 1998. "Why States Act through Formal International Organizations." *Journal of Conflict Resolution* 42(1): 3–32.

Bakke, Kristin M. 2015. *Decentralization and Intrastate Struggles: Chechnya, Punjab, and Quebec*. New York: Cambridge University Press.

Balch-Lindsay, Dylan, Andrew Enterline, and Kyle Joyce. 2008. "Third Party Intervention and the Civil War Process." *Journal of Peace Research* 45(3): 345–363.

Bloxham, Donald. 2005. *The Great Game of Genocide: Imperialism, Nationalism, and the Destruction of the Ottoman Armenians*. New York: Oxford University Press.

Brancati, Dawn. 2006. "Decentralization: Fueling the Fire or Dampening the Flames of Ethnic Conflict and Secessionism." *International Organization* 60(3): 651–685.

Butt, Ahsan. 2013. "Anarchy and Hierarchy in International Relations: Explaining South America's War-Prone Decade, 1932–1941." *International Organization* 67(3): 575–607.

Butt, Ahsan. 2017. *Secession and Security: Explaining State Strategy against Separatists*. Ithaca, NY: Cornell University Press.

Coggins, Bridgett. 2014. *Power Politics and State Formation in the Twentieth Century: The Dynamics of Recognition*. New York: Cambridge University Press.

Cunningham, Kathleen. 2011. "Divide and Conquer or Divide and Concede: How Do States Respond to Internally Divided Separatists?" *American Political Science Review* 105(2): 275–297.

Cunningham, Kathleen. 2014. *Inside the Politics of Self-Determination*. New York: Oxford University Press.

Downes, Alexander. 2007. *Targeting Civilians in War*. Ithaca, NY: Cornell University Press.

Elkins, Zachary, and John Sides. 2007. "Can Institutions Build Unity in Multiethnic States?" *American Political Science Review* 101(4): 693–708.

Fazal, Tanisha. 2007. *State Death: The Politics and Geography of Conquest, Occupation, and Annexation*. Princeton, NJ: Princeton University Press.

Fearon, James. 1995. "Rationalist Explanations for War," *International Organization* 49(3): 379–414.

Gilpin, Robert. 1981. *War and Change in World Politics*. New York: Cambridge University Press.

Gowa, Joanne, and Edward D. Mansfield. 1993. "Power Politics and International Trade." *American Political Science Review* 87(2): 408–420.

Griffiths, Ryan. 2015. "Between Dissolution and Blood: How Administrative Lines and Categories Shape Secessionist Outcomes." *International Organization* 69(3): 731–751.

Grigoryan, Arman. 2015. "Concessions or Coercion? How Governments Respond to Restive Ethnic Minorities." *International Security* 39(4): 170–207.

Hale, Henry. 2008. *The Foundations of Ethnic Politics: Separatism of States and Nations in Eurasia and the World.* New York: Cambridge University Press.

Hirschman, Albert O. 1969. *National Power and the Structure of Foreign Trade.* Berkeley: University of California Press.

Horowitz, Donald L. 2000. *Ethnic Groups in Conflict.* Berkeley: University of California Press.

Huth, Paul K. 1996. *Standing Your Ground: Territorial Disputes and International Conflict.* Ann Arbor: University of Michigan Press.

Jenne, Erin. 2007. *Ethnic Bargaining: The Paradox of Minority Empowerment.* Ithaca, NY: Cornell University Press.

Kalyvas, Stathis, and Laia Balcells. 2010. "International System and Technologies of Rebellion: How the End of the Cold War Shaped Internal Conflict." *American Political Science Review* 104(3): 415–429.

Kaufman, Stuart. 2001. *Modern Hatreds: The Symbolic Politics of Ethnic War.* Ithaca, NY: Cornell University Press.

Kramer, Mark. 1992. "The Czech-Slovak Rupture and European Security." Paper for the Security for Europe Project. Providence, RI: Center for Foreign Policy Development.

Kuperman, Alan. 2008. "The Moral Hazard of Humanitarian Intervention: Lessons from the Balkans." *International Studies Quarterly* 52(1): 49–80

Kydd, Andrew H., and Barbara F. Walter. 2006. "The Strategies of Terrorism." *International Security* 31(1): 49–80.

Mann, Michael. 2005. *The Dark Side of Democracy: Explaining Ethnic Cleansing.* New York: Cambridge University Press.

Mearsheimer, John. 2001. *The Tragedy of Great Power Politics.* New York: W.W. Norton and Company.

Melson, Robert. 1992. *Revolution and Genocide: On the Origins of the Armenian Genocide and the Holocaust.* Chicago: University of Chicago Press.

Moore, Will H., and David R. Davis. 1998. "Transnational Ethnic Ties and Foreign Policy." In *The International Spread of Ethnic Conflict: Fear, Diffusion, and Escalation,* edited by David A. Lake and Donald Rothchild. Princeton, NJ: Princeton University Press, pp. 89–104.

Mylonas, Harris. 2012. *The Politics of Nation-Building: Making Co-Nationals, Refugees, and Minorities.* New York: Cambridge University Press.

Olson, Mancur. 1993. "Dictatorship, Democracy, and Development." *American Political Science Review* 87(3): 567–576.

Petersen, Roger D. 2002. *Understanding Ethnic Violence: Fear, Hatred, and Resentment in Twentieth-Century Eastern Europe.* Cambridge: Cambridge University Press.

Posner, Daniel. 2005. *Institutions and Ethnic Politics in Africa.* Cambridge: Cambridge University Press.

Powell, Robert. 2006. "War as a Commitment Problem." *International Organization* 60(1): 169–203.

Reynolds, Michael A. 2009. "Buffers, Not Brethren: Young Turk Military Policy in the First World War and the Myth of Panturanism." *Past and Present* 203(1): 137–179.

Saideman, Stephen. 1997. "Explaining the International Relations of Secessionist Conflicts: Vulnerability versus Ethnic Ties." *International Organization* 51(4): 721–753.

Salehyan, Idean. 2009. *Rebels without Borders: Transnational Insurgencies in World Politics*. Ithaca, NY: Cornell University Press.

Singer, David J., Stuart Bremer, and John Stuckey. 1972. "Capability Distribution, Uncertainty, and Major Power War, 1820–1965." In *Peace, War, and Numbers*, edited by Bruce Russert. Beverly Hills: Sage, pp. 19–48. Dataset version 4.0 available at http://www.correlatesofwar.org/COW2%20Data/Capabilities/NMC_v4_0.csv.

Tilly, Charles. 1985. "War Making and State Making as Organized Crime." In *Bringing the State Back In*, edited by Peter B. Evans, Dietrich Rueschemeyer, and Theda Skocpol. Cambridge: Cambridge University Press, pp. 169–191.

Toft, Monica. 2003. *The Geography of Ethnic Violence: Identity, Interests, and the Indivisibility of Territory*. Princeton, NJ: Princeton University Press.

Walter, Barbara. 2009. *Reputation and Civil War: Why Separatist Conflicts Are So Violent*. Cambridge: Cambridge University Press.

Waltz, Kenneth. 1979. *Theory of International Politics*. Reading, MA: Addison-Wesley.

Chapter 5

Global Constitutional Strategies to Counter-Secession

Rivka Weill*

INTRODUCTION

U.S. presidents drew comparisons between marital and territorial relationships to either justify or reject secession. Thomas Jefferson expressed the American revolutionaries' sentiments when justifying secession of the colonies from Great Britain in terms of lost love to it. Abraham Lincoln, in contrast, utilized the comparison to reject the Southern States' secession from the Union: "A husband and wife may be divorced, and go out of the presence, and beyond the reach of each other . . . the different parts of our country cannot do this. They cannot but remain face to face; and intercourse, either amicable or hostile, must continue between them" (Levinson 2004, 466).

People often treat both types of unions as sanctified; they use an oath or a vow to attest to their loyalty, whether to the state or to the spouse. People depict both relationships as based on love, not just self-serving interests and reciprocity (Sollors 1986, 112). In both cases, reneging on an oath is considered treason, and in the case of secession it may even lead to imprisonment and death. The union between spouses and territories has at times merged historically to one in royal marriages, in which the marriage also cemented a union between two states (Thomas 2010). It was thus considered an act of treason against the state in the UK to have sex outside of marriage with the King's wife, his eldest son's wife, or the King's eldest unmarried daughter (Treason Act 1351). The aspiration to treat these unions of people and territories as sacred may reflect the fact that a union often proves too difficult to maintain over time. It may be more natural to stand alone, rather than take others' interests into account.

Secession lies at the intersection between international law and constitutional law. Increasingly, constitutional literature deals with secession, debating whether it is advisable for a state to legalize secession and even set the procedures of how to achieve it in the constitution. Those in favor of constitutionalizing secession suggest that it will prevent violence and may even indirectly prevent secession by setting high consensual standards for achieving it (Norman 2003). Those against argue that it may become a self-fulfilling prophesy or at least lead to strategic exploitations of threats to secede to gain a larger share of the limited resources of the state (Sunstein 1991).

Scholars debate the design question but seem to agree regarding the portrayal of the actual practice of countries. Common wisdom is that "in most cases, the constitution is simply silent on the matter" (Monahan and Bryant with Coté 1996, 4–6; see also Jackson 2016, 314; Coggins 2011, 37). Since constitutional democracies are typically based on the consent of the governed, this constitutional silence might be interpreted as tacit permission for secession. The Canadian Supreme Court, for example, interpreted the silence of the Canadian Constitution as permitting secession via a constitutional amendment (Reference *re* Secession of Quebec).

In contrast to the prevailing approach, my theoretical and empirical work on "Secession and the Prevalence of Both Militant Democracy and Eternity Clauses Worldwide" published in the *Cardozo Law Review* suggests that the overwhelming majority of world constitutions, including the constitutions of the overwhelming majority of democratic and semi-democratic states, prohibit secession in explicit but indirect manners (Weill 2018, 905).[1] In that work, I analyze the different constitutional treatments of secession existing in 192 constitutions of states that are members of the United Nations (UN) and the empirical findings regarding their prevalence. I use this chapter to sketch some of the themes, elaborate on others, and foster a discussion with political scientists and international relations scholars.

The second section defines secession. The third section introduces the two primary tools constitutions use to prevent secession and explains why scholarship has missed the prevalence of these tools in constitutions. The fourth section discusses militant democracy in the context of secession. The fifth section deals with the protection of territorial integrity through eternity clauses. The sixth section explains the nexus between militant democracy and eternity clauses. The seventh section argues that even when constitutions allow for secession, they intend to frustrate it. The eighth section concludes with strategic and normative explanations for constitutions' treatment of secession.

THE SECESSION THREAT

Secession, just like divorce, is thus an ever-present threat to the territorial integrity of states and the unity of their body citizenry. In fact, there are secessionist movements all over the world (Beary 2011): Scotland in the UK; Catalonia and Basque in Spain; Flanders in Belgium; Kurds in Turkey and Iraq; Vermont, Texas, and Alaska in the United States; Kashmir in India; and so forth. Wherever one places a finger on the map, one is likely to find a secessionist movement.

In 1945, the UN General Assembly was founded with fifty-one member states; today it has almost quadrupled its membership to 193 states. Almost three-quarters of new states formed in the twentieth century owe their births to secession (Coggins 2011, 27–28). This number includes decolonization cases that some scholars do not enumerate as part of the secessionist phenomena. But, in order to understand the rise in secessionist activity in the twentieth and twenty-first centuries, we must take into account decolonization.

When decolonization occurred, it occurred with the recognition of international law that it is legitimate and that colonized states have the right to self-determination (UN General Assembly Resolution 1514 titled the "Declaration on the Granting of Independence to Colonial Countries and Peoples"). But decolonization occurred under preexisting boundaries. The colonial powers were not primarily interested in respecting the national identities of the people in the particular territories that they were ruling. They were dividing the territory according to administrative needs and agreements between themselves. Thus, decolonization did not address the need of the ethnic national people within the territories for unity (Ratner 1996). After decolonization, the world has witnessed additional waves of territorial unrest, in which the people in existing states want to secede to better cater for their national identities.[2]

Internal autonomous arrangements within existing states are not considered secession. I define secession to include three types (cf. Buchanan 1997, 31; Brilmayer 1991, 177). The *classic* form of secession occurs when a group of citizens creates a new state in part of the territory of an existing state. This would have been the case had Scotland seceded from the UK, Catalonia from Spain, and so forth.

A *second* type is *irredentist* secession, in which part of the citizens depart with part of the territory in order to join another existing state. Typically, the majority of the citizens in the seceding area belong to the same ethno-national community as the majority in the neighboring state or the seceding area used to belong to the neighboring state and the secessionists want to restore the previous territorial distribution. This is how Russia tries to portray the situation in Crimea, while the Western world believes that this was a case of forceful annexation of Crimea by Russia.

A *third* form of secession ensues when an existing state dissolves and new states are formed in its place. For example, Czechoslovakia divided into the Czech and Slovak republics in 1993. In the first two forms of secession, the original state remains in a reduced form, but it completely dissolves in the third type. Should a situation in which no mother state is left be treated as secession? My aim is to look at the situation *ex-ante*, before secession occurs, from the viewpoint of how secession challenges the constitutional law of the mother state. Thus, this third type should be treated as part of the secessionist phenomenon.

The three types of secession may pose different challenges from an international law perspective because when the secessionists attempt to establish a new state, they need to gain the recognition of the international community. In contrast, when they join an existing state, then supposedly they enjoy the benefits of joining a state that is already recognized under international law. But, from a constitutional law perspective, what all three cases share in common is the fact that they challenge the very basic norm of the constitutional system, and that is the identity of the constitution-making body in the territory. I am arguing that popular sovereignty, in particular, is a territorial concept. It is not composed of people alone, as scholars traditionally think, but popular sovereignty is rather composed of people plus territory (cf. Ackerman 2014).

THE CONSTITUTIONAL TREATMENT
OF SECESSION

Countries employ primarily two nuclear constitutional weapons to fight against secession. The first is the ban on participation at elections of secessionist political parties, and the second is an eternity clause, which means treating the territorial integrity of the state and national unity as an eternal value that cannot be amended.[3] Both tools imply that secessionists cannot achieve their goal in an evolutionary manner but must resort to extra-constitutional means. They must initiate a new constitutional beginning in the Kelsenian sense (Kelsen 1945, 118, 435–437). Secession does not necessarily require force, but it does require a new constitutional beginning.

Why did the literature wrongly argue that constitutions are mostly silent on secession? First, to understand the extent of the fight of states against secession, one has to look at both bans on political participation and eternity clauses and understand the relationship between the two tools. Many scholars have looked at only one of the mechanisms rather than the two together.

Second, scholars have been looking only at explicit treatment of secession in the constitution, and constitutions typically do not even use the word secession in the constitution. They treat territorial integrity, national unity but not secession *per se* (Weill 2018). In addition, constitutions often address the topic in indirect ways. For example, when it comes to the ban on political parties, we find constitutions that ban regional political parties. Constitutions do not add the explanation that this is to prevent secession. Or, when it comes to an eternity clause, many times there are mere declarations of the inviolability of territorial integrity but not the added dimension that this provision may not be amended. One needs to derive that this declaration is intended to empower the courts to declare a contradictory amendment invalid. We need to look at both explicit and implicit provisions and read the constitution in its entirety to understand the extent of the fight against secession.

Third, democracies have developed a narrative that they fell in love with according to which the unconventional constitutional tools are available only to protect the democratic nature of the regime. Using these tools to prevent secession does not align with the narrative that democracies tell about themselves.

Fourth, the most important constitutional decision in comparative constitutional law on the subject of secession is the Canadian Supreme Court case from 1998 on secession of Quebec. That decision interprets the Canadian Charter that is silent on the topic of secession. Scholars assumed that this landmark decision is relevant to the world at large and missed the fact that it has limited bearing to the overwhelming majority of countries, whose constitutions are not silent on secession and treat secession very differently than the Canadian Charter.[4]

THE BAN OF SECESSIONIST POLITICAL PARTIES

One of the most important sources of democratic legitimacy is the fact that democracy is based on elections and majority rule. At the same time, it is widely accepted since World War II that democracies might need to ban political parties that threaten democracy itself. Karl Loewenstein developed the "militant democracy" theory in two breakthrough articles published in the *American Political Science Review* in 1937 on the eve of World War II to justify the ban on political parties in democratic terms. He fled Germany because he was a Jew, and from his exile in the United States, he enunciated the theory against the historical background of the rise of Nazism and fascism (Loewenstein 1937a, 638; Loewenstein 1937b, 417).

In his articles, Loewenstein warned democracies from committing suicide by adhering to democratic formalism and enabling those seeking to destroy democracy to use the tools of democracy for this aim. He warned that elections might serve as the Trojan horse through which the enemy enters and destroys democracy. He sought to impose restrictions on the access of threatening nondemocratic social forces to governmental power. He called for preventing their election to the legislature, preventing them from arming themselves and establishing military or private police forces, and preventing the bureaucratic officials from joining them. He argued that the more extreme are the tools used against these nondemocratic forces, the more democracies should restrict the use of these tools to states of emergency situations.

The conventional approach to militant democracy is both overinclusive and underinclusive, in comparison to Loewenstein's approach. It is overinclusive in the sense that courts and scholars may use the rhetoric of militant democracy to justify acts conducted to protect state security, including administrative detention and suspension of *habeas corpus*, even when the individuals subject to these measures do not pose a threat of overtaking government power. It is underinclusive in the sense that militant democracy is often used as an interchangeable term with ban on political parties, while Loewenstein intended to include other measures necessary to protect against the overtake of government power.

Ban on political parties became an acceptable democratic mechanism because its use is perceived as limited to the protection of the very existence of the democratic nature of the system. If a fascist or communist party assumes power, then democracy in a country might be destroyed, because of the principles that this nondemocratic party represents. However, secessionist parties do not necessarily destroy democracy. If they manage to gain power, they may begin the process of secession, but this can happen within the realm of a democratic system of governance with democratic procedures. This is why even when countries include in their constitution an explicit ban of secessionist political parties, scholars assume that these textual provisions are dead letter. They point to the fact that there are numerous secessionist political parties worldwide as proof that democracies allow for secession (Norman 2003, 207–208; Jovanović 2011, 357–358). Some scholars even theorize that since democracies allow for secessionist political parties, it is advisable to even establish a secession process in their constitutions (Mancini 2008, 575–579).

But the situation on the ground is different. Democracies target and ban secessionist political parties because of their secessionist agendas but justify the ban in the name of preserving the democratic regime alone. Democracies ban secessionist parties under the pretext of preventing racism, violence, and terrorism but the subtext is preventing secession. Even when the constitutional text of a given country allows banning a political party based on secession, the authorities oftentimes prefer to justify their actions in the name of the broader cause of protecting democracy. In this way democracies conceal their fight against secession.

The Spanish Constitution, for example, provides that political parties must respect the Constitution and that the Spanish nation is indissoluble. The Spanish Supreme Court banned the Batasuna Party in 2002, even though it participated in elections in the preceding twenty years. The Court based the ban on the fact that Batasuna was not condemning, not that it was endorsing, the Basque terrorist actions. More recently, the Spanish central authorities quashed Catalonian secessionist forces. They dismantled the Catalan legislature and executive branches of government. They called for new elections and jailed central figures of the secessionist movement. Banning secessionist political parties occurred in major European countries as well as in Asia, including in recent years (Weill 2018, 905).

States conceal the fact that they utilize the ban against secessionist political parties also because of the "peer pressure" of the international community. The European Court of Human Rights (ECHR), for example, overruled decisions of both Turkish and Bulgarian courts that banned secessionist political parties based on its position that a secessionist agenda is not a legitimate basis for bans, unless the parties' agendas are antidemocratic or they are associated with violence (*Case of the Socialist Party of Turkey (STP) and Others v Turkey, Case of the United Macedonian Organisation Ilinden – Pirin and Others v Bulgaria*). The ECHR's attitude encourages states, when banning secessionist activities, to articulate rationales other than self-preservation to avoid international criticism on their actions.

One might argue that democracies' fight against secessionists succeeded in creating an acoustic separation, where the secessionists understand that they are persecuted for their secessionist activities while the wider Western audience believes that they are banned to protect democracy (cf. Dan-Cohen 1984, 625). It is a rather easy task for democracies to convince their public that they utilize the ban against secessionist political parties to protect democracy alone. Why should not the public be persuaded? Do not these secessionist political parties have brothers and sisters in terrorist organizations? Do not they want to separate from the state because of their ethnic identity? Does not it sound like racism?

While scholars rely on the fact that there are many secessionist political parties across the entire democratic world, in fact, there is a delicate game between democratic states and secessionist forces. In many constitutional systems, the ban leads to a game of "cat and mouse," where the ban is implemented in a tailored manner, allowing a rebirth of the same secessionist party under a different name (Ayres 2004, 99; Bale 2007, 141; Bourne 2012, 196; Bligh 2013, 1321).[5] In this process, democracies try to dry secessionists' energy and resources. Democracies try to coerce these secessionist forces to soften and rephrase their agendas.

The game is very delicate and the picture is also blurred because democracies are very wise regarding whom they target. Democracies try to curtail secessionist political parties that are neither too small to be bothered with nor too big to be handled with through the ban. Allowing non-threatening secessionist parties to operate serves the purpose of steaming out their frustration within the confines of normal politics. But even when states allow secession-ist parties to operate despite a ban on the books, the parties know that they exist at the mercy of democracies, and not as a matter of right.

THE PROTECTION OF TERRITORIAL INTEGRITY
THROUGH ETERNITY CLAUSES

Constitutional democracies set limits on the power to amend the constitution as another lesson from World War II. Such limits on the amendment power are known as "eternity clauses." Eternity clauses mean that the constitution grants absolute entrenchment status to certain constitutional values and rights, so that they may not be amended and are treated as eternal. To protect this eternal status, courts developed the doctrine of the "unconstitutional consti-tutional amendment." This accompanying doctrine means that, even though a constitutional amendment is passed according to the procedure defined in the constitution for amendment, if its content runs against the basic values of the constitutional system as identified in an eternity clause, the courts may declare such an amendment invalid and unconstitutional (Fox and Nolte 1995, 1; Preuss 2011, 429). We justify this doctrine in the name of the protec-tion of democracy alone, just like with regard to the ban on political parties.

Scholars are aware that the constitutional texts of a few democratic coun-tries include declarations making the territory indivisible or making the unitary or federal structure of the state unamendable. But they treat these declarations as subject to the regular process of constitutional amendment (Radan 2011, 334–335). Yet I argue that these constitutional clauses are intended to trigger the "unconstitutional constitutional amendment" doctrine. Moreover, rather than being a negligible phenomenon, it is prevalent among constitutional democracies to treat their federal structure, unitary status, and territorial integrity as unamendable (Weill 2018). The German Constitutional Court, for example, ruled, in 2016, that Bavaria could not hold a referendum on independence as secession is forbidden under the Basic Law (BVerfG, 2 BvR 349/16, December 16, 2016). The Italian Constitutional Court issued a similar decision in 2015 preventing Veneto from holding a consultative referendum on independence (Corte Cost., 29 aprile 2015, n.118, 2015 (It.)).

Even when the constitution is silent on secession, the courts may read into the constitution an implied clause preventing secession. One of the most interesting cases is the U.S. case of *Texas v White* of 1868. Texas decided to secede during the civil war and join the confederation and the people of Texas ratified this decision in a referendum. The case arose during the Reconstruc-tion era and Texas was not yet readmitted to the Union. There was a question whether the U.S. Supreme Court could entertain the case at all, because if

Texas was not a state within the Union, then the Court had no jurisdiction over the case.

The Court held that even though Texas was not yet readmitted, it also never seceded. The reasoning of the Court is fascinating. The Court used a language that we typically attribute to the Indian Supreme Court. We typically think that the Indian Supreme Court is the inventor of the basic structure doctrine, the idea of an implied eternity clause. But the language of Chief Justice Chase in *Texas v White* sounds very much like the basic structure doctrine: "The Constitution in all its provisions looks to an indestructible Union composed of indestructible States" (*Texas v White*, 726). The Court was looking at the entire structure of the constitution to derive the eternal principle of unity and that secession is impossible under the U.S. Constitution, unless agreed between the seceding state and the rest of the states that form part of the Union.

Some constitutions contain seemingly contradictory provisions. At times, a constitution may declare the territorial integrity inviolable but then provide a procedure of achieving territorial change (Weill 2018). Courts, too, use doublespeak. When it came to Ukraine or Spain, the courts invalidated regional referenda or tried to prevent them from taking place, holding that secession was a national, not a regional, topic. Thus, only the national political bodies could hold a national referendum on the subject (Judgment of the Constitutional Court of Ukraine on all-Crimean Referendum). Rather than stating that secession could not be brought about by amendment, they referred the secessionists to processes that would frustrate their will. They knew that at the national level there was no support for secession. These decisions reflect the courts' understanding that it is better to intervene early in the process of secession, before a constitutional amendment is adopted. By the time the "unconstitutional constitutional amendment" could be applied, it may be too late, as the seceding area would no longer be under the jurisdiction of the constitutional court of the parent state.

It is rare to find a court invalidating secession based on the doctrine of the "unconstitutional constitutional amendment." Secessions are usually achieved through force and illegality rather than the orderly process of a constitutional amendment (Young 1994, 773). The existence of the doctrine of the "unconstitutional constitutional amendment" suggests to secessionists that they cannot achieve their aims through amendment and must thus resort to forceful, extraconstitutional means.

ON THE NEXUS BETWEEN ETERNITY CLAUSES AND MILITANT DEMOCRACY

There is a deep relationship between the two mechanisms that constitutional democracies use to prevent secession: the ban on secessionist political parties should be treated as the "front guard" of the constitutional system. It is intended to prevent the reformers from ever reaching the legislature and initiating constitutional change. It is customary in constitutions that to embark on constitutional change, one needs the consent of both the elites, and primarily the legislature, and the people. If the secessionists do not reach power, then they cannot trigger constitutional change. If the secessionists are not banned and do reach power, then the eternity clause and the accompanying doctrine of the "unconstitutional constitutional amendment" serve as the "rear guard" of democracy. It is intended to declare the amendment of the reformers invalid. Both tools are mirror images of one another. They kick in at different times for the protection of the constitutional *status quo*.

It is justified to see the tools as complimentary on theoretical, historical, and methodological grounds. Historically, both the ban on political parties and eternity clauses became prevalent after World War II. Theoretically, though militant democracy theory is identified with the ban alone, eternity clauses are about the same idea of using a militant stance against those who do not share the state's basic values. Methodologically, both are tools of absolute entrenchment. While this is more obvious with eternity clauses, ban on political parties express absolute entrenchment in the sense that if the secessionists do not reach the legislature, they will also not be able to trigger constitutional change. In a given country, the list of constitutional values protected under each of the mechanisms should be roughly the same, if the system is to have a coherent constitutional identity.[6]

Democracies told themselves the story that militant democracy and eternity clauses are about the protection of the democratic regime alone. It was important for them to tell this story because these two tools are on the verge of being nondemocratic. Many times statesmen use the rhetoric of militant democracy as an empowering rhetoric, not understanding that when they use this rhetoric, they are not only legitimizing the exercise of extreme powers but also admitting that they are on the verge of being nondemocratic. How democratic can a state be when it bans peaceful political parties from participating at elections? How democratic can a state be, when it declares a constitutional amendment unconstitutional, even though it was adopted according to the procedure set in the constitution for amendment? Scholars discuss the "counter-majoritarian" difficulty with regard to judicial review but explain that the decisions of courts may be overturned by constitutional amendment. But an eternity clause blocks the constitutional amendment track.

As democracies understand that these tools are so problematic, they justify them in the name of protecting the democratic regime. That democracy is not just majority rule but also individual rights. It is not just formal but also substantive. But if democracies admit that they are using these tools to protect against the dismantling of the state, then they must admit that they are using nondemocratic tools for nondemocratic goals. This is why democracies go into such great lengths to try and hide their fight against secession. I am not arguing that states do not have legitimate reasons to fight against secession.[7] I am only trying to explain why countries are conflicted on the topic of secession.

REFERENDA MECHANISMS FOR SECESSION

Even the minority of countries that have constitutional secession clauses use them not to promote orderly secession but to subvert secession. In some cases, countries constitutionalize secession only to attract smaller countries to join their federation. Once they achieve this goal of enlargement, they retract their promise to enable secession and treat the state as unitary. This explains the paradoxical situation in which constitutional secession clauses were found in nondemocratic countries like the former Soviet Union or China. Lenin was keen enough to admit that the Soviet Constitution enabled secession to enlarge the Soviet Union and not accommodate the smaller states. The Soviet constitutional secession clause did not articulate the procedure of secession. It could not even theoretically serve as a roadmap for the secession of the thirteen out of fifteen republics that led to the fall of the Soviet Union. China later abolished its secession clause (Weill 2018).

In other cases, the constitutional secession clauses impose such burdensome obstacles that secession becomes impossible to achieve in a constitutional manner. The obstacles may appear as a super-majority requirement, requiring that, even if a majority of the people approves secession in a referendum, no secession will take place. For example, the Constitution of Saint Kitts and Nevis requires the support of two-thirds of the Nevis electorate at a nationally organized referendum to achieve secession (Saint Kitts and Nevis Constitution, article 113, § 2). In 1998, 61.7% of the Nevis electorate approved secession, not meeting the threshold for secession (Radan 2011, 339).

In addition, secession referenda are typically treated as merely advisory, meaning that they are binding only if the result is negative. In fact, on more than one occasion, though the secession referendum produced a positive result, secession did not take place. Thus, for example, Western Australia voted in favor of secession in a referendum in the 1930s, but the Imperial British Parliament refused their petition to secede from Australia "except upon the definite request of the Commonwealth of Australia conveying the clearly expressed wish of the Australian people as a whole" (Mayer 1968, 63).

Referenda are the opening phase of a long process of negotiation, and the negotiations may fail, as the Canadian Supreme Court openly acknowledged (Reference *re* Secession of Quebec, 270–271, 278, 289–290). Characteristically, the central government decides the timing and conduct of the referendum, the phrasing of the question, and the interpretation of its results. Moreover, secession usually requires a constitutional amendment and that again grants veto power to the central government.

If no agreement is met, the rump state will oppose secession. The lack of agreement will also lead the international community to more easily side with the rump state to protect the international norm of territorial integrity. No state wants to encourage the secessionist phenomenon, as it may need to face similar challenges within its borders.

ON WE THE TERRITORIAL PEOPLE

My explanation for the prevalence of the constitutional ban against secession is both strategic and normative. Strategically, the ban is intended to minimize internal conflict by raising the costs of achieving secession. In this respect, international law and constitutional law seem to complement each other in their treatment of secession. International law, too, requires secessionists in contexts other than decolonization or alien occupation to resort of extra-legality to bring about change. This is my interpretation of the International Court of Justice's decision regarding Kosovo from 2010 ("Accordance with International Law of Unilateral Declaration of Independence in Respect of Kosovo," Advisory Opinion, 2010 I.C.J. 403 (July 22)). The Court held that Kosovo's unilateral Declaration of Independence did not violate international law because Kosovo was not trying to rely on international law to legitimate its unilateral declaration of independence, but quite the opposite. Kosovo declared that the intermediate regime of international law imposed in Kosovo failed, and this is why it was resorting to a unilateral declaration of independence.

Both international law and constitutional law thus cooperate in raising the stakes to the secessionists, by requiring them to resort to extra-legality and extra-constitutionality to achieve their goal. They raise the stakes to the secessionists to minimize world unrest. And the strategy succeeds at least according to the data we have with regard to international law. When international law recognizes the right to secede, which is true in cases involving decolonization or alien occupation, secessionists enjoy a high success rate of 77%. In contrast, in other contexts, secessionists' success rate is only 16% (Fazal and Griffiths 2008, 203; cf. Coggins 2011, 32). So, by not recognizing the right to secede, the law reduces the incentives to embark on secession.

States, too, prohibit secession in their constitution to deter secessionists from pursuing their goal and raise the stakes for the secessionists. The ban on political parties hinders their mobilization. Secessionists must feel strongly enough about their cause to risk violating the internal law of the state. They need to be committed enough to withstand the pressure of lost hopes in light of an eternity clause. By prohibiting secession, states hope that they will prevent secessionist movements from gathering momentum. And even if despite the militant stand, states will need to compromise, they hope that the prohibition will give them the upper hand in the negotiations with the secessionists.

The second explanation for the total prohibition of secession is that, in the overwhelming majority of cases, secession challenges the basic norm of who the sovereign body in the constitutional system is.[8] My argument is that constitutions' treatment of secession reveals that popular sovereignty is a territorial concept. This is not trivial. The literature by and large emphasizes that popular sovereignty is a notion that involves population alone. But what I am arguing is that constitutions are not so worried about the loss of people through emigration. They are also not so worried about the redrawing of boundaries. But constitutions use their most unconventional constitutional tools to prevent losing the combination of citizens plus territory.

This suggests to me that secession poses a unique challenge to constitutions. It is no coincidence that constitutions require that secession will be brought about by extra-constitutionality, revolution, and new beginnings in the Kelsenian sense. Constitutions in essence are telling the secessionists: when you challenge the very identity of the constitutional making body, when you challenge who "we the people" are, then you cannot rely on "we the people" of the current constitution to bring about change. You have to act from outside the system. Constitutions' treatment of secession reveals that "We the People" is truly "We the territorial people."

My argument does not rest on the distinction between the constitution-making body and the amending body. I do not treat the latter as inferior to the former, as is typically assumed in theoretical explanations of the "unconstitutional constitutional amendment" doctrine (Weill 2014). I argue the opposite: the body in charge of amending the constitution is on par with the body in charge of creating the constitution. The basic norm is situated not just in the process of constitutional adoption but also in the process of constitutional amendment. Rather, I distinguish between constitutional amendments that redefine the constitution-making body in the state and other types of constitutional amendments. When the constitution-making body is redefined, as occurs in secession, it amounts to an "annihilation" of the existing constitution and demands a new independent act of self-definition by both the departing and the remaining people, each people acting separately to constitute themselves (cf. Schmitt 1928, 151). They need to reach agreement to avoid competing claims to sovereignty over the same people and territory. This contrasts with the common approach that suggests that either only the seceding people should be consulted in a referendum or secession requires a national referendum that includes the secessionists. As long as states need the combination of citizens and territory to exist, both international and constitutional laws will most likely continue to ban secession.

NOTES

* Senior research scholar, Yale Law School (2018–2019); professor of Law, Harry Radzyner Law School, IDC. I expand on the themes of this chapter in "Secession and the Prevalence of Both Militant Democracy and Eternity Clauses Worldwide" 40 *Cardozo Law Review* 905 (2018). For discussion of some of these ideas, see https://podcasts.apple.com/us/podcast/secession-prevalence-both-militant-democracy-eternity/id1447304234?i=1000434719049. I thank the editors of this book and Argyro Kartsonaki for their helpful comments on this chapter.

1. I treat a country as nondemocratic if one or both the Democracy Index and Freedom House's Index found a country to be nondemocratic (authoritarian or not free). I treat the classification of democracies as based on a continuum rather than binary. The classification itself is debatable and political.

2. Decolonization, nationalism, globalization, democratization, the language of human rights, mass migration—have all contributed to the rise in secessionist activity in the twentieth and twenty-first centuries. See Weill (2018, 921–926).

3. I discuss other constitutional tools that states employ in their fight against secession in Weill (2018).

4. For full explanation why the Canadian Supreme Court case regarding Quebec should be distinguished rather than serve as a leading precedent in comparative constitutional law, see Weill (2018, 983–984).

5. For examples of this "cat and mouse" game, see Weill (2018, 944–946).

6. For further elaboration on the nexus between unamendability and the ban, see Weill (2018, 960–966; 2017).

7. The reasons why states may legitimately fight against secession are enumerated in Weill (2018, 926–928).

8. For cases in which secession does not challenge popular sovereignty and may be achieved via a constitutional amendment, see Weill (2018, 977–985).

REFERENCES

"Accordance with International Law of the Unilateral Declaration of Independence in Respect of Kosovo," Advisory Opinion, 2010 I.C.J. 403 (July 22).

Ackerman, Bruce. 2014. *We the People: The Civil Rights Revolution*. Cambridge, MA: Harvard University Press.

Ayres, Thomas. 2004. "Batasuna Banned: The Dissolution of Political Parties under the European Convention of Human Rights." *Boston College International and Comparative Law* 27(1): 99.

Bale, Tim. 2007. "Are Bans on Political Parties Bound to Turn Out Badly? A Comparative Investigation of Three 'Intolerant' Democracies: Turkey, Spain, and Belgium." *Comparative European Politics* 5(2): 141.

Beary, Brian. 2011, *Separatist Movements: A Global Reference*. Washington: CQ Press.

Bligh, Gur. 2013. "Defending Democracy: A New Understanding of the Party-Banning Phenomenon." *Vanderbilt Journal of Transnational Law* 46: 1321.

Bourne, Angela. 2012. "The Proscription of Political Parties and 'Militant Democracy': The Problem with Militant Democracy." *Journal of Comparative Law* 7(1): 196.

Brilmayer, Lea. 1991. "Secession and Self-Determination: A Territorial Interpretation." *Yale Journal of International Law* 16: 177.

Buchanan, Allen. 1997. "Theories of Secession." *Philosophy and Public Affairs* 26(1): 31.

BVerfG, 2 BvR 349/16, December 16, 2016.

Case of the Socialist Party of Turkey (STP) and Others v Turkey, App. No. 26482/95, Eur. Ct. H.R. Rep. (2003).

Case of the United Macedonian Organisation Ilinden – Pirin and Others v Bulgaria, App. No. 59489/00, Eur. Ct. H.R. Rep. (2005).

Coggins, Bridget L. 2011. "The History of Secession: An Overview." In *The Ashgate Research Companion to Secession*, edited by Aleksandar Pavković and Peter Radan. Great Britain: Ashgate, 23–37.

Corte Cost., 29 aprile 2015, n. 118, 2015 (It.)

Dan-Cohen, Meir. 1984. "Decision Rules and Conduct Rules: On Acoustic Separation in Criminal Law." *Harvard Law Review* 97(3): 625.

Fazal, Tanisha, and Ryan Griffiths. 2008. "A State of One's Own: The Rise of Secession since World War II." *The Brown Journal of World Affairs* 15(1): 199.

Fox, Gregory H., and Georg Nolte. 1995. "Intolerant Democracies." *Harvard International Law Journal* 36(1): 1.

G. A. Res. 1514 (XV). "Declaration on the Granting of Independence to Colonial Countries and Peoples" (December 14, 1960).

Jackson, Vicki C. 2016. "Secession, Transnational Precedents, and Constitutional Silences." In *Nullification and Secession in Modern Constitutional Thought*, edited by Sanford Levinson. Kansas: University Press of Kansas, 314–342.

Jovanović, Miodrag A. 2011. "To Constitutionalize or Not? Secession as Materiae Constitutionis." In *The Ashgate Research Companion to Secession*, edited by Aleksandar Pavković and Peter Radan. Great Britain: Ashgate, p. 357.

Judgment of the Constitutional Court of Ukraine on all-Crimean Referendum, No. 1–13/2014 (March 14, 2014); S.T.C., Oct. 17, 2017, No. 4334–2017 (Ukraine).

Kelsen, Hans. 1945. *General Theory of Law and State*. Translated by Anders Wedberg. Cambridge, MA: Harvard University Press.

Levinson, Sanford. 2004. "Perpetual Union, Free Love, and Secession: On the Limits to the Consent of the Governed." *Tulsa Law Review* 39: 457–484.

Loewenstein, Karl. 1937a. "Militant Democracy and Fundamental Rights, I." *American Political Science Review* 31(4): 638.

Loewenstein, Karl. 1937b. "Militant Democracy and Fundamental Rights, II." *American Political Science Review* 31(4): 417.

Mancini, Susanna. 2008. "Rethinking the Boundaries of Democratic Secession: Liberalism, Nationalism, and the Right of Minorities to Self-Determination." *International Journal of Constitutional Law* 6: 575–579.

Mayer R. A. 1968. "Legal Aspects of Secession." *Manitoba Law Journal* 3: 61.

Monahan, Patrick J., and Michael J. Bryant, with Nancy C. Coté. 1996. "Coming to Terms with Plan B: Ten Principles Governing Secession." *C.D. Howe Institute Commentary* 83: 1.

Norman, Wayne. 2003. "Domesticating Secession." In *Secession and Self-Determination*, edited by Stephen Macedo and Allen Buchanan. New York: NYU Press, p. 207.

Preuss, Ulrich K. 2011. "The Implications of 'Eternity Clauses': The German Experience." *Israel Law Review* 44(3): 429.

Radan, Peter. 2011. "Secession in Constitutional Law." In *The Ashgate Research Companion to* Secession, edited by Aleksandar Pavković and Peter Radan. Great Britain: Ashgate, p. 333.

Ratner, Steven R. 1996. "Drawing a Better Line: *Uti Possidetis* and the Borders of New States." *American Journal of International Law* 90: 590.

Reference *re* Secession of Quebec, [1998] 2 S.C.R. 217 (Can.).

Saint Kitts and Nevis Constitution, article 113, § 2.

Schmitt, Carl. 1928 [2008]. *Constitutional Theory*. Translated by Jeffrey Seitzer. Durham: Duke University Press, 151.

Sollors, Werner. 1986. *Beyond Ethnicity: Consent and Descent in American Culture*. Oxford: Oxford University Press.

Sunstein, Cass R. 1991. "Constitutionalism and Secession." *University of Chicago Law Review* 58: 633.

Texas v White, 74 U.S. 700 (1868).

Thomas, Elizabeth. 2010, "'We Have Nothing More Valuable in Our Treasury': Royal Marriage in England, 1154–1272." A Thesis Submitted for the Degree of PhD at the University of St Andrews, https://research-repository.st-andrews.ac.uk/handle/10023/2001.

Treason Act 1351, 1351 Chapter 2 25 Edw 3 Stat 5. http://www.legislation.gov.uk/aep/Edw3Stat5/25/2.

Weill, Rivka. 2014. "The New Commonwealth Model of Constitutionalism Notwithstanding: On Judicial Review and Constitution-Making." *American Journal of Comparative Law* 62: 127.

Weill, Rivka. 2017. "On the Nexus of Eternity Clauses, Proportional Representation, and Banned Political Parties." *Election Law Journal* 16(2): 237.

Weill, Rivka. 2018. "Secession and the Prevalence of Both Militant Democracy and Eternity Clauses Worldwide." *Cardozo Law Review* 40(2): 905.

Young, Robert A. 1994. "How Do Peaceful Secessions Happen?" *Canadian Journal of Political Science* 27(4): 773.

Part II

EMPIRICAL CASE STUDIES OF SECESSION AND COUNTER-SECESSION STRATEGIES

Chapter 6

Democratic Institutions, Secessionist Strategy, and the Use of Violence: An Empirical Analysis

Faruk Aksoy and Melike Ayşe Kocacık-Şenol

This chapter is reserved for exploring the relationship between democracy and the tactical choices of secessionists. Even though there has been mushrooming research in the literature on secessionist movements overall, the role of institutions and components of democracy on tactical decisions of secessionist groups have been neglected. This is the lacuna which we attempt to fill in this chapter. We discuss the extent to which different institutions which entail democracy might affect the tactical choices of secessionist movements. For this purpose, we look at democracy through a different lens by decomposing the concept into its components. These components are deduced in light of causal arguments which have been offered by related literature about how democracy alters the behavior of rebel groups. Considering this practice, we focus on three components of democracy, namely constraints on government, civil and political liberties, and free and fair elections. Thus, the central task of this chapter is to analyze discrete effects of each component of democracy using the Varieties of Democracy (V-Dem) dataset on the four possible tactics of secessionists, which we measure by using the dataset of Cunningham, Dahl, and Frugé (2017). As an empirical strategy, we will investigate democracy indicators as latent variables alongside the change in the level of democracy indicators in terms of their effect on the tactical choices of secessionists.

What we expected from these analyses was threefold. First, we hoped to find that these three components of democracy affect the tactical decisions of secessionists separately. Second, we looked for the different patterns for the relationship of each of these three components with secessionist tactics. Our third and last expectation was that these relationships exist in a different form in anocracies in comparison to democracies and autocracies. What we found in our descriptive analyses roughly corresponds with these expectations. First, the low level of each of the three components is a harbinger of violence as a secessionist tactic. Our findings also show that what matters for tactical choices of secessionists seems to depend on changes in the levels of constraints on government and levels of free and fair elections but not on the changes in the levels of civil and political liberties. Also, the effect of a change in the constraints on government is different in anocracies in comparison to democracies and autocracies; additionally, changes in the level of free and fair elections has a remarkable impact only in anocracies.

Before starting, it is worth emphasizing that these results cannot be conclusive and they are not sufficient to make causal inference. Note that the central task of this chapter is merely to present the patterns, thereby turning the attention to the multifaceted nature of democracy which is, we think, worth to be considering while analyzing the tactical choices of secessionist groups. To this end, the remainder of this chapter is structured as follows. First, we present a review of the literature on the relationship between democracy and secessionist tactics. After that, there is a section in which we search for potential causal mechanisms for this relationship by delving into the literature of civil war, terrorism, and protest. Next, we present our analyses. There is a description of the relationship between the four tactics of secessionists and three components of democracy. Subsequently, more elaborated evaluations of two of these tactics, violence and protest, present a vivid picture. We conclude this chapter with a discussion on the findings of our study which might give a hint for future research on the relationship between democracy and secessionist tactics.

SECESSIONIST TACTICS AND DEMOCRACY

As Cunningham (2013) stated, the tactical choice of secessionist groups depends on which of those tactics has a higher probability in succeeding with a lower expected cost. Therefore, it is essential to examine the conditions which might impact cost and benefit expectations of using different tactics. Among these conditions, political institutions have a special status, since the primary function of institutions is to set the rules of the game, which shapes the decisions of actors by altering the cost and/or benefit of any particular behavior. By doing so, they constrain the choices of actors and shape human interaction (North 1990). Therefore, it is plausible to argue that secessionists' cost-benefit calculations for tactical choices need to be discussed considering political institutions of the polity that they emerged from. In this respect, the very first institutions that come to mind are those which have originated from the regime type of the country. Perhaps institutions of political regimes shape the playing field for secessionists, who are expected to adjust their tactics accordingly. In the light of cost-benefit calculations, for instance, the cost of organizing a protest is probably higher in a regime in which freedom of association has been circumvented. This condition might affect the tactical choices of secessionist groups so that they may refrain from organizing this collective action or they might prefer a violent tactic because of the difference between the cost of assembling a protest and the cost of violent action declines. In a similar vein, the institutions of a regime might multiply the probability of violence. For example, Lacina (2006) found that for rebel groups in an autocracy, deadly tactics might be more feasible to employ, since they need a military victory or to topple the regime to achieve their goals. On the other hand, democracies have institutions to make concessions in response to rebel group demands and are more open to feeling pressure to protect the state order in the process of settling the dispute.

In this respect, among the studies focusing on the relationship between democracy and secessionism (Walter 2006; Svensson and Lindgren 2010; Cunningham 2011; Griffiths 2015), there are studies in which the relationship between regime type and secessionists' tactics has been discussed. It is worth emphasizing that, in the extant literature, the reference point to evaluate other political regimes is a democracy. For example, Gleditsch and Rivera (2017) argued that nonviolent campaigns are more likely to diffuse to neighboring countries if the affected country is a nondemocracy rather than a democracy. Also, if a country has more democratic neighbors, the likelihood of contagion increases. They use the Polity 4 dataset to construct a dummy variable for measuring democracy. On the other hand, Cunningham's (2013) study on the determinants of secessionist movements' preference for strategies defined two variables to measure democracy. The first one is the binary democracy variable based on Polity 4. Also, she constructed a variable for political instability, which is coded as 1 if there has been a three or higher-level change in Polity 4 score for the past two years and otherwise is coded as 0. She found that nonviolent campaigns, compared to conventional politics, are more likely to occur in nondemocracies. Also, political instability has no statistical and substantive significant effect on tactical decisions of secessionists. In another study, Cunningham, Dahl, and Frugé (2017) attempted to understand why secessionist movements prefer specific nonviolent tactics. They added the Polity 2 score into the statistical analysis by which they try to ascertain the correlates of seven tactics. They found that there is a correlation between the level of democracy and the usage of protest, but an insignificant relationship between the level of democracy and political noncooperation was reported. Last, Griffiths and Wasser (2019) argued that secessionists who struggle with democratic regimes are less likely to be successful than secessionist who targets nondemocracies. Moreover, they suggested that violence is a more preferred strategy in nondemocracies. The authors also indicated that a claiming proto-state is a more effective strategy in nondemocracies. To measure democracy, they constructed a dummy variable using the Polity 4 dataset.

The lacuna which we observed in the previously mentioned literature is the lack of attention on institutions of democracy which may alter the tactical choices of secessionist groups. Also, most of the studies employ binary or continuous variable to measure democracy with a single indicator. Nonetheless, democracy is a combination of different institutions, each of which might affect the diverse set of behavior of actors in the polity. Therefore, to unveil the causal link between democracy and the tactical choices of secessionist movements, we need to turn our focus to each institution of democracy, which constitutes components of it, as the building blocks of a regime. In other words, the question waiting to be discussed concerns which components of democracy influence secessionists' decisions to employ specific tactics. Since the operationalization of democracy in the literature of secessionism has not considered this possibility enough, it is not sufficient to narrow the theoretical expectation with this literature. Therefore, the search for the causal link between democracy and secessionists' tactics is required to pursue an alternative strategy. For this purpose, it might be plausible to turn our focus to the cousin literature of secessionism in which the effects of democracy on civil war, terrorism, and protest—as potential strategies—has been discussed. Pieces in these literati might help us to nominate discrete components of democracy as candidates which affect the tactical choices of secessionists. To this end, the next section is reserved for this task before our analysis in the subsequent section.

SEARCH FOR CAUSAL EXPECTATIONS

Let us start with the literature on the civil war. The relationship between democracy and the choice of rebel groups to resort to violence has been discussed through two causal arguments. Regardless of the operationalization of democracy or the model of analysis, the effect of democracy on the choice of violence has been explained through the existence of institutions *facilitating freedoms and liberties and constraining the government*. Nevertheless, for both arguments, studies provided contrary mechanisms and results. There have been some studies which argue that freedoms and liberties alleviate the probability of civil war, since they provide potential rebels an opportunity to express their demands without resorting to violence (Gurr 1970; Keefer 2008; Getmansky 2013), whereas other studies have suggested that by helping dissident groups to organize, freedom and liberties increase the likelihood of civil war (Saideman et al. 2002). A similar pattern can be detected in the case of constraints on government as well. Some studies have pointed out the function of constraints on the government as deterring the government from using extreme actions that might trigger a civil war (Merom 2003; Walter 2015). On the other hand, the literature contains arguments that constraining government increases the opportunity of rebel groups for organization and mobilization by narrowing the policy set of government (Morgan and Campbell 1991; Davenport and Armstrong 2004; Carey 2010).

Along with studies in which the relationship between civil war and democracy is reported as linear, there is a vast amount of literature which has proposed a quadratic pattern for this relationship (Hegre et al. 2001; Reynal-Querol 2002; Fearon and Laitin 2003). Nevertheless, the causal arguments do not differ from the studies mentioned in the previous paragraphs. Anocracies, as middle-level democracies, are more fragile for experiencing a civil war because they do not provide enough freedom and liberties to potential rebels for expressing their grievances while they leave the door half open for rebels to organize and mobilize support for their cause. Also, this quadratic relationship leads us to think further on how different components of democracy, a lack of which causes a regime to turn into an anocracy, incentivize secessionist groups to use distinct tactics for self-determination.

Similar causal arguments can be found in the literature on terrorism and protest as well. For instance, Young and Dugan (2011) argued that when there are more legal constraints to changing the *status quo*, it is harder for governments to handle terrorism. In other words, more veto players in the political system make the polity more vulnerable to terrorism. A similar finding was reported by Li (2005) in the case of transnational terrorist attacks and by some other scholars regarding domestic terrorism (Eyerman 1998; Chenoweth 2010). In a similar vein, Saideman et al. (2002) found that both protests and rebellions are more likely to occur in democracies. Potential protesters and rebels have more opportunity to organize and collaborate in democracies which ensure political and civil liberties.

As this brief review of the literature shows, the discussion on the effects of components of democracy on conflict, far from being smooth, have pointed out contrary directions in terms of the impact of the same components. Note that our self-assigned task does not tackle with these inconsistent results. Nevertheless, this review steers us to two potential causal links between democracy and tactical choices of secessionists: the constraints on government and civil and political liberties. Therefore, institutions which constitute these two components will be our variables of interest. But this is not all; there is one more component of democracy that we want to address in terms of its potential effect on secessionists' tactics.

THE LAST COMPONENT: FREE AND FAIR ELECTIONS

In addition to constraints on government and civil and political liberties, we will include another component of democracy to the analysis: free and fair elections. Let us first define each concept separately. Free elections refer to providing an unrestricted opportunity to voters and candidates in terms of being able to participate in the election free from any coercion (Elklit and Svensson 1997). In a similar vein, fair elections require that the rules of the game, that is, election rules, constitution, and other regulations, are applied impartially to everyone, and candidates alongside voters need to have similar opportunities to express themselves during the electoral process (Elklit and Svensson 1997).

The reason behind our choice to include free and fair elections into the analysis is twofold. First, all definitions of democracy contain free and fair elections as a prerequisite; in fact, this component is the minimal definition of democracy (Schumpeter 2010; Schmitter and Karl 1991). In other words, it is *the necessary condition* for having a democratic regime. Any composite indicator of democracy directly or indirectly measures how much the elections are free and fair. In addition to the centrality of free and fair elections in the definition of democracy, the nexus between the literature on civil conflict and the hybrid regimes gives us a hint that free and fair elections might be one of the components of democracy which affects the tactical choices of secessionists. As we discussed in the previous section, one of the main findings of the civil war literature is the vulnerability of anocracies for experiencing civil war. The literature indicates the constraints on government and civil and political liberties as the causal links for this relationship. However, the comparative politics literature offers us another hybrid regime type, anocracy, whose definitive characteristic is the lack of sufficient level of free and fair election, competitive authoritarianism. In competitive authoritarian regimes, governments abuse their power to undermine the chance of the opposition to win the elections, thereby undermining the principle of the free and fair elections. Examples for incumbent behavior include a wide range of violations by incumbents, which affects the level of free and fair elections, such as using state resources for their electoral campaign, electoral fraud, censorship, imprisonment, and assassination of opposition leaders (Levitsky and Way 2010). Under these circumstances, it is plausible to expect that such an unfair playing field might affect the tactical choices of secessionists. Therefore, this is our second reason for including free and fair elections in the analysis.

Thus, we have now three components of democracy, namely the constraints on government, civil and political liberties, and free and fair elections, as potential candidates for influencing the tactical choices of secessionists.

It is important to note that our aim is neither to make a causal inference nor to find a causal direction for these components. In fact, we will attempt to investigate:

(1) whether these components of democracy affect the tactical choices of secessionists;
(2) how patterns in the relationships of each of the three components of democracy with tactical choices of secessionists differ from each other; and
(3) whether these relationships are different in anocracies in comparison to democracies and autocracies.

In the following sections, we will attempt to find descriptive evidence for these expectations. But before the analysis, we will explain the data and measures, which is the next task of this chapter.

DESCRIPTION OF THE DATASET

The dataset that we employed to measure our three components of democracy is the V-Dem dataset. This dataset choice depends on two reasons. First, V-Dem decomposes the components of democracy, which is necessary for our analysis. Also, it uses the Bayesian method for the aggregation rule, which has been presented as a better way to construct a composite index (Treier and Jackman 2008). For each of the three components of democracy, we employed an index from V-Dem into our analysis to evaluate the impact of our three components of democracy on secessionist tactics. In this respect, for the level of constraint on government, we used the Horizontal Accountability Index of V-Dem. This index includes judicial and legislative constraints on the executive and the level of authority and power of other state agencies to check the actions of the executive. Additionally, for the level of civil and political liberties, we use the Diagonal Accountability Index of V-Dem, which contains variables measuring media freedom, characteristics of civil society, freedom of expression, and the political engagement of citizens Coppedge et al.. Last, we used the Clean Election Index of V-Dem for the level of free and fair elections in which the extent to which the elections are free and fair is measured.

Meanwhile, for secessionist tactics, we used Cunningham, Dahl, and Frugé's (2017) dataset. The advantage of using this dataset is its unit of analysis which is the factions within secessionist groups and the availability of data for different nonviolent tactics used by these factions. Other datasets on secessionist movements (Cunningham 2013; Chenoweth and Stephan,

2011; Sambanis, Germann, and Schädel 2018) defined different actions based on whether these groups used any violent means for establishing a sovereign state or not. However, particularly, nonviolent actions can vary in aim and scope in using different nonviolent tools. In this respect, Cunningham, Dahl, and Frugé (2017) presented five different nonviolent resistance types of secessionist movements. The protest and demonstration category includes incidences such as rallies, protests, and demonstrations. Nonviolent interventions, on the other hand, involve sit-ins, occupations, and blockades. Nonviolent tactics, which are more individualistic and lower in cost, might encompass as economic, social, and political noncooperation. Economic noncooperation includes incidences such as strikes, tax refusals, and consumer boycotts. Social noncooperation refers to actions such as hunger strikes, self-immolation, or other kinds of self-harm. Political noncooperation includes withdrawals from political office or coalitions in the government.

After explaining the datasets which we employed, we can now turn to a general description of the first tactics employed by a faction, which is our variable of interest.[1] Using different tactics as the first action is diverse among different states. Table 6.1 shows the number of factions which engaged in different tactics in the year of their emergence. A total of 845 factions did not use any tactics, whereas 279 factions used at least one of the violent or nonviolent tactics in the year that they arose. It means that approximately 75% of the secessionist groups had not employed a tactic in the year of their emergence but only announced their intention for self-determination.

When we compare decisions of secessionist groups on their first tactic in any year after their emergence rather than only in the year of their emergence, we also observe divergence in their tactical choices. Table 6.2 represents the first tactics that these secessionist groups have employed. A total of 183 factions chose to use violence against the state, whereas 129 of them decided to protest. In total, 148 factions conducted institutional actions. These are the factions that only used one of these tactics. In some cases, the secessionist groups decided to use more than one tactic. Fifty of them used only mixture of nonviolent tactics, while fifty of them mixed violent and nonviolent tactics.

Table 6.1.   Number of Different Action Types During Emergence

Institutional	101
Violence against the state	65
Protests and nonviolent intervention	78
Noncooperation (economic, social, and political)	35
No action	845

Table 6.2.   Number of Different Action Types as the First Action Taken

Institutional	148
Violent	183
Protests and nonviolent intervention	129
Noncooperation (economic, social, and political)	54
Nonviolent tactics mixed	50
Violent and nonviolent mixed	50

After the description of the data on secessionist tactics, the next step will be the presentation of our analyses and their results. Our strategy in assessing the relationship between secessionist tactics and democracy is twofold. First, we will present a description of the relationship between the first tactics utilized by a faction and the level of three democracy indicators. Then, we will focus on two tactics, namely violence against the state and protest, to analyze the relationship between the change in the level of democracy indicators after the emergence of the secessionist movement and the preference of secessionist about using or not using violence/protest as a strategy.

ANALYSES

The preliminary descriptive data described earlier indicate that there is a variation in the use of nonviolent versus violent tactics as the first action toward secession. To evaluate whether there is a relationship between the levels of our three components of democracy and the tactical decisions of secessionist groups, we introduce the following tables. Our purpose is to track whether any variation among the tactical choices of factions emerges in different institutional settings. Note that this is merely a descriptive depiction of the relationship rather than a causal argument, albeit with the claim of dealing with endogeneity. Aside from eliminating endogeneity, causal linkage requires testing the effects of a variety of confounding variables on the hypothesized relationship. However, we do not conduct a statistical analysis by which potential confounding variables are detected. Instead, we aim to provide a general picture of the relationship rather than to offer conclusive evidence for a causal relationship. Therefore, our results should be evaluated in this light.

Table 6.3 shows the number of tactics used at different levels of diagonal accountability. We created the categorical variable of diagonal accountability using the continuous variable in the V-Dem dataset. We composed three categories by using the same coding schemes[2] provided in the dataset. The

Table 6.3.   Number of Tactics at Different Levels of Diagonal Accountability

	Violence against the State	Protest	Nonviolent intervention	Institutional
Low	48 (75%)	4 (6.25%)	3 (4.69%)	9 (14.06%)
Medium	35 (21.60%)	47 (29.01%)	15 (9.26%)	65 (40.12%)
High	100 (25.77%)	118 (30.41%)	52 (13.40%)	118 (30.41%)
Total	183 (29.80%)	169 (27.52%)	70 (11.40%)	192 (31.27%)

distribution of the use of specific tactics for secessionist purposes as the first action is different in countries with weak civil society and freedom of speech. In countries in which diagonal accountability is at the lowest levels, only sixteen factions employed nonviolent tactics such as protests, institutional actions, and noncooperation, whereas 75% of factions engaged in violent methods. The frequency of using violence against the state as the first action, however, was different in countries with higher levels of diagonal accountability. Countries with middle levels of diagonal accountability were more likely to experience protests or institutional activities, similar to the countries with strong civil society and freedom of speech.

Tables 6.4 and 6.5 show similar ratios of tactical diversity at different levels of democracy indicators. At lower levels of governmental constraints and free and fair elections, violence against the state was a more common method (54.90% and 42.44%, respectively), while the rate of using protest as the first action toward secession was higher for the countries which are better in these different components of democracy.

One salient finding of this analysis is about the tactical decision of factions in competitive authoritarian countries. Table 6.5 shows that in countries with medium levels of free and fair elections, nearly 50% of the tactics consist of institutional actions. Hence, half of the factions targeting secession from states with low levels of free and fair elections contest the state by appearing in the national elections as a political party rather than conducting violent attacks. In addition to these, another finding that is worth underlining is that the ratio of violent actions in countries with high levels of governmental constraints is higher compared to those with relatively lower levels. About 18.48% of the factions used violence in the countries with mid-level governmental constraints, whereas the ratio of violence as the first tactic in countries with high governmental constraints is around 29%.

As the next step of our inquiry, to capture the relationship from a different angle, we now turn our focus to the relationship between the overall change

Table 6.4.   Number of Tactics at Different Levels of Governmental Constraints

	Violence against the State	Protest	Nonviolent intervention	Institutional
Low	56 (54.90 %)	17 (16.67%)	7 (6.86%)	22 (21.57%)
Medium	39 (18.48%)	73 (34.60%)	18 (8.53%)	81 (38.39%)
High	88 (29.24%)	79 (26.25%)	45 (14.95%)	89 (29.57%)
Total	183 (29.80%)	169 (27.52%)	70 (11.40%)	192 (31.27 %)

Table 6.5.   Number of Tactics at Different Levels of Free and Fair Elections

	Violence against the State	Protest	Nonviolent intervention	Institutional
Low	73 (42.44%)	43 (25.00%)	18 (10.47%)	38 (22.09%)
Medium	24 (20.51%)	27 (23.08%)	8 (6.84%)	58 (49.57%)
High	86 (26.46%)	99 (30.46%)	44 (13.54%)	96 (29.54%)
Total	183 (29.80%)	169 (27.52%)	70 (11.40%)	192 (31.27%)

in the level of these three components of democracy after secessionist movements emerged and their tactical choices for self-determination. We look at two specific tactics, violence against the state and protest, which have privileged attention in the literature. Our method is a comparison between the countries in which the tactic has been applied and countries in which the tactic has not been employed in terms of the change in the level of each democracy indicator.

For this purpose, we will operationalize the change in the levels of each democracy indicator as two variants. As the first variant, we will measure the change in components of democracy by using the average change in these components between the year that the secessionist group emerged and the year that they employed the first violent action/protest. We will apply this procedure for the countries in which the secessionist group has at any time applied violence/protest.[3] On the other hand, for the countries in which the group has never used violence/protest, we will use the value of democracy indicators in the past year of the observation instead of the year that they employed the first violent action/protest. This procedure constitutes the second variant of our operationalization for the change in democracy indicators.[4] Note that these calculations were conducted for violence and protest separately. Figure 6.1 represents a timeline to make the operationalization clearer for the readers, and figure 6.2 shows the formulas for calculating the change in the level of democracy indicators.

The year that the
secessionist movement

emerged

$(t{\downarrow}emerge)$

The last year of

observation

$(t{\downarrow}last)$

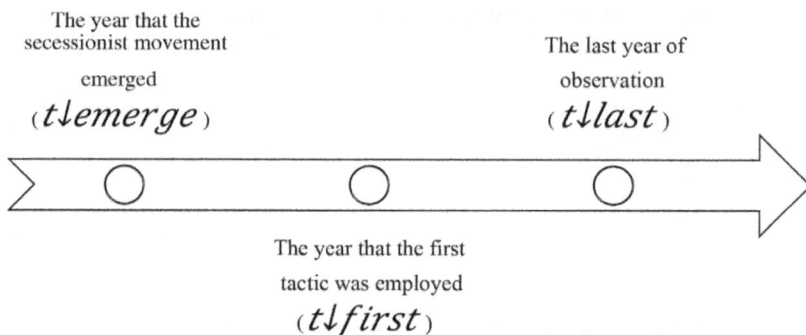

The year that the first

tactic was employed

$(t{\downarrow}first)$

Figure 6.1. Timeline to Illustrate Which Periods Are Used for Calculating the Change

For countries in which the tactic was emloyed:

$$-\frac{(\text{The level of the democracy indicator at } (t_{emerge}) - \text{The level of democracy indicator at } (t_{first}))}{t_{emerge} - t_{first}}$$

For countries in which the tactic has never been employed:

$$-\frac{(\text{The level of democracy indicator at } (t_{first}) - \text{The level of democracy indicator at } (t_{last}))}{t_{first} - t_{last}}$$

Figure 6.2. The Formulas for Calculating the Change in the Level of Democracy

As the last step before the analysis, we categorized countries with respect to their regime type at the time when the secessionist movement emerged. Countries fell into one of three regime types, namely autocracy, anocracy, and democracy, with respect to their Polity score in the year that the secessionist movement emerged.[5] As we have already indicated, the reason behind this categorization is the expectation that the effect of the change in democracy indicators on the tactical choices of secessionists might differ in the different regime types. In fact, since there is a specific focus on anocracies in the literature, as we discussed in previous sections, it might be enlightening to see how the effect of the change in the level of components of democracy differs in anocracies in comparison to democracies and autocracies. For this purpose, in the following paragraph we look at the cross and within regime-type trends for violence and protest as secessionist tactics with respect to change in each of the three democracy indicators.

Let us now turn to present the analyses and their results. Figure 6.3 depicts the relationship between the three indicators of democracy and the employment of violence. The first row on the graph displays the results for the countries in which the secessionist faction has resorted to violence as the first

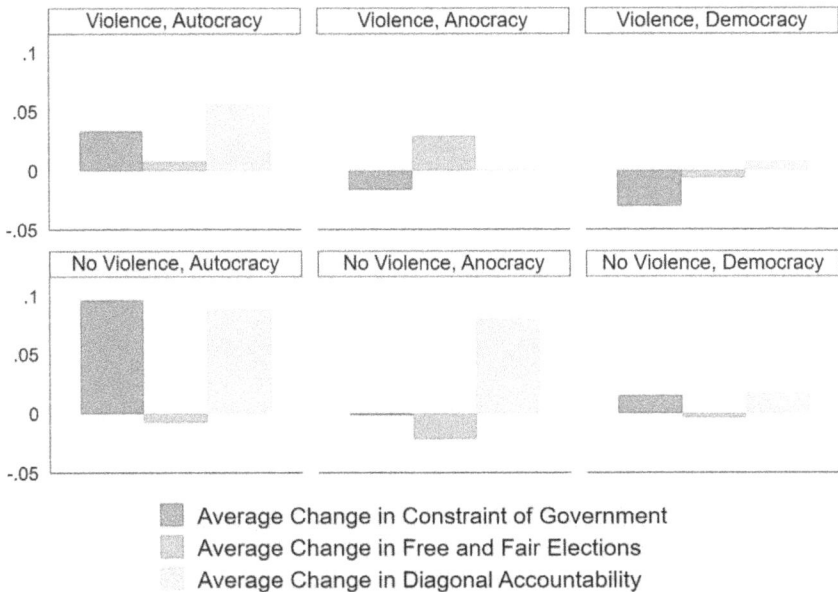

Figure 6.3. The Relationship between the First Violence and Change in Democracy

tactic. Meanwhile, the second row gives the results for the countries in which secessionist factions have never employed a violent tactic. Also, countries are categorized with respect to their original regime type which is represented as the columns on the graph. Two salient patterns on the graph should be underlined. The first is that in democracies in which secessionist factions employed violence as the first tactic, the level of constraints on government had been decreasing before the usage of this violent tactic. On the other hand, the level of constraints on government had been increasing in democracies in which secessionists had never employed violent tactics. The second finding worth emphasizing is that the level of free and fair elections had been increasing before the violence, as the first tactic, in anocracies in which violence was employed. Nevertheless, in anocracies in which violence was never applied, the level of the free and fair election had been decreasing.

Figure 6.4 also illustrates the average annual change in indicators of democracy with respect to the regime types of countries in which the faction emerged. This time, however, the countries are categorized in terms of whether the secessionist groups have ever preferred protest as a tactic. The first row on the graph presents the results for the countries in which the secessionist faction has preferred protest as the first tactic. Meanwhile, the second row shows the results for the countries in which

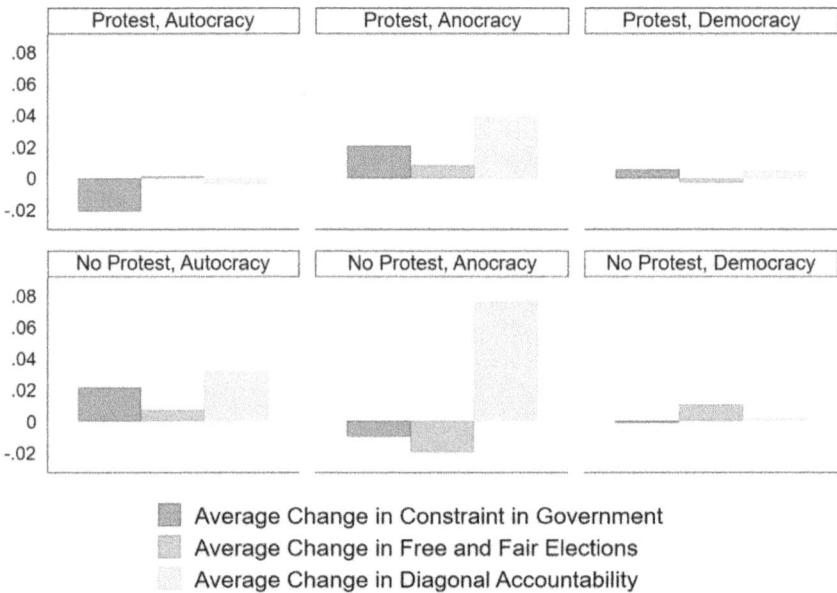

Figure 6.4.   The Relationship between the First Protest and Change in Democracy

secessionist factions have never preferred protest as a tactic. As in the first graph, countries categorized with respect to their original regime type are represented as the columns on the graph. Three patterns are worth emphasizing about this graph. The first is that in autocracies in which secessionist faction preferred protest as the first tactic, the constraints on government had been decreasing before the first protest. On the other hand, the constraints on government had been increasing in autocracies in which secessionists have never preferred protest as a tactic. The second finding which we want to underline is that the level of free and fair elections had been increasing before the first protest in anocracies in which protest was preferred as the first secessionist tactic. Nevertheless, in anocracies in which protest has never been employed, the level of the free and fair election had been decreasing. Last, in anocracies in which secessionist faction preferred protest as the first tactic, the level of constraint on government had been weakening before the first protest. Nonetheless, the level of constraint on government has been increasing in anocracies in which secessionists had never preferred protest as a tactic.

Before discussing the results and concluding the chapter, lets clarify the previously highlighted findings of analyses on violence and protest (see table 6.6).

Table 6.6. Summary of Findings

	Regime type: Autocracy	Regime type: Anocracy	Regime type: Democracy
The first tactic: **Violence**		↑Free and fair election	↓Constraints on government
The first tactic: **Protest**	↓Constraints on government	↑Free and fair election ↑Constraints on government	

DISCUSSION

Throughout the chapter, we have discussed how different institutions of democracy might influence the decision of secessionist movements to employ specific tactics. For this purpose, we decomposed democracy into its components, which were deduced from the related literature's causal arguments on how democracy affects the behavior of rebel groups. We specified three components of democracy, namely, the constraints on government, civil and political liberties, and free and fair elections. We used the V-Dem dataset to measure components of democracy, whereas for secessionist tactics, we used the dataset of Cunningham, Dahl, and Frugé (2017).

On the relationship between democracy and the tactical choices of secessionist, we proposed three expectations. Our first expectation was to find a link between these three components of democracy and tactical decisions of secessionists for self-determination. We also expected that patterns for the relationship between each of the three components and secessionist tactics might be different. Last, we expected to find that in anocracies in comparison to democracies and autocracies, these relationship patterns display a different form. To investigate these expectations, we conducted two sets of descriptive analysis. In the first one, we looked at the overall relationship between the level of three democracy indicators and four secessionist tactics. In the second, we investigated how changes in the level of components of democracy alter the tactical choices of secessionists.

The most prominent finding in the first analysis in which we analyzed the relationships between four potential tactics of secessionists and three components of democracy at different levels of these components are that violence, as a secessionist tactic, is preferred more in political regimes in which each component of the democracy is at the lowest level. At the same time, the analysis by which we investigated the choices of secessionist groups to resort to violence and to organize protest yield several additional substantial findings. The first notable pattern is that not civil and political liberties but changes in the level of constraints on government and the level of free and fair elections seem to have an effect on the tactical choices of secessionists. More specifically, changes in the level of constraints on government have an impact on the tactical decisions of secessionists in each regime type. However, it seems that, as we expected, the relationship between the change in the constraints on government and the tactical choices of secessionist groups show a different pattern in anocracies in comparison to democracies and autocracies.

In addition, the results of the analyses are in line with our expectation about the critical place of free and fair elections in anocracies. It seems that improving the level of free and fair elections does not help anocracies to avoid violence and protest from secessionist groups. On the contrary, anocracies in which the level of free and fair elections increases after the secessionist movement emerged are more vulnerable to facing secessionist tactics of violence and protest.

The task of this chapter is merely to understand general patterns but not to offer a causal inference which would require a rigorous statistical model by which the necessary conditions of causal inference are satisfied. Nevertheless, the patterns highlighted in this chapter give us a reason to believe that analyzing the relationship between secessionist tactics and democracy requires more attention to the discrete effects of each component of democracy. In future researches, such an attitude on the operationalization of democracy might shed further light on the complex relationship between tactical choices of secessionists and democracy.

NOTES

1. Since we investigate the relationship after the emergence of the secessionist movement while introducing the analysis, we need to also account for a possible endogeneity problem in which the tactical choices can impact components of democracy. Tactics used by secessionists might incentivize governments to act which, in turn, cause a fluctuation in democracy. For example, the government might attempt to get rid of the institutional constraints or circumvent liberties vis-a-vis to violent secessionists. On the other side, any change in components of democracy might shape the preference of secessionists. For instance, secessionists might incline to prefer protest as a response to an increase in diagonal accountability, since it makes easier to organize a protest. Under these circumstances, the causal direction is not easy to determine. This is the very reason why we use "the firsts." In the former part, to control for the endogeneity problem we will analyze only the very first actions by each secessionist faction. In the latter part, we only include the faction which used violence/protest for the first time in a country.

2. The range of continuous diagonal accountability measure ranges from -2 to 2; we coded every one-third of the ranking as a group. We applied a similar coding scheme to the level of governmental constraints and free and fair elections. Only the

continuous free and fair elections variable ranks between 0 and 1; hence, the limits of the categorical variable are different.

3. The year of the emergence of a secessionist group and the year that they employ the first action are not generally the same in the dataset. We exploited this opportunity to measure the effect of democracy. However, the trade of this procedure is the exclusion of the countries in which the year of the emergence of a secessionist group and the year that they employ the first action are the same. For violence, approximately 4% of the cases fall under this category, whereas the same indicator is 6% for protest. Nevertheless, these countries do not present different patterns which would change the results of our analysis.

4. For the first variant, which contains the countries in which the present strategy is applied by secessionists, we subtracted the value of democracy indicator in the faction's year of emergence from the value of the same democracy indicator in the year that the present strategy was first applied in this country. Note that for each country, only the faction which applied the present strategy first was included in the analysis. The reason behind this decision is that some countries encountered several factions, all or several of which applied the present strategy. Except for the faction which used present strategy first, all other factions operated in a polity where the present strategy had been already applied. However, as was discussed, this increases the risk of endogeneity—our primary concern. Another problem is that the number of years between the emergence of a faction and application of the present strategy varied across countries. Therefore, the difference between two values of democracy indicators depended on the time span. To solve this problem, we standardized the subtraction by dividing it to the number of years between the emergence of the faction and the year that the present strategy was used. Also, like the first variant, to standardize the variable, we divided the subtraction to the number of total years that the faction was presented in the data. Since some secessionist movements divided into more factions than others, this may mean that some countries represented the sample more than others, which in turn may have affected the results of the descriptive analysis. Additionally, we differentiated the current democracy level so we can evaluate whether the impact of being a democratic country is different when one of the democracy measures changes the tactical decisions of secessionist groups.

5. This is the conventional method in the literature of civil conflict to categorize the regimes. For a detailed description, see Fearon and Laitin (2003).

REFERENCES

Carey, Sabine C. 2010. "The Use of Repression as a Response to Domestic Dissent." *Political Studies* 58(1): 167–186.

Chenoweth, Erica. 2010. "Democratic competition and Terrorist Activity." *The Journal of Politics* 72(1): 16–30.

Chenoweth, Erica, Maria J. Stephan, and Maria J. Stephan. 2011. *Why Civil Resistance Works: The Strategic Logic of Nonviolent Conflict*. New York: Columbia University Press.

Coppedge, Michael, John Gerring, Staffan II Lindberg, Svend-Erik Skaaning, Jan Teorell, Joshua Krusell, Kyle L. Marquardt et al. 2017. V-Dem methodology v7.

Cunningham, Kathleen Gallagher. 2011. "Divide and Conquer or Divide and Concede: How Do States Respond to Internally Divided Separatists?" *American Political Science Review* 105(2): 275–297.

Cunningham, Kathleen Gallagher. 2013. "Understanding Strategic Choice: The Determinants of Civil War and Nonviolent Campaign in Self-Determination Disputes." *Journal of Peace Research* 50(3): 291–304.

Cunningham, Kathleen Gallagher, Marianne Dahl, and Anne Frugé. 2017. "Strategies of Resistance: Diversification and Diffusion." *American Journal of Political Science* 61(3): 591–605.

Davenport, Christian, and David A. Armstrong. 2004. "Democracy and the Violation of Human Rights: A Statistical Analysis from 1976 to 1996." *American Journal of Political Science* 48(3): 538–554.

Elklit, Jorgen, and Palle Svensson. 1997. "What Makes Elections Free and Fair?" *Journal of Democracy* 8(3): 32–46.

Eyerman, Joe. 1998. "Terrorism and Democratic States: Soft Targets or Accessible Systems." *International Interactions* 24(2): 151–170.

Fearon, James D., and David D. Laitin. 2003. "Ethnicity, Insurgency, and Civil War." *American Political Science Review* 97(1): 75–90.

Getmansky, Anna. 2013. "You Can't Win If You Don't Fight: The Role of Regime Type in Counterinsurgency Outbreaks and Outcomes." *Journal of Conflict Resolution* 57(4): 709–734.

Gleditsch, Kristian S., and Mauricio Rivera. 2017. "The Diffusion of Nonviolent Campaigns." *Journal of Conflict Resolution* 61(5): 1120–1145.

Griffiths, Ryan D. 2015. "Between Dissolution and Blood: How Administrative Lines and Categories Shape Secessionist Outcomes." *International Organization* 69(3): 731–751.

Griffiths, Ryan D., and Louis M. Wasser. 2019. "Does Violent Secessionism Work?" *Journal of Conflict Resolution* 63(5): 1310–1336.

Gurr, Ted Robert. 2016. *Why Men Rebel.* New York: Routledge.

Hegre, Håvard. 2001. "Toward a Democratic Civil Peace? Democracy, Political Change, and Civil War, 1816–1992." *American Political Science Review* 95(1): 33–48.

Keefer, Philip. 2008. "Insurgency and Credible Commitment in Autocracies and Democracies." *The World Bank Economic Review* 22(1): 33–61.

Lacina, Bethany. 2006. "Explaining the Severity of Civil Wars." *Journal of Conflict Resolution* 50(2): 276–289.

Levitsky, Steven, and Lucan A. Way. 2010. *Competitive Authoritarianism: Hybrid Regimes after the Cold War.* New York: Cambridge University Press.

Li, Quan. 2005. "Does Democracy Promote or Reduce Transnational Terrorist Incidents?" *Journal of Conflict Resolution* 49(2): 278–297.

Merom, Gil.2003. *How Democracies Lose Small Wars: State, Society, and the Failures of France in Algeria, Israel in Lebanon, and the United States in Vietnam.* New York: Cambridge University Press.

Morgan, T. Clifton, and Sally Howard Campbell. 1991. "Domestic Structure, Decisional Constraints, and War: So Why Kant Democracies Fight?" *Journal of Conflict Resolution* 35(2): 187–211.

North, Douglass C. 1990. *Institutions, Institutional Change and Economic Performance.* New York: Cambridge University Press.

Reynal-Querol, Marta. 2002. "Ethnicity, Political Systems, and Civil Wars." *Journal of Conflict Resolution* 46(1): 29–54.

Saideman, Stephen M., David J. Lanoue, Michael Campenni, and Samuel Stanton. 2002. "Democratization, Political Institutions, and Ethnic Conflict: A Pooled Time-Series Analysis, 1985–1998." *Comparative Political Studies* 35(1): 103–129.

Sambanis, Nicholas, Micha Germann, and Andreas Schädel. 2018. "SDM: A New Data Set on Self-Determination Movements with an Application to the Reputational Theory of Conflict." *Journal of Conflict Resolution* 62(3): 656–686.

Schmitter, Philippe C., and Terry Lynn Karl. 1991. "What Democracy Is . . . and Is Not." *Journal of Democracy* 2(3):75–88.

Schumpeter, Joseph A. 2010. *Capitalism, Socialism and Democracy.* Oxon: Routledge.

Svensson, Isak, and Mathilda Lindgren. 2010. "Community and Consent: Unarmed Insurrections in Non-Democracies." *European Journal of International Relations* 17(1): 97–120.

Treier, Shawn, and Simon Jackman. 2008. "Democracy as a Latent Variable." *American Journal of Political Science* 52(1): 201–217.

Walter, Barbara F. 2006. "Building Reputation: Why Governments Fight Some Separatists But Not Others." *American Journal of Political Science* 50(2): 313–330.

Walter, Barbara F. 2015. "Why Bad Governance Leads to Repeat Civil War." *Journal of Conflict Resolution* 59(7): 1242–1272.

Young, Joseph K., and Laura Dugan. 2011. "Veto Players and Terror." *Journal of Peace Research* 48(1): 19–33.

Chapter 7

The European Union in the Narratives of Secessionist Parties: Lessons from Catalonia, Flanders, and Scotland

Bart Maddens, Gertjan Muyters, Wouter Wolfs, and Steven Van Hecke

INTRODUCTION

About a month after former President of the Government of Catalonia Carles Puigdemont had fled to Brussels, he said, 'the European Union [EU] is a club of decadent and obsolescent countries, ruled by a happy few linked to disputable economic interests'. In the same interview, Puigdemont argued in favour of a Catalan referendum on EU membership (Cymerman 2017). This anti-EU discourse gave rise to some consternation, as it stood in sharp contrast to the almost emphatically Euro-enthusiastic stance that Catalan separatists had taken up to that moment. The U-turn also led to some criticism among the separatist rank and file, as a result of which Puigdemont was obliged to qualify these statements and reaffirm his European creed (Gorriarán 2017).

Nevertheless, this sudden outburst of criticism seems indicative of a growing frustration among separatist movements with the EU. While this unease may have been growing for some time, the Catalan crisis of October 2017 appears to have functioned as a catalyst for anti-EU feelings among separatists. This crisis made it abundantly clear that the EU makes the so-called internal enlargement impossible without the consent of the respective member state, that is, the home state. It, therefore, does not come as a surprise that separatists became increasingly sceptical about the EU. Of course, it could be argued that it is only natural for separatists to be averse to political integration at a supranational level. Yet this is belied by the fact that, in the past, secessionists have embraced European integration.

In this chapter, we focus on political parties that as substate actors strive for independence within existing EU member states. These parties incorporate or have incorporated EU membership within their secessionist strategies. In other words, they have used this particular kind of the international community, the EU, as a strategic field to realize their ultimate goal: secession. Through the EU arena and European public opinion, secessionist parties could put pressure on their home state. If the home capital was not convinced by the legitimacy of secession, perhaps it could be realized through EU membership. Politically speaking, 'going Brussels' became an alternative strategy for going national, although legally speaking the EU was never entitled to engage in domestic constitutional affairs, in particular the territorial integrity of its member states (Introduction chapter in this volume, 7).

First, we will start from the abundant literature which tries to explain the seemingly contradictory love affair between separatism and European integration. Next, we will investigate how this pro-European attitude takes shape in the European elections' manifestoes of three secessionist parties: the Nieuw-Vlaamse Alliantie (N-VA, Flanders/Belgium), the Scottish National Party (SNP, Scotland/UK), and Esquerra Republicana de Catalunya (ERC, Catalonia/Spain). On the basis of a number of interviews with members of the European Parliament (MEPs) from these parties, we will analyse to what extent recent events in Scotland and Catalonia have triggered a more critical stance, and how pro-European themes and arguments in secessionist narratives of the past dovetail with this new position.

WHY SECESSIONISTS EMBRACE(D) THE EU

Autonomist or secessionist parties can respond in roughly three different ways to European integration (Nagel 2004, 61). First, they can oppose European integration and opt for a Eurocritical stance. Second, they can play the 'regional game', making use of the opportunities which the EU offers to substate actors and seeking to enlarge these opportunities within the existing state order. Finally, they can opt for an 'independence in Europe' strategy, which involves supporting the EU while seeking to become a full-fledged member state. The line between these strategies is often fuzzy, and they are also not mutually exclusive. For instance, a party can attempt to strengthen the institutional position of the region in the short term, while aiming at independence in the long term.

While most secessionist or autonomist parties were initially very sceptical about European integration, during the 1980s, they become more positive and even quite enthusiastic. By the end of the 1990s, an expert survey showed that the regionalist party family was the most pro-European of all European party families (De Winter 2001, 26). Even though this enthusiasm about Europe has waned somewhat during the past decade, as will be seen later in this chapter, secessionist and autonomist parties have until recently never taken an overtly anti-EU stance. In other words, EU membership by the home state was seen as a means to an end that was not supported by the home state: secession. There is extensive literature which explains why this is the case. The explanations are related to the strategic and discursive advantages of European integration, on the one hand, and the institutional opportunity structure, on the other. We will very briefly discuss these explanations in that order.

Regarding the strategic and discursive advantages, first of all, European integration has undermined the doctrine of exclusive state sovereignty linked to a specific territory (Keating 2004, 368–370). It has given rise to the notion that we are now living in a 'post sovereignty' world, where sovereignty is shared within a complex multinational structure. This fuzziness surrounding the notion of sovereignty has opened up a discursive space for autonomist and secessionist movements. These can now choose a vaguely defined third way between 'mere regionalism' and 'radical secession'. The post-sovereignty perspective allows secessionists to make their claim more palatable and less menacing to moderate voters outside their ethnic core group (Keating 2001, 56–57). Secession can now be presented as a mere reshuffle of partitioned sovereignty. Additionally, this line of reasoning helps to defuse the criticism that separatism involves parochialism or *Kleinstaaterei* and will isolate the region from the rest of the world (Tarditi 2010, 18).

The post-sovereignty discourse also has implications for the institutional options regarding the EU. As will be shown later, secessionist parties vacillate between a 'federal' and a 'confederal' vision of a future EU. This ambiguity can also be seen as a reflection of the increasing fluidity surrounding the notion of state sovereignty, which is evident in the scientific literature. In the traditional literature – mostly inspired by German constitutional law – a clear-cut line is drawn between a federation and a confederation, based on the notion of sovereignty. According to this approach the constituent parts of the confederation are sovereign states which are directly governed by rules of international public law. The *Kompetenz-Kompetenz* (i.e., the power to allocate competences) belongs to these constituent parts which decide by treaty to jointly exercise a number of competences (Velaers 2013, 2015, 20–21). More recent approaches put more emphasis on the hybridity and contingency of the sovereignty concept and hence the existence of a grey zone between federalism and confederalism (Loughlin 2015, 12; Keating 2015, 54; Sottiaux 2011; 2014).

This theme of post-sovereign hybridity is a bit at odds with a second EU-related discursive topos, that is, the so-called pincer movement argument. This is based on a rather strict distinction between various levels of government. If more and more competences are devolved to a lower substate level, on the one hand, and a higher European level, on the other, it is argued, the intermediate level of the traditional nation-state will eventually become redundant due to a lack of competences (De Winter and Gomez-Reino 2002, 497; Elias 2008). Maintaining such a hollowed-out state is portrayed as inefficient, costly, and irrational. Arguably, envisaging a federal EU adds to the persuasiveness of this reasoning. This is so because it is difficult to imagine a 'triple-layered' European federation, consisting of member states which themselves are subdivided into entities with legislative competences. Also, a federal perspective allows for an additional de-dramatization, as secession would take place within the EU and merely involve the issue of how the United States of Europe is subdivided into member states. An additional rhetorical bonus of such a federal perspective on the EU is that it defuses the criticism that a fragmentation of the EU into more member states would impede efficient decision-making.

Finally, the EU provides secessionists with the safety net argument. According to Alesina and Spolaore (2003), its single market has decreased the costs of being a small state. The economies of scale, from which large states profit, are now realized at the European level. In this way, the EU facilitates secession. The same applies to the North Atlantic Treaty Organization (NATO), which guarantees small states a level of security which is normally only available for large countries. In this way, both NATO and the EU provide a safety net for seceded states and help to make secession a more acceptable and less daunting venture.

Apart from these rhetorical advantages, it also has to be taken into account that the EU has provided a political opportunity structure for autonomist and secessionist parties. To start with, in various countries, the more proportional election system for the European Parliament made it easier for these parties to obtain a seat than was the case in their national parliament (De Winter 2001, 19–23). In 1981, the European Free Alliance (EFA) was created as a forum for cooperation for these parties (Lynch 1998). In this way, the EU provided an external support system to autonomist parties, which were often marginal within their national political system.

Particularly since the coming into force of the Maastricht Treaty in 1993, substate entities obtained direct access to the EU level. The Committee of the Regions was created, and it became possible for regions to directly represent their state in the Council of Ministers. The regions were recognized as the key actors in the EU cohesion policy and had to interact directly with the European Commission. Also, the Interreg program provided a stimulus for cross-border collaboration between regions, bypassing the state. This also incentivized regions to engage in European paradiplomacy, for instance, by establishing regional delegations in Brussels (Keating 2001, 150–159; Hooghe and Keating 2004). The rise of the 'new regionalism' also involved various forms of cooperation between strong regions (Nagel 2004, 61–64). These institutional devices buttressed the post-sovereigntist discourse and gave it credibility.

However, the hype of the 'new regionalism' in Europe was short-lived. It rapidly became clear that the states remained the dominant actors in the EU and that the manoeuvring space for regions was small (Nagel 2004, 73; Hepburn 2008; Elias 2008, 557–560). This was even more the case in the wake of the 2004 enlargement. The new Central and Eastern European member states lacked a tradition of strong regions or autonomist parties, which led to a further marginalization of, for instance, the EFA parliamentary (sub)group. More in general, the enlargement strengthened the intergovernmental tendencies within the EU, making the post-sovereignty narrative less credible and appealing to secessionists. Also, there was a growing awareness that transferring sovereignty to the EU eroded the competences of the regions. As a consequence, for EU-related matters, the regions have to implement EU directives which are negotiated between the states (Lynch and De Winter 2008, 602–603). These factors appear to have led to a more lukewarm attitude of autonomist or secessionist parties towards the EU, mainly resulting in less emphasis on the issue (Elias 2008).

The question is whether this tepid attitude will now turn into an outright Eurocritical stance as a result of the response of the EU to the 2014 Scottish independence referendum and the 2017 Catalan crisis. Of course, the EU has always been reticent towards secession and has developed a strategic culture involving a clear preference for accommodation of territorial conflicts on the basis of self-government (Coppieters 2010, 254–256). But the 2014 Scottish referendum appears to even have sharpened this anti-secessionist stance. The absence of clear rules regarding 'internal enlargement' made it possible to foster uncertainty regarding EU membership of an independent Scotland, although the European Commission had taken a clear stance long in advance (Schmidt 2014, 7–8). If the EU had taken the position that an independent Scotland would remain in the Union, one way or another, the yes and no votes would probably have been even, according to survey research (Keating 2017, 116–118).

The perception that the EU actively opposes secession has been strengthened by the 2017 Catalan crisis. The violence on occasion of the unconstitutional referendum of October 1 initially led to a request by the Catalan government for international mediation. Various attempts were made to let the European Commission play a mediating role. This was vehemently opposed by Spanish authorities who feared an internationalization of the conflict. The Commission immediately took sides with Madrid and argued that the Catalan crisis was an internal matter in which it could not interfere (Juliana 2017). But the president of the Commission, Jean-Claude Juncker, went further than this legal position and explicitly condemned the Catalan separatists, describing nationalism and separatism in Europe as a 'venom' (Del Riego 2017).

RESEARCH QUESTIONS, RESEARCH DESIGN, AND CASE SELECTION

In this chapter, we investigate to what extent these recent events have changed the discourse of secessionist parties with regard to the EU, both from an institutional and a strategic perspective. As regards the institutional component, we focus on two questions: (1) do secessionists prefer a federal or a confederal/intergovernmental EU? and (2) do they prefer a transfer of more competences to the EU or a renationalization of certain competences? With regard to the strategic component, we will investigate how these institutional positions relate to the three key arguments outlined earlier: the post-sovereignty argument, the pincer movement argument, and the safety net argument.

These research questions require a qualitative design with, for practical reasons, a limited number of cases. As we want to map the discourse for a longer period, we limit the analysis to parties that have been overtly secessionist since at least the turn of the century. This excludes the Catalan CiU/CDC/PDeCAT, which only recently opted for outright separatism. We selected three parties within three different EU member states which have been separatist since their foundation: the N-VA, the SNP, and the ERC. Admittedly, the SNP case has diverged since the Brexit referendum. We, nevertheless, opted to include it, partly because the SNP plays such a central role in the literature on secessionism and the EU, and partly because the Scottish independence referendum is one of the events that may have pushed secessionists in a Eurocritical direction.

The most obvious data source for an in-depth qualitative analysis of party positions on the EU are party manifestoes for European Parliamentary elections. We will analyse all these manifestoes from the 1990s onwards. For the N-VA, which was only founded in 2001, we will start with the 2004 European manifesto. For the developments after 2014, we have conducted five in-depth interviews with MEPs from the three parties: two from N-VA, two from ERC, and one from SNP. In what follows, we will discuss each case separately.

NIEUW-VLAAMSE ALLIANTIE

The centre-right N-VA initially consisted of the separatist wing of the centrist Volksunie, which fell apart in 2001. The attitude of the N-VA towards European integration is rooted in the way of thinking of the Volksunie (Brack, Wolfs, and Van Hecke 2017, 12). At first, the latter party was lukewarm about European integration but did not give it much attention. It was only during the 1970s that the party warmed to Europe and developed a distinctive vision: the 'Europe of the peoples' (Brown 2017, 128–136). This notion also formed the ideological foundation of the EFA, of which the Volksunie was the driving force. Even though the 'Europe of the peoples' was largely a vague and romantic idea, the party took care to put its proposals for a federal reform of Belgium in a European perspective. The Volksunie has always been in favour of a federal Europe and viewed the federalization of Belgium as a model for Europe. The logical implication was that Belgium was nothing more than a temporary structure, which would – according to the classical 'pincer movement' reasoning – become superfluous as Flanders and Wallonia became member states of a federal Europe. The Volksunie position can thus be summarized as 'Flanders as a member state of a federal Europe'.

Even though the Volksunie had gradually radicalized, it remained ambivalent about independence. The N-VA, in contrast, immediately highlighted this aim in the first article of its statutes: 'An independent Flemish republic as a member state of a democratic Europe' (Beyens et al. 2015, 4–5). In line with the Volksunie, the N-VA was initially enthusiastic about European integration. This was symbolically underscored by the use of both the EU and the Flemish flags at party rallies and victory celebrations. But the party was ambiguous with regard to the institutional architecture of the EU. In 2004, the party, on the one hand, argues that the EU should develop from a confederal to a federal model *sui generis* in the long term (N-VA 2004, 4). On the other hand, it also envisages the EU as a bond of sovereign states (N-VA 2004, 5), while in the 2009 manifesto the EU is viewed as a confederal model *sui generis*.

In its 2004 and 2009 electoral programmes, the party argues against the intergovernmental method and favours more power and competences for the supranational EU institutions (N-VA 2009, 73–74). In its 2009 manifesto, the N-VA also argues that all competences which require a supranational approach should be dealt with at the macro-EU level: monetary union, defence, security, migration, asylum, internal market, energy, and climate. The most adequate micro-level is Flanders, for those competences that need to be implemented as close to citizens as possible (N-VA 2009, 68–69, 75–76, 88). According to traditional 'pincer movement' reasoning, little room is left for a Belgian intermediate level in such a scenario. The party also explicitly applies Alesina and Spolaore's safety net argument. The choice for the most suitable level to conduct a policy field should be guided by a trade-off between economies of scale and costs of heterogeneity, it is argued. According to the N-VA, Belgium does not provide many economies of scale but has enormous costs of heterogeneity. Incidentally, in 2006, the party invited author Enrico Spolaore at a congress about 'Flanders, state in Europe' (Maddens 2017).

The N-VA did not adopt the romantic notion of a 'Europe of the peoples' from the Volksunie and the EFA (even though the party remained a member of the EFA). Nevertheless, in the short run, as a mere 'region', Flanders should have a stronger direct representation at the EU level. Regions should be directly involved at the European level for all policy fields that fall within their competences, according to the '*in foro interno, in foro externo*' principle (N-VA 2004, 5–6).

In 2014, the party's enthusiasm about European integration clearly wanes. The party now explicitly describes its position as 'Eurorealist', entailing a critical approach towards the EU and an unambiguous stance in favour of a confederal model. In line with this stance, the earlier institutional proposals to reduce intergovernmental decision-making are dropped. While the party still supports the transfer of some competences to the EU (such as foreign and security policy), based on more majority voting, it also argues that it might be better to renationalize other competences (N-VA 2014, 83, 89).

This new Eurorealist position was one of the reasons why, after the election, the N-VA joined the European Conservatives and Reformists parliamentary group (contrary to SNP and ERC, who remained in the Greens/EFA group). Nevertheless, in 2014, the N-VA took, for the first time, a strong stance in favour of 'internal enlargement'. The party wants more recognition for the development of nations without a state like Scotland, Catalonia, the Basque Country, and Flanders and argues that they should be automatically an EU member when they become independent and that they only need to fulfil the membership criteria after a transition period (N-VA 2014, 85).

The interviews with two N-VA MEPs indicate that the party will continue to follow this Eurorealist course, without turning to an outright anti-EU position. True, the Catalan crisis gives rise to some emotional anti-European comments: 'Once you are a member of the [European] club, you are trapped. You are a prisoner in a cage' (Interview B, 21 February 2018). Recent events in Scotland and Catalonia have shown that the EU impedes rather than facilitates secession. The EU should have played a more proactive role in Catalonia, encouraging the government in Madrid to start a dialogue with a Catalan government (Interview B, 21 February 2018).

But this resentment is directed towards the EU's policy and the incumbent EU leaders, and in particular the European People's Party, rather than towards the EU polity as such. The current N-VA discourse still concurs in large part with the 2014 manifesto. The MEPs emphasize that the EU should remain confederal. According to one of them, the essence of confederalism is that the member states retain the 'Kompetenz-Kompetenz': the member states decide on the decision-making procedures and the division of competences in an (international) treaty, and they can freely resign from the EU (Interview A, 21 February 2018). Interestingly, for the N-VA, confederalism does not preclude qualified majority voting. The positions taken by the interviewees contain no traces of the post-sovereignty or shared-sovereignty discourse of the 1990s. This is also reflected in the fact that the MEPs are quite derogatory about earlier proposals to strengthen the role of the regions in the EU. These are now brushed aside as simplistic and totally unrealistic in a confederal Europe dominated by states (Interview A, 21 February 2018; Interview B, 21 February 2018).

The N-VA takes a very pragmatic approach concerning competences. Some national competences, particularly in the field of defence and foreign policy, should be transferred to the Union (Interview A, 21 February 2018; Interview B, 21 February 2018). It is pointed out, according to the pincer movement logic, that these are the competences that the N-VA wants to retain at the Belgian confederal level as long as Flanders is not independent. At the same time, the N-VA is drafting a list of competences that should be returned to the member states. It does not seem to bother the party that this may strengthen Belgium and slow down the 'evaporation' of this level. The party also does not appear to be troubled about the role of Belgium as an interface between the regions and the EU. Belgium merely functions as a post office, adding up the regional positions and transferring them to the EU level, it is said (Interview A, 21 February 2018).

While the post-sovereignty topos is completely absent in the discourse, and the pincer movement reasoning only applied half-heartedly, the N-VA still explicitly invokes the 'safety net' argument. In spite of everything, the EU facilitates Flemish independence, because it provides Flanders with the economies of scale needed for competences such as security and migration: 'We need a Europe which works, because an independent Flanders cannot stand on its own in a globalised world' (Interview A, 21 February 2018).

But interestingly, this narrative is now primarily instrumental to defend European integration against increasing Eurocriticism, rather than to defend secession. In fact, since 2014, the party appears caught between reaping some electoral profit from the lack of popularity of the EU and rejecting outright 'populist Euroscepticism'. The safety net discourse now mainly serves the latter purpose. The inhibition to go for an outright anti-EU position is partly due to the inheritance of the Europhile Volksunie in N-VA (Brack, Wolfs, and Van Hecke 2017). Another factor is the participation of the party in the Belgian government (2014–2018), which is traditionally a staunch proponent of European integration. It appears that, in this complex strategic calculus, the relationship between the EU and Flemish independence is only of secondary importance.

SCOTTISH NATIONAL PARTY

The SNP has gone through various phases of love and hate in its relationship with European integration. Initially pro-European, during the 1950s, the party adopted a rather favourable stance towards the European Coal and Steel Community. In this way, it could distance itself from the British government. However, when this government applied for membership, during the 1960s, the SNP changed course and vehemently opposed European integration. It portrayed the European Community as centrist, bureaucratic, and elitist, and it resented that Scotland was not involved in the membership negotiations. Again, the SNP position was driven by a strategy to antagonize Westminster. In the 1970s, this anti-European stance became more outspoken and, in the 1975 UK European Communities membership referendum, the party campaigned against membership (Tarditi 2010, 10–11). During the 1980s, there was a gradual moderation of hostility towards European integration. This culminated in 1988, when the party adopted its new 'independence in Europe' strategy and turned towards Europhilia. Nevertheless, after some discussion, the party made it clear that it envisaged a confederal Europe, rejecting a federal 'United States of Europe' (Hepburn 2010, 76–77).

This is also made clear in the manifesto for the 1989 European election, which states that the party's aim is a 'confederal family of nations working together to improve the quality of life of its constituent peoples' (SNP 1989, 2). 'Independence in a confederal Europe' is the main theme throughout all the manifestoes of the 1990s (Jolly 2007, 123; Tarditi 2010). At the end of the 1990s, the party pushes this pro-European stance even further. It appears to move away from mere intergovernmentalism when it defends a Europe-wide voting system for the European Parliament and extending its power (Tarditi 2010; Jolly 2007). Also, it wants Scotland to adopt the euro as soon as possible (SNP 1999, 3). This is in line with the 'pincer movement' argument, a metaphor which appears to be invented by SNP: 'I admit that I am attracted by the idea – I make no secret of it – of this place losing powers to the European Parliament, to European institutions and to the people of Scotland. I want to see the Parliament of Westminster squeezed between those two elements' (Alex Salmond in 1992, cited in Brown 2017, 125).

The SNP has never embraced the 'new regionalism' or the notion of a Europe of the regions or the peoples, championed by the Flemish Volksunie and EFA (Brown 2017, 125), even though the SNP has been a member of EFA since 1989. The party has from the outset taken the position that was later adopted by the N-VA: the states are the main actors in the EU; therefore, we have to obtain statehood.

After the 1999 election, the SNP gradually becomes more critical towards the EU. While the general pro-European gist remains, the party now explicitly argues against devolution of certain competences to the EU and even takes a stand for renationalizing competences (SNP 2004, 12). The party also opposes the Constitutional Treaty among other reasons because 'it entrenches an exclusive power over fishing in the hands of the EU institutions' (SNP 2004, 18). From 2004 onwards, there is also a growing discontent about the way Westminster defends Scottish interests in Europe. This frustration is fuelled by the 2004 enlargement and the accession of various small states. At the same time, this enlargement is welcomed as a barrier against a future United States of Europe (SNP 2009, 2–3). It buttresses the confederal position of the party and makes it more credible that a small nation such as Scotland could become a separate member state (Tarditi 2010, 31–35). The strong emphasis in the 2009 manifesto on having an own voice in Europe coincides with the push towards an independence referendum, after the SNP's accession to power in 2007.

The 2014 European election takes place when the campaign for this independence referendum is already in full swing. The SNP manifesto first and foremost tries to convince voters that a 'smooth and seamless transition to EU membership as an independent state' will be possible. This pro-European narrative is now also linked to the threat of Scotland being pushed out of the EU against its will if Westminster would give in to the growing pressure of UK Independence Party. Nevertheless, the manifesto explicitly rejects membership of the Schengen area or the Eurozone, in contrast to the 1999 position (SNP 2014, 3, 7). While the main emphasis is on the advantages of EU membership, the criticism towards the EU is retained, although phrased in more subdued terms. With regard to fishery, for instance, 'European policy has to date, however, not worked in our interests' (SNP 2014, 9).

Of course, the 2014 and 2016 referendums have fundamentally changed the contours of the debate on Scottish independence and the EU. In the run-up to the 2014 independence referendum, Commission president José Manuel Barroso made it very clear that an independent Scotland could not continue being part of the EU, which did not help to convince hesitant pro-independence voters (*The Scotsman*, 11 December 2012). Later, however, the initial shock of the 2016 Brexit victory caused some EU leaders to express their sympathies for a Scottish 'remain' scenario, and hence, implicitly, for Scottish secession. Immediately after the referendum, Scottish prime minister Nicola Sturgeon visited the European Commission and Parliament with a view to 'preserve Scotland's relationship and place within the EU' (Euractiv, 29 June 2016). But the president of the European Council, Donald Tusk, refused to meet Sturgeon because 'it was not the right time' (Crisp, 29 June 2018). The idea of a Scottish remain scenario was short-lived. During the following months, both the Spanish prime minister and the French president insisted that the EU could only negotiate with the UK about Brexit. It did not help that, in this period, Catalan separatists were already heading for a unilateral declaration of independence (*The Irish Times*, 29 June 2016).

Nevertheless, our interview with the SNP MEP yields a more ambivalent discourse on the EU and Brexit. The 'Norway option' would be in our interest, economically speaking, the MEP admits, 'but politically and democratically . . . I don't want us to be a client state'. The idea that the UK or Scotland would be a rule-taker instead of a rule-maker is not met with enthusiasm, to put it mildly. Neither is there a consistent discourse about possible alternative solutions for the border between Scotland and England, apart from: 'We are looking carefully at the Northern Ireland situation' (Interview C, 27 February 2018).

A possible accession of an independent Scotland to the EU appears to become something increasingly remote in the SNP discourse. Entering the EU after Brexit will be much more complex than before, the MEP admits. In case of a yes gain in 2014, it would have been easy. You would have seen both the UK and the EU turn pragmatic. After Brexit 'we will have more issues to deal with' (Interview C, 27 February 2018). But one also cannot escape from the impression that enthusiasm about the EU is on the wane. There remain hard feelings about the way particularly the Commission has surreptitiously influenced the independence referendum. 'We have a memory about that in Scotland. . . . OK, maybe we could go to someone else. . . . We have Ireland at one side but we also have close links with Norway, Denmark, Iceland as well. There are other options' (Interview C, 27 February 2018). In spite of the 'independence in Europe' rhetoric, independence without the EU has always remained conceivable for SNP (Brown 2017, 145) and after the 2014 and 2016 referendums, this seems more the case than ever.

ESQUERRA REPUBLICANA DE CATALUNYA

Unlike the centrist Convergència i Unió (CiU), the leftist ERC has favoured secession since its foundation in 1931. But the party has always oscillated between full-fledged separatism and a more pragmatic, autonomist course. The disenchantment with Catalan autonomy under the new 1978 Constitution led to a radicalization at the end of the 1980s. In this way the party could distance itself from the more moderate CiU. This is reflected in new statutes, approved in 1992, which describe the ERC as a party 'which strives for the territorial unity and the independence of the Catalan nation through the construction of a separate state within the European framework' (Culla 2013, 377).

Proposals for such a 'European framework' are elaborated in the 1994 European election manifesto. 'We want a European government of a federal nature which will be an umbrella for sovereign peoples and a factor of coordination and solidarity', the party argues (ERC 1994, 13). The ERC opposes an intergovernmental Europe, where each state has a veto. Throughout the manifesto, the party pleads for transferring more competences to the EU, in the field of social policy, taxes, and defence, for instance.

Nevertheless, the party does not unequivocally envisage Catalonia as a separate member state of this future federal Europe. ERC follows a double track. On the one hand, it argues in favour of a more direct involvement of Catalonia in European decision-making. It wants to be included in the Spanish delegation to the Council of Ministers (as made possible by the Treaty of Maastricht). It also proposes to create a second chamber, next to the European Parliament: a 'Senate of the nations', with equivalent competences, composed of 'sovereign territories' such as Catalonia (ERC 1994, 18; 1999, 12). The second 'independence in Europe' track is much less prominent in the ERC discourse. It is formulated more as a threat to Madrid than as a first choice option. If Spain would refuse to give Catalonia a say in European decision-making, then 'no other solution will remain than independence' (ERC 1994, 15).

At the end of the 1990s, ERC returned to a more moderate strategy focussing on its left-wing goals and primarily focused on government participation (Argelaguet 2011, 163). The party now abided by the Spanish constitutional framework and even promoted a dual Spanish-Catalan identity (Culla 2013, 479, 505). This pragmatic turn culminated in the 2003 entry in the tripartite Catalan government, together with the socialists and the greens. ERC also supported the socialist minority government of José Luis Zapatero from 2004 onwards. The party negotiated a new statute of autonomy with its government partners and strived for a constitutional reform in the longer run (Argelaguet 2006, 155; 2011, 164–167).

Still, this pragmatic turn did not fundamentally change the ERC's discourse on the EU, as evident from the 2004 manifesto. The manifesto remains emphatically Euro-enthusiastic and resumes demands for more EU competences. The ERC rejects the proposed European Constitutional Treaty and will also join the no-campaign in the 2005 referendum (Culla 2013, 615–617). One reason for this position is that it does not involve a federal reform of the Union. But the main objection against the Constitutional Treaty is that it does not provide channels for the 'nations without a state' to participate directly in EU decision-making. The Committee of the Regions remains mainly 'decorative' (ERC 2004, 10). Also, the idea of a second chamber is now developed more in detail (ERC 2004, 13–14). 'Independence in Europe' is mentioned almost as an afterthought and again as a threat, this time directed to Europe: if the EU should remain a union of states, 'the only alternative for the nations without a state to obtain recognition at the European level will be to become independent states in Europe' (ERC 2004, 11, 17).

The pragmatic strategy of the ERC backfired when, in 2006, the PSOE negotiated with CiU to get a watered-down version of the new statute of autonomy through the national parliament (van Houten 2009, 176–181). It was under the pressure of its rank and file that ERC eventually campaigned for a no-vote in the 2006 referendum on the new statute. Although the tripartite government was reinstated after the 2006 regional elections, these events set the party on a more secessionist course (Argelaguet 2011, 164–167).

This radicalization is already apparent in their 2009 European manifesto. Much less emphasis is now put on institutional devices to involve 'nations without a state' in EU decision-making. These are still mentioned, but at the same time dismissed as wishful thinking: 'We cannot forget that the European model which is now being constructed is a Europe of the states. Therefore, in order to exist, to have a direct channel to Europe, and to participate in the construction of Europe, it is necessary to be a state' (ERC 2009, 30). The arguments in favour of more EU competences remain. But the notion of a federal Europe has disappeared from the discourse. When the Spanish Constitutional Court abrogated important parts of the new Statute of Autonomy in 2010, this radicalization gained momentum. It was mainly driven by civil society mass mobilizations and also dragged along CiU (which was later reduced to CDC after Unió split off). In coalition with CiU, ERC organized a first quasi-referendum in November 2014.

The 2014 European election took place in the run-up to this referendum. The manifesto now fully embraces the idea of the Catalan Republic as a new EU state. But interesting, this EU is now envisaged as confederal rather than federal. A European constitution should be designed 'on a confederal base' (ERC 2014, 16). The idea of replacing the Council of Ministers into a Second Chamber 'of territorial and plurinational representation' is retained but now 'on a confederal base' (ERC 2014, 17). At the same time, this novel confederal stance is somewhat half-hearted as the party also wants to strengthen the powers of the European Parliament and is against the unanimity rule in European decision-making. The discourse remains pro-European and in favour of more EU competences. The manifesto claims that the EU will be pragmatic with regard to accepting Catalonia as a new member state. Nevertheless, if access would be denied, there are other ways for Catalonia to remain integrated in Europe. Thus, EU membership is not seen as a necessary condition for secession (ERC 2014, 7).

The interviews with two ERC MEPs confirm that the ERC has not made an unequivocal switch to confederalism. In fact, one of them quite emphatically defends a federal model, with less intergovernmental decision-making and more powers for the European Parliament and the Commission (Interview E, 21 March 2018). This implies that sovereignty has to be shared, but in order to be able to do so, Catalonia first has to obtain the right to decide its own future, it is argued. The other MEP is more aloof with regard to 'the F-word' but still defends positions that go in that direction (Interview D, 02 March 2018). Both defend without reserve more EU competences.

The ERC MEPs are less condescending towards earlier proposals to strengthen the position of the regions, but nevertheless do not consider these as a solution for Catalonia. A Senate for the regions or a stronger Committee of the Regions would be useful for stateless nations which do not want to be independent, it is argued. But even if this could be realized, Catalonia would still pursue independence. According to these ERC MEPs, this is primarily due to domestic factors, such as the unwillingness of Madrid to negotiate or to consider confederal or plurinational options for Spain.

More generally, the secessionist discourse is very much focused on Spain, while the EU is hardly instrumentalized to defend independence. The pincer movement argument is not used, probably because there is a tendency to downplay the autonomy already obtained within Spain. The stance in favour of shared sovereignty within a more federal EU is not linked to the secessionist narrative, and the opportunities which such a post-sovereignty federalist discourse offers to de-dramatize secession are not used. When asked, the MEPs acknowledge that the EU facilitates secession, as it provides a safety net, particularly because of European integration and the euro (Interview E, 21 March 2018). But at the same time – and in line with the 2014 manifesto – they emphasize that EU membership is not a precondition to independence. 'There is life outside the European Union', they say or a possible bilateral agreement with the EU (Interview D, 02 March 2018).

It does not come as a surprise that the MEPs do not mince their words when criticizing the EU, and more in particular the Commission, for taking sides with Madrid in the Catalan conflict and allegedly applying double standards with regard to human rights abuses. But even though they admit to having become more critical towards the EU, they also take pains to dissociate themselves from 'populist Euroscepticism' (Interview E, 21 March 2018). Overall, they show a more pro-European attitude than the N-VA MEPs whose 'Euro-realistic' discourse is more detached and cerebral.

DISCUSSION

This chapter assessed the position of three secessionist parties vis-à-vis the EU. Secessionist parties have traditionally been in favour of European integration. Recently, however, attitudes seem to have changed due to the reluctance of EU institutions to embrace secessionist movements. The 2014 Scottish independence referendum and especially the 2017 Catalan crisis made it clear that, for the EU, it is impossible for seceding regions to automatically gain membership. Therefore, the question is how this development is reflected in secessionist parties' attitudes towards the EU and in the way they instrumentalize the EU for their strategic purpose: secession.

The party manifestoes show that N-VA, SNP, and ERC have more or less gradually abandoned a federal perspective on the EU. After a brief discussion, SNP opted for a confederal model right away, that is, at the moment when it switched to a pro-EU stance in 1988 and launched its 'independence in Europe' narrative. The N-VA has inherited a federal approach from its successor, the Volksunie. The initial narrative of the party about the EU is ambiguous and contains both federal and confederal elements. It is only from 2009 onwards that the party unambiguously defends a confederal model for the EU and develops a similar 'intergovernmental' discourse as SNP. ERC is the party which appears to be lagging behind in this development. The party unequivocally defended a federal EU until 2004. The 'F-word' disappears in 2009 and in 2014 the term 'confederalism' starts to trickle into its discourse, even though this is not quite in alignment with the institutional proposals of the party. The interviews confirm that this more confederal approach of ERC is still rather half-hearted.

To a certain degree, ERC takes a more traditional pro-European stance, such as many parties in Spain. In contrast, the SNP has been more critical, even making a plea for a confederal Europe, in line with the overall British attitude towards European integration. Only the N-VA seems to deviate from its direct competitors. Whereas Flemish parties are still in favour of more European integration, the N-VA adopts, mainly for strategic reasons, a much more critical approach, including a plea for an intergovernmental EU.

Originally, however, the federal narrative of the 1990s (of ERC and Volksunie) dovetailed with the ideas of post-sovereignty and multilevel governance which prospered in the wake of the 1993 Maastricht Treaty. The proclaimed end of the sovereign nation-state made it possible for secessionists to de-dramatize separatism. These rhetorical opportunities were enhanced in a federalist narrative, which allowed for downplaying secession as a mere split-up of a member state. But in the heyday of 'post-sovereignty', the Flemish and Catalan autonomists were following a more moderate regionalist course and therefore could not fully grasp this strategic opportunity. When they switched to a more radical secessionist stance, the window of opportunity had already closed and prospects of a federal multilevel Europe became increasingly unrealistic due to, among other reasons, the 2004 enlargement.

A second way to use the EU in secessionist discourse is the so-called pincer movement argument. This reasoning implies a stance in favour of hollowing out the state by transferring more competences to the EU. The N-VA initially did adopt such a position, aiming at a gradual 'evaporation' of the Belgian state. Yet, in 2014, the party switched to a so-called Eurorealistic position and is now drafting a list of competences that should be devolved to member states, possibly reinforcing the federal level within Belgium. The SNP already made this turn towards renationalization in 1999. ERC is the only party which has remained enthusiastic about a one-way transfer of competences to the EU. But the party does not use the pincer argument to the same extent as SNP and N-VA did, probably because it wants to downplay the competences which Catalonia already obtained within the Spanish framework.

Finally, European integration can be useful to secessionist parties because it arguably reduces the cost of independence. It is mainly the N-VA which explicitly uses this safety net argument. But this discourse is now primarily instrumental to defend maintaining the EU in the context of the party's Euro-realistic discourse. This argument does not play a major role in the discourse of SNP and ERC. While it is acknowledged in the interviews that a European safety net facilitates secession, it is also argued that EU membership is not a precondition for Catalan or Scottish independence. The idea that there is life outside the EU was already present in the 2014 ERC manifesto. For the SNP, since Brexit, it has become even more inconceivable. This attitude is also evident from interviews, which show that recent events in Scotland and Catalonia have fuelled unease about the EU. Yet this is not yet translated into a full-fledged Eurocritical stance, let alone independence outside the EU.

In sum, the tendency of secessionists to distance themselves from the EU predates the recent crises. This tendency can partly be explained on the basis of the internal context of the three countries. The fact that the European dimension is less central to the secessionist discourse of SNP than in the case of Volksunie and N-VA and that SNP has opted for confederalism at an early stage is arguably related to the more peripheral position of both Scotland and the UK in the EU and the more Eurocritical stance of public opinion, even in Scotland. It is because of a growing Eurosceptical sentiment in public opinion (Eurostat 2018) that the N-VA has switched to its 'Eurorealist' discourse in 2014, abandoning some strategic advantages of a more pro-European discourse. But at the same time, being a member of the pro-EU Belgian government from 2014 until 2018, the party had to keep a brake on this anti-EU tendency. Finally, the recent emphasis of ERC on a new Catalan Republic in (or outside of) a more or less confederal Europe is obviously driven by the escalating political conflict with Madrid.

Nevertheless, the stance towards the EU and the way the EU is used in secessionist discourse appears also in large part determined by the broader development of the Union. During the 1990s, it rapidly became clear that notions of 'post-sovereignty' and 'new regionalism' were overblown. In the context of the 2004 enlargement and the rejection of the European Constitution, the notions of a 'United States of Europe' or a 'Europe of the regions' became increasingly ephemeral. This imposed a shift towards confederalism in the narrative of secessionists and also robbed them of some EU-related rhetorical advantages. The EU is still a strategic playing field for secessionist parties, but Brussels is now perceived to be on the other side: the wrong one, the one of the home state. In a more state-centred and intergovernmental perceived EU, opting for independence has again become a radical choice.

REFERENCES

Alesina, A., and E. Spolaore. 2003. *The Size of Nations*. Cambridge: MIT Press.

Argelaguet, J. 2006. 'Esquerra Republicana de Catalunya: The Third Pole within Catalan Politics'. In *Autonomist Parties in Europe: Identity Politics and the Revival of the Territorial Cleavage*, edited by L. De Winter, M. Gómez-Reino, and P. Lynch. Vol. I. Barcelona: Institut de Ciències Polítiques i Socials, pp.143–165.

Argelaguet, J. 2011. 'Esquerra Republicana de Catalunya'. In *From Protest to Power. Autonomist Parties and the Challenge of Representation*, edited by A. Elias and F. Tronconi. Wien: Wilhelm Braumüller, pp. 147–169.

Beyens, S., K. Deschouwer, E. van Haute, and T. Verthé. 2015. 'Born Again, or Born Anew: Assessing the Newness of the Belgian Political Party New-Flemish Alliance (N-VA)'. *Party Politics* 23(4): 1–11.

Brack, N., W. Wolfs, and S. Van Hecke. 2017. 'Breaking the Consensus. How Real Is the N-VA's Eurorealism?' Paper presented at the UACES 47th Annual Conference, Jagiellonian University, Krakow.

Brown, C. 2017. 'The Art of the Possible. Framing Self-Government in Scotland and Flanders'. Unpublished Ph.D., University of Edinburgh.

Coppieters, B. 2010. 'Secessionist Conflict in Europe'. In *Secession as an International Phenomenon. From America's Civil War to Contemporary Separatist Movements*, edited by D. H. Doyle. Athens: University of Georgia Press, pp. 237–258.

Culla, J. B. 2013. *Esquerra Republicana de Catalunya 1931–2012. Una història política*. Barcelona: La Campana.

Cymerman, E. 26 November 2017. 'Puigdemont cree que Catalunya debería votar si quiere seguir en la UE'. *La Vanguardia*.

Del Riego, C. 9 November 2017. 'Juncker advierte contra el "veneno" para Europa de los nacionalismos y separatismos'. *La Vanguardia*. https://www.lavanguardia. com/politica/20171109/432743200383/juncker-veneno-europa-nacionalismos-separatismos.html

De Winter, L. 2001. 'The Impact of European Integration on Ethnoregionalist Parties'. Working paper nr. 185. Barcelona: Institut de Ciències Polítiques i Socials.

De Winter, L., and M. Gomez-Reino Cachafeiro. 2002. 'European Integration and Ethnoregionalist Parties'. *Party Politics* 8(4): 483–503.

Elias, A. 2008. 'From Euro-Enthusiasm to Euro-Scepticism? A Reevaluation of Minority Nationalist Party Attitudes towards European Integration'. *Regional & Federal Studies* 18(5): 557–581.

Esquerra Republicana de Catalunya (ERC). 1994. 'Països Catalans, Unió Europea. Per l'Europa de les Nacions'. Programa electoral eleccions al Parlament Europeu.

Euractiv (29 June 2016). *Sturgeon in Brussels to Push Scotland's Remain Case*. [17 February 2018, *Euractiv*. https://www.euractiv.com/section/uk-europe/news/ sturgeon-in-brussels-to-push-scotlands-remain-case/].

ERC. 1999. 'Lliures dins una Europa sense fronteres'. Programa electoral eleccions al Parlament Europeu.

ERC. 2004. Programa eleccions al Parlament Europeu juny 2004.

ERC. June 2009. 'Próxima estació, Europa'. Programa electoral eleccions al Parlament Europeu.

ERC. 2014. 'Comencem el #noupaís. Ara, a Europa. Eleccions al Parlament Europeu 2014'. Programa electoral.

Eurostat. 2018. 'Level of Citizens' Confidence in EU Institutions'. [29 March 2018. http://ec.europa.eu/eurostat/tgm/table.do?tab=table&init=1&language=en&pcode =tsdgo510&plugin=1].

Gorriarán, R. 28 November 2017. 'Puigdemont recula en su discurso antieuropista al comprobar su soledad'. *Las Provincias*. https://www.lasprovincias.es/elecciones/catalanas/puigdemont-recula-discurso-20171128095512-ntrc.html

Hepburn, E. 2008. 'The Rise and Fall of a 'Europe of the Regions'. *Regional & Federal Studies* 18(5): 537–555.

Hepburn, E. 2010. *Using Europe. Territorial Party Strategies in a Multi-Level System*. Manchester: Manchester University Press.

Hooghe, L., and M. Keating. 2004. 'The Politics of European Union Regional Policy'. In *Regions and Regionalism in Europe*, edited by M. Keating. Cheltenham: Edward Elgar, pp. 466–492.

The Irish Times. 29 June 2016. 'Blow Dealt to Scotland's Hopes of Separate EU Talks' [17 February 2018. https://www.irishtimes.com/news/world/uk/blow-dealt-to-scotland-s-hopes-of-separate-eu-talks-1.2704270].

Jolly, S. K. 2007. 'The Europhile Fringe? Regionalist Party Support for European Integration'. *European Union Politics* 8(1): 109–130.

Juliana, E. 26 November 2017. 'La mediación que no llegó'. *La Vanguardia*. https://www.lavanguardia.com/politica/20171126/433202123811/mediacion-catalunya-espana-generalitat.html

Keating, M. 2001. *Plurinational Democracy. Stateless Nations in a Post-Sovereignty Era*. Oxford: Oxford University Press.

Keating, M. 2004. 'European Integration and the Nationalities Question'. *Politics and Society* 32(3): 367–388.

Keating, M. 2015. 'The Rescaling of States and Political Communities'. In *(Con)federalism: Cure or Curse?* Re-Bel e-book 18, edited by K. Deschouwer and J. Poirier. http://www.rethinkingbelgium.eu/rebel-initiative-ebooks/ebook-18-con-federalism-federalism-cure-or-curse, pp. 53–54.

Keating, M. 2017. 'The European Question'. In *Debating Scotland. Issues of independence and Union in the 2014 Referendum*, reedited M. Keating. Oxford: Oxford University Press, pp. 102–118.

Loughlin, J. 2015. 'Federalism, Federations and Confederations: Towards Hybridity'. In *(Con)federalism: Cure or Curse?* Re-Bel e-book 18, edited by K. Deschouwer and J. Poirier. http://www.rethinkingbelgium.eu/rebel-initiative-ebooks/ebook-18-confederalism-federalism-cure-or-curse, pp. 4–16.

Lynch, P. 1998. 'Co-Operation between Regionalist Parties at the Level of the European Union. The European Free Alliance'. In *Regionalist Parties in Western Europe*, edited by L. De Winter and H. Türsan. London: Routledge, pp. 190–203.

Lynch, P., and L. De Winter. 2008. 'The Shrinking Political Space of Minority Nationalist Parties in an Enlarged Europe of the Regions'. *Regional and Federal Studies* 18(5): 583–606.

Maddens, B. 2017. 'Secessionist Strategies: The Case of Flanders'. In *Secession and Counter-Secession. An International Perspective*, edited by D. Muro and E. Woertz. Barcelona: CIDOB, pp. 55–62.

Nagel, K.J. 2004. 'Transcending the National/Asserting the National. How Stateless Nations like Scotland, Wales and Catalonia React to European Integration'. *Australian Journal of Politics and History* 50(1): 57–74.

N-VA. 2004. *Verkiezingsprogramma N-VA: Europese verkiezingen 13 juni 2004*, Brussel: Nieuw-Vlaamse Alliantie.

N-VA. 2009. *Afrit Vlaanderen Uitrit Crisis: Verkiezingsprogramma 7 juni 2009 Europa Vlaanderen Brussel*. Brussel: Nieuw-Vlaamse Alliantie.

N-VA. 2014. *Verandering voor Vooruitgang: Verkiezingsprogramma Vlaamse, federale en Europese verkiezingen 25 mei 2014*. Brussel: Nieuw-Vlaamse Alliantie.

Schmidt, P. 2014. 'Secession: Member States, Aspiring States and the European Union, KU Leuven Center for Global Government Studies'. Policy Brief No. 22 https://ghum.kuleuven.be/ggs/publications/policy_briefs/pb22-schmitt.pdf

Scottish National Party (SNP). 1989. 'Scotland's Future – Independence in Europe'. SNP Manifesto. European Elections 15 June 1989, Edinburgh: Scottish National Party.

SNP. 1999. 'Standing Up for Scotland. Independence in Europe'. Scottish National Party Manifesto for the European Parliamentary Elections, 10 June 1999, Edinburgh: Scottish National Party.

SNP. 2004. 'Vote for Scotland'. European Manifesto, Edinburgh: Scottish National Party.

SNP. 2009. 'We've Got What It Takes'. Manifesto '09 SNP, Edinburgh: Scottish National Party.

SNP. 2014. *Make Scotland's Mark on Europe*. Edinburgh: Scottish National Party.

Sottiaux, S. 2011. *De Verenigde Staten van België. Reflecties over de toekomst van het grondwettelijk recht in de gelaagde rechtsorde*. Mechelen: Kluwer.

Sottiaux, S. 2014. 'De zevende staatshervorming: van federale staat naar Verenigde Staten van België?' In *Het federale België na de zesde staatshervorming*, edited by A. Alen a.o. Brugge: die Keure, pp. 635–651.

Tarditi, V. 2010. 'The Scottish National Party's Changing Attitude towards the European Union'. SEI Working Paper No 112, EPERN Working paper No 22. Sussex European Institute.

The Scotsman. 11 December 2012. 'Scottish Independence: New Setback for SNP over EU Membership as Jose Manuel Barroso Blocks Automatic Entry' [28 March 2019. https://www.scotsman.com/news/politics/scottish-independence-new-setback-for-snp-over-eu-membership-as-jose-manuel-barroso-blocks-automatic-entry-1-2683922].

van Houten, P. 2009. 'Authority in Multilevel Parties: A Principal-Agent Framework and Cases from Germany and Spain'. In *Territorial Party Politics in Western*

Europe, edited by W. Swenden and B. Maddens. Houndmills: Palgrave MacMillan, pp. 167–182.

Velaers, J. 2013. *Confederalisme/federalisme . . . En de weg ernaartoe. KVAB-standpunten nr. 20.* Brussel: KVAB-Press.

Velaers, J. 2015. 'The Belgian Federalism/Confederalism Debate in Light of Classic Constitutional Theory'. In *(Con)federalism: Cure or Curse?* Re-Bel e-book 18, edited by K. Deschouwer and J. Poirier, http://www.rethinkingbel gium.eu/rebel-initiative-ebooks/ebook-18-confederalism-federalism-cure-or-curse, pp.17–26.

Interviews

Interview A: Loones, S. (Brussels, 21 February 2018). *N-VA and the European Union.* [Sander Loones is an N-VA MEP in the ECR Group and vice president of the N-VA.]

Interview B: Demesmaeker, M. (Brussels, 21 February 2018). *N-VA and the European Union.* [Mark Demesmaeker is an N-VA MEP in the ECR Group and N-VA delegation leader.]

Interview C: Smith, A. (Brussels, 27 February 2018). *SNP and the European Union.* [Alyn Smith is an SNP MEP in the Greens/EFA Group and member of the SNP's National Executive Committee.]

Skype Interview D: Terricabras, J. M. (Brussels, 02 March 2018). *ERC and the European Union.* [Josep-Maria Terricabras is an ERC MEP in the Greens/EFA Group.]

Skype Interview E: Solé, J. (Brussels, 21 March 2018). *ERC and the European Union.* [Jordi Solé is an ERC MEP in the Greens/EFA Group.]

Chapter 8

The Two Québec Independence Referendums: Political Strategies and International Relations

André Lecours*

Independence referendums in multinational democracies are high stakes, emotionally charged events that feature debates over the desirability, legitimacy, and feasibility of secession (Lecours 2018). These debates feature a strategic playing field where many different actors operate at distinct territorial levels: within the minority national community, where the dominant issue tends to be the desirability of independent statehood; involving the central government, where desirability arguments are also part of the debate but where the legitimacy question is often present; and on the international scene, where the feasibility of establishing a new state, that is, the international recognition of independent statehood, is a central question.

This paper analyses the strategies of secessionist forces in the context of independence referendum campaigns as they unfold along these three territorial levels using the case of Québec. Québec is exceptional among all cases of nationalist movements in liberal democracies, as governments formed by the secessionist Parti québécois (PQ) have organized two independence referendums. Thus, the Québec case offers particularly fertile ground for examining how a secessionist party seeks to convince, through normative appeals, a majority of voters to support independence in a referendum campaign while a host of other actors (within the province, across the country, and around the world) make a case against secession. More specifically, the unique Québec experience with two independence referendums allows for an in-case comparison that can illuminate differences and similarities in campaign dynamics and point towards potential explanatory factors in the event that significant differences are identified between the two referendums.

The chapter is divided into three main sections. The first section discusses briefly how secessionist actors typically interact with non-secessionist forces within the minority national community, in the rest of the country and beyond the state's borders. The second section looks at the two cases of independence referendums in Québec, in 1980 and 1995. The third section examines the consequences of the Clarity Act (2000) on the potential recognition dynamics stemming from any future independence referendum in Québec.

INDEPENDENCE REFERENDUM CAMPAIGNS: SECESSIONIST POLITICS WITHIN THE MINORITY NATIONAL COMMUNITY, AT THE STATE-WIDE LEVEL AND INTERNATIONALLY

A central aim of secessionist actors during an independence referendum campaign is to convince members of the minority national community of the desirability of secession. In advanced industrialized liberal democracies, this is not a simple argument to make, since there typically does not exist issues of security, systemic oppression, or extreme poverty. Yet a wide variety of arguments (and counterarguments) are made in independence referendum campaigns. For the purpose of analytical clarity, I distinguish among four types of arguments.

The first are identity arguments. All independence referendums feature, to some degree, the notion that the community for whom independence is sought is a nation, distinct from the one projected by the state. Additionally, if the minority nation is closely associated with specific cultural markers like language, an identity argument for secession can be that independence will transform a cultural or linguistic minority into a majority. Overall, pro-secession arguments tend to include the notion that independence will be beneficial to the culture, the identity, and indeed the nationhood of a minority national community.

The second are public policy arguments. An argument for secession can be that independence would allow the minority national community to implement public policies in tune with the societal preferences of the minority national community. In other words, the secessionist movement may claim that the minority national community prefers policies other than those implemented by the central government (and over which it has no veto). Of course, such arguments about public policies are often tied to national identity (Béland and Lecours 2008), so the division between policy and identity considerations in analysing secessionist arguments is somewhat artificial.

The third are societal project arguments. This type of arguments encompasses both identity and policy dimensions but has broader ideological and political meaning. Indeed, secessionist movements often make the argument that independence can allow for the creation of a different type of society, presumably built upon the dominant values and preferences of the minority national community, as well as a different (presumably better) way of doing politics. For example, at the most basic level, secessionist actors can argue that independence can lead to a more progressive and egalitarian society or to one where autonomy and entrepreneurship is fully maximized.

The fourth type of secessionist arguments involves grievances against the state. Such grievances are always present in some way within an argument for secession. These grievances tend to be multifaceted; the central government, or the state, is typically said to have slighted the minority national community is multiple ways. Such perceived slights can include issues of fiscal redistribution, political centralization, marginalization, and the (non)recognition of nationhood or distinctiveness. Overall, accusations of unfair or discriminatory treatment against the minority national community tend to be powerful discursive tools for promoting secession during a referendum campaign.

From a strategic perspective, secessionist movements tend to want to downplay the radical nature of their project. Indeed, their leaders seek to reassure citizens that the process of gaining independence will not drastically, and certainly not adversely, change their daily life. In the European context, for example, secessionist leaders have argued that secession from the host state can occur with a minimum of disruption, since the European Union (EU) acts as a safety net, as chapter 7 suggests. Also, as this chapter suggests, these leaders often present secession as involving the acquisition of a greater measure of sovereignty, though not complete sovereignty, since some have been and will remain delegated to the EU. In other words, secessionist movements typically look to portray independence as something other than an all-or-nothing proposition.

Secessionist politics also often involves secessionist actors tackling the question of the legitimacy of an independence referendum. This question sometimes pits secessionists and nonsecessionists within the minority national community, but it is most often debated between secessionist leaders and the central government. In some cases, central governments may not question the legitimacy of holding an independence referendum, and it may not even look to establish, or negotiate, some parameters for the consultation exercise. More likely, however, is that the central government will look to specify what a legitimate independence looks like: who gets the right to vote, when does the vote takes place, what question is asked, what majority is required for a secessionist win, and so on. Secessionist leaders can then choose to negotiate some kind of an agreement with the central government or choose to have all the parameters set unilaterally by the political institutions of the minority national community. The latter choice involves a substantial risk, since a win of the secessionist option might not be recognized by the central government, which leaves secessionists with the very difficult task of seeking recognition of statehood against the wishes of the state. The central state may also choose to reject the legitimacy (and even the legality and constitutionality) of an independence referendum and may actively work to prevent it from happening. In such a case, the issue of legitimacy is likely to permeate the whole referendum campaign and only supporters of secessionists may turn out to vote.

Ultimately, the feasibility of independence hinges strongly on the international recognition of statehood. When there is an agreement in place on the parameters of the referendum between secessionist leaders and the central government, presumably including a commitment on the part of the central government to recognize that a secessionist win will lead to independent statehood, secessionists may not view it as crucial to look to secure international support for their independence project; the eventual recognition of independence by the state whose existence is questioned by the referendum is expected to open the door for a generalized recognition by the international community. In cases where no such agreement exists, however, it becomes crucial for secessionist leaders to seek out potential support internationally for an eventual declaration of independence. Hence, in such circumstances, these leaders 'go abroad' to explain their project and elicit some sympathy for it. They use the international arena in an attempt to put some pressure on their state to recognize the eventual independence of their minority national community if not to get outright assurances that some other states will offer such recognition. Of course, this is a tall order. States defend the principle of territorial integrity, and those who have to manage nationalist movements do it particularly strongly. As multinational democracies such as Canada, the United Kingdom, Spain, and Belgium offer measures of autonomy (in addition to the protection of basic individual rights) to their minority national communities, states consider that these communities have achieved an acceptable level of self-determination. In this context, the democratic will and self-determination arguments of secessionist leaders tend to fall flat. Sometimes, historical and/or cultural connections between the minority national community and some foreign states can provide an apparent opening for secessionist leaders to persuade these states to support an eventual declaration of independence. As we will see in the next section, it is exactly what Québec's PQ government sought to do in both 1980 and 1995.

THE QUÉBEC INDEPENDENCE REFERENDUMS

Nationalism in advanced industrialized liberal democracies was considered dead by many scholars in the 1960s. Modernist thinking held that processes of economic, cultural, social, and political diffusion from centre to periphery would definitively complete the integration of Western states (Deutsch

1966). Yet, in Canada, the rise of Québécois nationalism led to a referendum on independence in 1980 and yet another one in 1995. Although held only fifteen years apart, these referendums featured quite different secessionist strategies but exhibited similar dynamics on legitimacy questions as well as international engagement.

The 1980 Referendum: The Societal Project of Francophone Emancipation and Social-Democracy

The 1980 Québec referendum came on the heels of a process of modernization in the province known as the Quiet Revolution. Engineered by Québec governments beginning in the 1960s, the Quiet Revolution featured, among other things, measures to improve the socioeconomic status of Francophones, rendered difficult by decades of mostly conservative politics and strong Church influence, and legislation to promote the French language and culture at a time when English was the dominant language at the highest echelons of the province's economy (McRoberts 1993). The (Liberal) Québec governments of the Quiet Revolution also argued that they shouldered the special burden of looking after the only mainly French-speaking society in North America and that, as a result, Québec should enjoy extensive autonomy within the Canadian federation and be recognized as different within its constitutional framework. The PQ, formed in 1968, went a step further and argued that the full emancipation of Francophones required Québec to be a sovereign state (Fraser 1984). Its majority government in 1976 gave the secessionist party the opportunity to organize a referendum on independence.

The PQ recognized the radical nature of its project and sought to reassure Quebeckers by adopting a so-called gradualist approach (*l'étapisme*). Indeed, in 1980, the PQ asked Quebeckers for a mandate to negotiate a 'sovereignty-association' arrangement with Canada. In the event of a 'yes' answer, a second referendum would be held to ratify whatever 'association' had been negotiated. In other words, Quebeckers would have a chance to confirm their decision to become independent after they initially granted the Québec government permission to begin secession negotiations with Canada. Also in recognition of the hurdles it faced in convincing Quebeckers to support secession, the PQ opted to use the concept of 'sovereignty' (rather than independence, which arguably sounded more like a rupture) coupled with the notion of an association with Canada. Such association remained ill-defined but, to the extent it was discussed at all, the focus was on an economic rather than a political association (although the latter was not formally excluded). These two elements (the gradualist, two-referendum approach and the use of the concept of sovereignty association) made for a 'softer' question viewed as more likely to garner a majority of 'yes' votes than a short, straightforward question on independence.[1]

The PQ government never sought to obtain the consent of the federal government for holding a referendum on independence. In the absence of constitutional barriers to secession, the federal nature of Canada, which involves a division of sovereignty, combined with the prominence in the province of political ideas such as the right to self-determination most likely contributed to the PQ taking for granted that Québec could become independent. The legitimacy of an independence referendum and, indeed, of the possible secession of Québec, was never challenged by federal government. Perhaps the fact that, as per the gradualist approach, a 'yes' vote in the first referendum would need to be followed by another 'yes' result in a second referendum made it easier for the federal government to tacitly accept the legitimacy of such a self-determination exercise by fully engaging in the campaign, as did the fact that it was confident that the 'no' would win rather handily. Moreover, the federal government never seriously objected to the question posed nor did it question that 50% + 1 would be a sufficient majority to trigger secession negotiations. In sum, even in the absence of a negotiated agreement between Québec and Canadian governments, there was virtually no debate, or even discussion, on the legitimacy of the referendum.

The PQ deployed two main arguments during the 1980 referendum campaign, both very broad in nature and anchored into the developing Québécois nationalism that was pushing aside notions of French-Canadian solidarity (Balthazar 2013).

The first argument was that a sovereign Québec could fully emancipate Francophones. For the PQ, independence was a project for the province's Francophone majority, as it was argued that an independent state could best protect and promote its socioeconomic, cultural, and linguistic interests. At that time, there was virtually no effort made to convince Anglophones and new immigrants, who were overwhelmingly in favour of Québec remaining part of Canada, to support independence. Not only did the PQ judge that there was basically no chance to change the views of even a handful of members of these communities but also running a campaign centred on the notion of giving Francophone Quebeckers 'a country' was not widely viewed as a problematic idea. Hence, the cultural content of the campaign was very substantial. French, in all its dimensions, was central to the argument for independence, and singers, artists, and poets were at the forefront of the 'Yes' campaign.

The second broad argument made by the PQ was that independence could be used to create a fairer, more egalitarian society where the state would be used extensively to bridge the gap between rich and poor. The PQ was created as a social democratic party and, during its government years preceding the referendum (1976–1980), implemented many progressive measures, particularly on the labour market. Trade unions were close to the PQ and supportive of independence, which they saw as a way to improve the socioeconomic status of Francophones and to create a more labour-friendly environment. The PQ argued that Québec independence would be used to create a different type of society, one inspired by the social democracies of Scandinavia (Béland and Lecours 2008).

To counter these arguments, the federal government used a two-pronged strategy. First, the then Prime Minister Pierre Trudeau articulated a strong defence of Canada, emphasizing that the country belonged to Quebeckers as much as it did to other Canadians. For many Quebeckers, especially older ones whose formative years pre-dated the Quiet Revolution and strongly identified as 'French-Canadians', this was a powerful argument. Second, the federal government predicted that independence would come with dire economic and financial consequences and that Québec would be a small, isolated, and poor sovereign state. The international context of the time gave these economic arguments some credibility. Indeed, at a time where economies were still (state) national, Québec's trading was very much oriented towards the rest of Canada.

In the international politics of Québec independence, there are two significant actors: France, historically and culturally the most meaningful external state for the province, and the superpower neighbour, the United States. In the 1960s, France expressed support for Québec independence, as demonstrated by General de Gaulle's *Vive le Québec libre!* pronouncement on the balcony of Montreal's city hall in 1967. General de Gaulle's strategy was in part motivated by his desire to 'break the Anglo-American domination of the North Atlantic Alliance and give France an independent Francophone ally in North America' (Nossal, Roussel, and Paquin 2015, 357).

Although such enthusiasm had tempered under Valéry Giscard d'Estaing, in his visit to France in 1977, Premier René Lévesque was welcomed with the diplomatic formalities usually reserved for heads of state and government. In fact, there remained enough sympathy for the PQ's project in the French government to have France develop a specific formula to designate the country's position towards secessionist politics in Québec: *non-ingérence, non-indifférence* (non-meddling, non-indifference) (Bastien 1999).

This stood in sharp contrast to the United States, which took an unambiguous position in favour of a united Canada. The PQ government recognized that the American opposition to Québec independence could deter some Quebeckers from voting 'yes', and so it launched the so-called Operation America to explain their independence project to Americans (Nossal, Roussel, and Paquin 2015: 362). When Premier René Lévesque and his Minister of Finance Jacques Parizeau went to New York in 1977, where they called the province's independence 'inevitable', they encountered mostly negative reactions on the part of the business communities that feared nationalizations and potential debt defaults (Nossal, Roussel, and Paquin 2015, 361). Indeed, the idea of independence was really badly received in the United States where the socio-democratic ideology of the secessionist movement led some to suggest independence would transform the province to a 'Cuba North', an unwelcome proposition in a United States still in the middle of the Cold War. Moreover, despite Premier René Lévesque's attempt to compare its project to the American War of Independence when speaking to an American audience, secessionist politics brought up memories of the Civil War instead.

Yet the federal government was not taking the United States' position on the issue of Québec independence lightly, fearing that even a few words of sympathy by American diplomats or even commentators could embolden more Quebeckers to vote 'yes'. Prime Minister Pierre Trudeau secured an invitation to speak to a joint session of the U.S. Congress where he warned that the secession of Québec would have more serious consequences for the United States than the Cuban missile crisis (Nossal, Roussel, and Paquin 2015, 362). He also said the breakup of Canada would be 'a crime against the history of mankind' (Nossal, Roussel, and Paquin 2015, 362). The position of the US government during the 1980 referendum remained consistent. President Carter expressed the idea that Canada's stability was of crucial importance and that, although the question of Québec's political future was a matter internal to Canada, the United States preferred a united Canada (Nossal, Roussel, and Paquin 2015, 362).

Although the impact of international factors on the 1980 referendum is impossible to assess with any precision, it was most likely marginal. The French and American positions largely conformed to the expectations of the actors involved in the referendum. For the PQ, convincing post-de Gaulle France to support clearly Québec's independence was always a long shot, while getting any kind of sympathy from the United States was even less likely.

The 1995 Referendum: Grievances against the Federal Government

The second referendum on Québec independence was the product of a very different political dynamic than the first. By the mid-1990s, Francophone Quebeckers by and large no longer felt like they required 'emancipation' or 'liberation'. Language legislation had helped to both strengthen the position of French and further the socioeconomic status of Francophones. Although the PQ still presented itself as social-democratic, the party appeared much more business-friendly than before. The nature of nationalist mobilization in Québec had changed but arguably reached new height in the early 1990s when constitutional negotiations aiming at meeting demands of Québec governments (after a new constitution act was adopted in 1982 without its consent) ultimately failed (Laforest 1995). These failures were interpreted by Quebeckers as a rejection of the province and, more specifically, of its distinctiveness. The PQ capitalized on, and fed, these feelings of rejection, arguing it was now time to make Québec an independent country. The secessionist party competed in the 1994 Québec elections with the promise of holding a second referendum on independence if it won. After winning a majority of seats and forming the government, the PQ announced a referendum would be held on 20 October 1995.

The federal government reacted placidly to this announcement. Much like in 1980, and despite polls having shown majority support for independence just a couple of years earlier, the expectation was for a similar result to the first referendum. Moreover, the 1980 referendum served as an important precedent, one that would have made it difficult for the federal government to challenge the legitimacy of a vote on independence fifteen years later. There was an important difference between the 1995 and the 1980 referendum processes: in 1995, the gradualist approach was abandoned and there was to be only one vote, which presumably gave the PQ government a mandate to negotiate a final secession settlement with Canada. Yet the federal government made no issue of this change, perhaps believing that asking for a second, post-negotiation confirmation vote in the event of a 'yes' result would have made it easier for Quebeckers to support independence in a first vote. Moreover, although some dismay was expressed by opponents of secession at the wording of the question, there was never any attempt on the part of the federal government to argue, before the referendum, that the wording rendered the exercise illegitimate. Of course, the question's wording was designed to maximize the chances of a 'yes' result. Like in 1980, the 'yes' side spoke of sovereignty rather than independence and stated that there would be an offer of economic and political partnership (never specifically defined) made to Canada once Quebeckers had voted for secession. All of this was reflected in the question.[2] Moreover, the question referred to an agreement between various parties. Indeed, by the early 1990s (and contrary to 1980), there was also a secessionist party operating at the federal level (the Bloc québécois, BQ) and a small nationalist party in the Québec party system (Action démocratique du Québec, ADQ) that chose to support independence. This multiparty support was referenced in the question (the PQ, BQ, and ADQ had signed an agreement to seek the independence of the province through a referendum), most likely in the hope that independence be seen as more than just the PQ project.

The failed constitutional negotiations of the 1980s and early 1990s constituted the essence of the argument of the 'yes' camp in 1995. Independence was best, according to 'yes' side leaders, because Québec's minimal conditions for a constitutional accord (including, most importantly, a recognition of its distinctiveness) had been too much for the rest of Canada to accept. These leaders deployed a narrative of exhaustion, similar to that of present-day Catalonia (Basta 2018), which stated that Québec governments had tried everything to make it work within Canada but to no avail, and that in these circumstances independence was the only option. The constitutional odyssey of the 1980s and early 1990s was presented as a rejection of Québec by Canada. Its main actors were vilified and/or presented as traitors (e.g., the then Prime Minister Jean Chrétien, himself a Quebecker). The leaders of the 'yes' side remained vague about what independence would mean, only arguing that with a 'yes' anything would be possible. In other words, secessionist arguments in the 1995 referendum were primarily about grievances held against the federal government; the societal project involved in the first referendum (emancipation of Francophones and establishment of a social democracy) was virtually absent.

For its part, the federal government seemed content to keep a low profile for the longest time, believing that a 'yes' vote was impossible. There was virtually no appeal to the Canadian identity of Quebeckers, something which prominent federalists in the province later said had been a major mistake (Hébert and Lapierre 2014). Arguments about the economic and financial risks of secession were less effective than they had been in 1980. The free-trade agreement with the United States, of which the PQ had been supportive in part for strategic reasons, had made the Québec economically less dependent on the rest of Canada (Martin 1995).

The PQ government was extremely active internationally in seeking support for a unilateral declaration of independence that would follow a 'yes' win (an exercise dubbed *le grand jeu*). Unsurprisingly, the main international protagonist of this game was France. Publicly, the French government mostly stuck to its non-meddling, non-indifference formula, stating that it would accompany Québec in whichever path it chose. This seemed to be neutral enough for the Canadian government, but 'yes' side leaders took it to mean that France would recognize Québec as an independent state following a declaration of independence. In fact, sometime in 1995, the Québec and French governments agreed on the following statement, to be released by the French government in the event of a 'yes' victory:

> France takes note of the democratic will expressed by the Québec people, on October 30 1995, to become sovereign after having formally offered Canada a new political and economic partnership. When Québec's National Assembly proclaims the sovereignty of Québec following the process laid out in the referendum question and now approved by the Québec people, France will amicably draw the consequences. Concerned that the process occurs in the best conditions,

France wants to reaffirm its friendship for Canada and its government. They can be assured of our willingness to maintain and deepen the excellent relations that bind us. (Nossal, Roussel, and Paquin 2015, 366, my translation)[3]

Québec's Premier Jacques Parizeau always expressed great confidence that France would recognize Québec as a sovereign state after the province's National Assembly proclaimed independence following 'yes' win and the offer of a partnership to Canada. France's prospective recognition was the centrepiece of the PQ's international strategy and would have become especially important had Canada hesitated to accept secession, for example, in the event of a very slim 'yes' win. The PQ government was hopeful that France would convince other French-speaking countries as well as other EU member states to follow suit (Nossal, Roussel, and Paquin 2015, 366). Hence the idea was that momentum would build towards a broad recognition of Québec as a sovereign state within the international community, including by the United States.

Just like in 1980, the United States clearly preferred that Québec remained within Canada. In his visit to Ottawa in February 1995, President Bill Clinton made a speech to the House of Commons that heralded Canada as a model for the world on how different cultures can live together in peace (Nossal, Roussel, and Paquin 2015, 367). On the North American Free Trade Agreement, the Clinton administration made it a point to say that an independent Québec would not automatically be part of the free-trade area (Nossal, Roussel, and Paquin 2015, 367). In short, all signs pointed to the United States not recognizing Québec's independence if Canada did not. In this context, the strategy was to place the U.S. government before a *fait accompli* by getting France, other French-speaking countries, and some other European states to recognize an independent Québec. Ultimately, the hope was that the United States would not want to be too far behind France in recognizing a new country in North America and that it would follow suit.

Interestingly there was no sense during the campaign that the prospects of recognition was affecting Quebeckers' choice, most supporters of independence taking it for granted that it would materialize after a referendum win.[4] Moreover, the position of international actors seemed to have had little effect on the campaign, although the new international context might have helped the 'yes' side. Although, the United States took position against Québec independence, in the post–Cold War era characterized by the liberalization of trade, there was no reference to 'Cuba North' coming from the American government, and independence did not seem to imply isolation and poverty. In other others, arguments against independence based on economic and financial concerns seemed to have weakened between 1980 and 1995, partly as a result of the liberalization of trade. In the end, the result was very close.

The 'yes' side picked up steam late in the campaign (after charismatic BQ leader Lucien Bouchard was given a bigger role in the campaign – evidence of the importance of agency in these events) and 'no' camp barely hung on, winning 50.6% of the vote.

POST-1995 DEVELOPMENTS: THE CLARITY ACT

A third referendum on independence is extremely unlikely in the short-to-medium term, as support for secession is at its lowest point in decades. Indeed, contrary to expectations secessionists have long had, young Que-beckers (eighteen- to thirty-four-year olds) cannot be counted on to support independence today and even within the generation that carried the project beginning in the 1970s support for secession is below 40%. Moreover, the more recent Québec elections, held in 2018, yielded for the first time in almost sixty years a government formed by a party other than the Liberals or the PQ. Indeed, the Coalition Avenir Québec has depicted itself as a nation-alist party with an autonomist agenda seeking to supersede the old cleavage between supporters and opponents of independence. In these same elections, the PQ had its worst showing in over forty years, finishing a distant third.

However, in the years immediately following the second referendum, there was a general expectation, considering the very close results, that the PQ (which formed another majority government after the 1998 Québec elections) would organize a third vote on independence. In this context, the federal government decided to establish a legal framework for independence referendums in the country. It first asked the Supreme Court of Canada if Québec could secede unilaterally from Canada under Constitution. The Court answered as follows:

> Quebec could not, despite a clear referendum result, purport to invoke a right of self-determination to dictate the terms of a proposed secession to the other par-ties to the federation. The democratic vote, by however strong a majority, would have no legal effect on its own and could not push aside the principles of feder-alism and the rule of law, the rights of individuals and minorities, or the opera-tion of democracy in the other provinces or in Canada as a whole. Democratic rights under the Constitution cannot be divorced from constitutional obligations. Nor, however, can the reverse proposition be accepted: the continued existence and operation of the Canadian constitutional order could not be indifferent to a clear expression of a clear majority of Quebecers that they no longer wish to remain in Canada. The other provinces and the federal government would have no basis to deny the right of the government of Quebec to pursue secession should a clear majority of the people of Quebec choose that goal, so long as in doing so, Quebec respects the rights of others. The negotiations that followed

such a vote would address the potential act of secession as well as its possible terms should in fact secession proceed. There would be no conclusions predetermined by law on any issue. Negotiations would need to address the interests of the other provinces, the federal government and Quebec and indeed the rights of all Canadians both within and outside Quebec, and specifically the rights of minorities. (Supreme Court of Canada 1998)

In other words, the Court found that the secession of Québec from Canada is neither legal nor illegal from a Canadian constitutional perspective but that, if a clear majority of Quebeckers supported independence, all the partners of the federation would have a duty to negotiate in the respect of specific principles.[5]

The federal government also asked if international law gives Québec the right to unilaterally secede from Canada. After answering 'no' to this question, finding that Québec is neither a colonized nor an oppressed people, the Court stated:

Although there is no right, under the Constitution or at international law, to unilateral secession, the possibility of an unconstitutional declaration of secession leading to a *de facto* secession is not ruled out. The ultimate success of such a secession would be dependent on recognition by the international community, which is likely to consider the legality and legitimacy of secession having regard to, amongst other facts, the conduct of Quebec and Canada, in determining whether to grant or withhold recognition. Even if granted, such recognition would not, however, provide any retroactive justification for the act of secession, either under the Constitution of Canada or at international law. (Supreme Court of Canada 1998)

The court thus confirms that secession is a political act whose ultimate success is dependent upon international recognition, and it presumes that recognition would hinge at least in part on the extent to which secession is considered legitimate and legal by international actors.

In 1980 and 1995, the federal government had not questioned the legitimacy or legality of the referendums nor had it spoken on the conditions upon which it would recognize an independent Québec after a 'yes' win. In the aftermath of the Supreme Court Reference on the Secession of Québec, the federal government proceeded to lay out such conditions in legislation, the so-called Clarity Act (formally *an Act to give effect to the requirement for clarity as set out in the opinion of the Supreme Court of Canada in the Quebec Secession Reference*).[6] The 2000 Clarity Act incorporates some content from the secession reference while, as some observers have pointed out (Rocher and Verrelli 2003), adding brand new elements to the question of the secession of a province.

First, the Clarity Act acknowledges that 'the government of any province of Canada is entitled to consult its population by referendum on any issue and is entitled to formulate the wording of its referendum question' (preamble). It also states that 'the Supreme Court of Canada has determined that the result of a referendum on the secession of a province from Canada must be free of ambiguity both in terms of the question asked and in terms of the support it achieves if that result is to be taken as an expression of the democratic will that would give rise to an obligation to enter into negotiations that might lead to secession'.

The Clarity Act then states that the House of Commons will judge, within thirty days after the referendum legislation has been tabled by a province, whether the question is clear or not (article 1–1). This judgement serves as one of the bases of the federal government's response to a 'yes' win: 'The Government of Canada shall not enter into negotiations on the terms on which a province might cease to be part of Canada if the House of Commons determines, pursuant to this section, that a referendum question is not clear and, for that reason, would not result in a clear expression of the will of the population of that province on whether the province should cease to be part of Canada' (article 1–6).

The second basis for the federal government's post-'yes' vote response is an evaluation of the clarity of a will to secede: 'The Government of Canada shall not enter into negotiations on the terms on which a province might cease to be part of Canada unless the House of Commons determines, pursuant to this section, that there has been a clear expression of a will by a clear majority of the population of that province that the province cease to be part of Canada' (article 4). No figure is presented or suggested as to what a 'clear majority' is, which means that the House of Commons would have great latitude, after the referendum, to assess if a clear will to secede has been demonstrated. In other words, the Clarity Act seems to make it easier, constitutionally but also politically, for the federal government of Canada to say that a 'yes' vote may not lead to secession. The notion that the federal government has any kind of right of oversight on the referendum question and the majority required for a 'yes' win to lead to independence is opposed by all Québec political parties.

Of course, if the federal government were to not consider that a 'yes' victory in an eventual third referendum on independence not lead to secession, the likelihood is that virtually all other states would do the same. This is especially true because the international context is presently less conducive to the recognition of an independent Québec, at least in the absence of such recognition by Canada, than in 1995. Perhaps most importantly, French governments have been less supportive of Québec self-determination in the past decade or so than ever before. The PQ used to enjoy strong networks with French politicians, which could be used to elicit sympathy for its project, but these days are largely gone. President Nicolas Sarkozy seemed downright hostile to the notion of Québec independence and the new generation of French politicians, including current President Emmanuel Macron, most likely do not have the sensibilities of their predecessors towards this type of self-determination claims. Indeed, the hostile reaction of France and all other European states towards the Catalan secessionist project (Le Parisien 2017) is inauspicious for any future Québec declaration of independence. Moreover, the traditional preference of the U.S. government for Canadian unity might be exacerbated by the contemporary importance of border control and immigration issues, among other things.

CONCLUSION

The story of the Québec referendums shows that secessionist and counter-secessionist strategies are contextual: they are inseparable from the political dynamics of the previous decade or so. In other words, the nature of debates over the desirability of secession is time-specific. Each of the Quebec referendums had its own political dynamic, featuring its own set of arguments on independence. Indeed, the political dynamics of the referendums of 1980 and 1995 were shaped by the preceding fifteen- to twenty-year period. These 'slices of history' informed how secessionist actors sought to prevail in each of the referendums as well as how opponents of independence promoted the 'no' option'. The question of legitimacy was more stable across the two Quebec referendums, as the position of the federal government in 1980 (accepting that a vote on secession was constitutional and legitimate) may have established a precedent from which it would have been politically difficult to stray. Internationally, the reactions of the two most important foreign states to the question of independence (France and the United States) were fairly similar across the two referendums, although a more developed and aggressive international relations strategy by the PQ government in 1995 seemed to have engaged the French government more substantially than fifteen years earlier. However, the question of the feasibility of an independent Québec nation in terms of international recognition remains to this day an unknown, as it most likely hinges on the reaction of the federal government to a 'yes' victory.

Of course, there is some agency involved in referendums; they are not strictly the product of their 'slice of history'. From this perspective, strategies used in the Québec referendums may present some lessons for both secessionists and their political adversaries elsewhere. For secessionists, the greater support for independence in the second Québec referendum suggests that focusing the argument on the state's refusal to acknowledge, symbolically and institutionally, the existence of an internal nation may be a more fruitful strategy (certainly one around which more people can rally) than attaching to independence some grand social project (to which many can find various faults). Secessionist leaders need to find a delicate balance between sparking some enthusiasm for independence and reassuring citizens that not all that much will change following secession. The Québec case shows how extremely difficult it is to convince citizens of an advanced industrialized liberal democracy that secession can occur without substantial costs or disruption, and that it does not constitute a complete rupture or a 'divorce'. For counter-secessionists, the Québec referendums recall the importance of actively speaking to the merits of the country and the history of the internal nation in it as a way to counter the narratives of rejection, dysfunction, and exhaustion mobilized by supporters of independence.

The Québec referendums were important precedents for nationalist movements elsewhere in liberal democracies. For the Scottish National Party (SNP), which formed a majority government in Scotland in 2011, and for the Catalan nationalist party Convergència I Unió, which took a secessionist turn in 2010–2011, the referendum was viewed as the centrepiece of an independence process. Québec was instrumental in showing the potential power of referendums in the context of self-determination politics. Its referendums, especially the one in 1995 with its 49.4% 'yes' result, provided an exemplar for both Scottish and Catalan secessionists of what could be. Moreover, for the SNP, which was allowed to proceed with an independence referendum by the British state, the Québec referendums were cases to be studied for the strategies deployed by both sides. For Catalan secessionists, the Québec (and Canadian) case served as support to the argument that a liberal democratic state should recognize an independence referendum as the exercise of a democratic right to speak to a collective future (Lecours 2018).

The Québec experience does not contain real insight on gaining international recognition for independence against the wishes of the state since both of the referendums failed to produce a majority for the 'yes' side. The PQ always felt it had a secret weapon because of Québec's so-called privileged relationship with France, but the exact response of the French government following a 'yes' win remains unknown. In all likelihood, international recognition of Québec independence would have greatly hinged on the reaction of the federal government. Although the federal government campaigned against independence in both referendums, thereby informally accepting its legitimacy, a short 'yes' vote would have posed quite the dilemma. The Clarity Act does not eliminate such dilemma in the event (unlikely in the short term) of a 'yes' vote in an eventual third referendum, but it seems to provide greater latitude for the federal government in deciding upon its response, from which the international community would most likely take its cue.

NOTES

* The author would like to thank the Research Group on Plurinational Societies/ Groupe de recherche sur les sociétés plurinationales (GRSP) for its support.

1. The question was as follows: 'The Government of Quebec has made public its proposal to negotiate a new agreement with the rest of Canada, based on the equality of nations; this agreement would enable Quebec to acquire the exclusive power to make its laws, levy its taxes and establish relations abroad – in other words, sovereignty – and at the same time to maintain with Canada an economic association including a common currency; any change in political status resulting from these negotiations will only be implemented with popular approval through another referendum; on these terms, do you give the Government of Quebec the mandate to negotiate the proposed agreement between Quebec and Canada?'

2. The question was as follows: 'Do you agree that Quebec should become sovereign after having made a formal offer to Canada for a new economic and political partnership within the scope of the bill respecting the future of Quebec and of the agreement signed on 12 June 1995?'

3. The original French is as follows:

> La France prend acte de la volonté démocratiquement exprimée par le peuple du Québec, le 30 octobre 1995, de devenir souverain après avoir formellement offert au Canada un nouveau partenariat politique et économique. Lorsque l'Assemblée Nationale du Québec en viendra à proclamer la souveraineté du Québec selon la démarche prévue par la question référendaire et maintenant entérinée par le peuple québécois, la France en tirera amicalement les conséquences. Soucieuse que ce processus se déroule dans les meilleures conditions, la France tient à réaffirmer son amitié pour (sic) au Canada et à son gouvernement. Ils peuvent être assurés de notre volonté de maintenir et d'approfondir les excellentes relations qui nous lient. (Nossal, Roussel, and Paquin 2015, 366)

4. The 'no' side chose not to discuss the issue of recognition, for fear that it would represent some type of an acknowledgement that a majority 'yes' vote was possible.

5. As such, the Secession Reference was generally satisfying to both supporters and opponents of Québec independence.

6. The political rationale for the Clarity Act was to provide some footing for the federal government if it decided not to recognize a hypothetical 'yes' majority vote in a future referendum on Québec independence, either because it did not view the question as clear or the result as sufficiently convincing. At the same time, the presence of legal parameters empowering the federal government to review the referendum question and evaluate the result would presumably hinder international recognition as foreign states acknowledge the prerogative of Canada to decide if secession happens.

BIBLIOGRAPHY

Balthazar, Louis. 2013. *Nouveau bilan du nationalisme au Québec*. Montréal: VLB.

Basta, Karlo. 2018. 'The Social Construction of Transformative Political Events'. *Comparative Political Studies* 51(10): 1243–1278.

Bastien, Frédéric. 1999. *Relations particulières. La France face au Québec après le Général de Gaulle*. Montréal: Boréal.

Béland, Daniel, and André Lecours. 2008. *Nationalism and Social Policy. The Politics of Territorial Solidarity*. Oxford: Oxford University Press.

Deutsch, Karl. 1966. *Nationalism and Social Communication. An Inquiry into the Foundations of Nationality*. Cambridge: MIT Press.

Fraser, Graham. 1984. *PQ: René Lévesque and the Parti Québécois in Power*. Toronto: Macmillan.

Hébert, Chnatal, and Jean Lapierre. 2014. *Confessions post-référendaires. Les acteurs politiques de 1995 et le scénario d'un oui*. Montréal: Édition de l'Homme.

Laforest, Guy. 1995. *Trudeau and the End of a Canadian Dream*. Montreal and Kingston: McGill-Queen's University Press.

Lecours, André. 2018. 'The Political Consequences of Independence Referenda in Liberal Democracies: Quebec, Scotland, and Catalonia'. *Polity* 50(2): 243–274.

Le Parisien. 2 October 2017. 'Référendum en Catalogne: Macron soutient le gouvernement espagnol'. Accessed 19 January 2019. http://www.leparisien.fr/politique/referendum-en-catalogne-macron-soutient-le-gouvernement-espagnol-02-10-2017-7302768.php.

Martin, Pierre. 1995. 'When Nationalism Meets Continentalism: The Politics of Free-Trade in Québec'. *Regional and Federal Studies* 5(1): 1–27.

McRoberts, Kenneth. 1993. *Quebec. Social Change and Political Crisis*. Toronto: Oxford University Press.

McRoberts, Kenneth. 1997. *Misconceiving Canada. The Struggle for National Unity*. Toronto: Oxford University Press.

Nossal, Kim Richard, Stéphane Roussel, and Stéphane Paquin. 2015. *The Politics of Canadian Foreign Policy* (4th edition). Montreal and Kingston: McGill-Queen's University Press.

Rocher, François, and Nadia Verrelli. 2003. 'Questioning Constitutional Democracy in Canada: From the Canadian Supreme Court Reference on Secession to the Clarity Act'. In *The Conditions of Diversity in Multinational Democracies*, edited by Alain-G. Gagnon, Montserrat Guibernau, and François Rocher. Montréal: IRPP and McGill-Queen's University Press, pp. 207–240.

Supreme Court of Canada. 1998. 'Reference Re Secession of Quebec'. Accessed 9 February 2019. https://scc-csc.lexum.com/scc-csc/scc-csc/en/item/1643/index.do.

Chapter 9

Business as a Political Actor: Mapping the Role of the Private Sector in Independence Referenda

Karlo Basta

While secession can be achieved with little popular support, many secessionist movements seek mass backing in order to strengthen their hand in confrontations with the central state. The key challenge in the strategy of mobilization is to convince the potential constituents for independence that secession is both necessary and feasible. The issue of feasibility in developed democracies such as Canada, the UK, and Spain, where the path to independence passes through a referendum, tends to revolve primarily around the economic consequences of independent statehood. Once one convinces a sufficient number of compatriots that independence is necessary, the second part of the challenge is to convince them that the economic costs will not be onerous. Scholarship on secession recognizes the importance of the economic dimension, but it pays little explicit attention to the *discursive strategies* deployed to persuade the voting public on the risks (or benefits) of independent statehood. Moreover, to the extent to which extant literature does address the framing of the costs and benefits of political divorce, it reduces the strategic field to just two actors – the secessionist movement and the central state. In this chapter, I take on both of these issues by foregrounding big business discursive strategies prior to independence referenda.

This chapter maps the strategic discursive field in Quebec, Catalonia, and Scotland. It theorizes the role of business (as individual enterprises, an organized actor, and as a class) and its strategies of public engagement on secession. It also examines the strategies secessionist actors deploy to undermine business attempts to shape the debate. Big business in particular, in all three of these jurisdictions, is a major political actor in its own right.[1] It has the incentive, the power, and the legitimacy to participate in public debates on secession. Both secessionist and counter-secessionist actors believe that the stance big business takes on the issue of political divorce has significant political implications. This is why the discursive action by big business tends to provoke significant counterefforts by secessionist actors.

The chapter makes three distinctive contributions to the study of secession. First, it underscores the role of persuasion as a strategic activity in shaping interests and preferences of the general public in secessionist contests. Second, in addition to the content of the debates, it emphasizes the importance of the *agent* that articulates particular messages – with the business community being particularly important for both secessionist and anti-secessionist political elites. Third, the chapter seeks to broaden our understanding of the secessionist strategic playing field by including actors that are normally left out of theoretical accounts of the politics of secession. To my knowledge, this is the first effort to theorize and conceptualize the role of business in independence referenda.

The following section briefly examines the existing scholarship on the economic dimension of secession. I then focus on the strategic considerations of business community with respect to secessionist contests. I foreground the interests, resources, and patterns of political practice of business under these circumstances. In the fourth section, I outline secessionist attempts to engage with the counter-secessionist practice of big business. The concluding section considers what the next steps ought to be in the study of the role of business in secession. I also suggest how the strategic playing field might be broadened not only in Western cases considered here but also in other regions where independentist movements operate.

ECONOMIC DIMENSIONS OF SECESSION IN EXISTING LITERATURE

Most scholarship on self-determination includes at least some discussion of the economic aspect of secession. Yet, in most cases, the *concrete process of persuasion* (particularly about the economic risks and benefits of independence) is not a prominent feature of theoretical work and often does not make it in the empirical material either. There are broadly two approaches to the economic dimension of the politics of independence. The first is to examine, either through small-n comparisons or multivariate analysis, the relative weight of various economic factors in accounting for the likelihood of secession (either the mobilization/demands, or success in obtaining independent statehood). Works in this tradition normally analyse a broad range of cases across time and space. The second approach is to probe the various determinants of voting behaviour in secession referenda, normally in a single case. The majority of these contributions are confined to the more recent and information-rich referenda in the West.

A number of studies explain secession by reference to the socioeconomic characteristics of multinational states, potential secessionist regions, and the international system. The key factor in accounting for both the timing and likelihood of secession in Horowitz's seminal work is the relative economic position of potentially secessionist regions and the titular 'groups' that inhabit them (Horowitz 1985, ch. 6). Sorens's study of secessionism in developed democracies reveals that the economic benefits of independence correlate strongly with support for secessionist parties, with the cost-benefit calculus being dependent on the relative wealth of the region in question (Sorens 2005). Regional patterns of economic inequality feature prominently in Sambanis and Milanovic's, as well as Collier and Hoeffler's, papers on secession, in ways similar to those flagged by Sorens (Collier and Hoeffler 2006; Sambanis and Milanovic 2011). Griffiths, by contrast, turns to the international arena, noting that the liberal international economy lowers the costs of independence and thus makes secession less costly (Griffiths 2014). All of these studies hover above the actual politics of secession and focus instead on broad, structural features and their correlation with the patterns of independence.

Scholars of voting behaviour have also been attentive to the economic aspects of secession. Most such work attributes at least some of the opposition to secession to its potential costs, though each contribution examines a different aspect. In his study of Quebec, Young argues that anti-secessionists must make the threat of post-independence non-cooperation credible in order to dissuade a sufficient number of potential secessionists from voting for independence (Young 1994). Yet he posits that this is not a credible option, given the costs of even a mild loss of gross domestic products for the rump state. Mendelsohn concludes that, while economic costs are not the decisive factor in determining opposition to secession, medium- and short-term economic risks do have an effect (Mendelsohn 2003). This is further echoed by Muñoz and Tormos' study of Catalan attitudes towards independence. The authors find that the expectations of economic consequences of secession do have an independent effect on voters' preferences (Muñoz and Tormos 2015). Liñeira, Henderson, and Delaney find that uncertainty on key economic matters may have influenced voting in Scotland's 2014 referendum (Liñeira, Henderson, and Delaney 2017). On a different note, Nadeau, Martin, and Blais estimated the importance of personal psychological profile of voters (their risk-proneness), but even here, the conclusion is that economic considerations matter (Nadeau, Martin, and Blais 1999). In their study of Scotland and Catalonia, Muro and Vlaskamp show that the prospects of European Union (EU) membership for the seceding territory might impact voters' preferences, though only moderately so (Muro and Vlaskamp 2016). Underpinning their argument are, again, the potential political and economic costs of secession.

Despite their differences, these studies share a central concern with parsing out the relative weight of various independent variables on voting patterns. This is in part why most do not provide conceptual or theoretical treatment of the *politics* of secession – that is to say, the struggles that the actors in the secessionist strategic field wage over the framing and counter-framing of both the necessity and the potential costs and benefits of independence. And yet voters do not form their opinions on the economic consequences of secession by coldly accessing and assimilating statistical information. Rather, the information they receive is shaped by at least two sets of factors. The first is framing, something critical for the success of any particular political message, given just how pervasive it is in politics.[2] The second is the legitimacy of the agent articulating a particular message. Discursive politics, after all, is not only about what is being said but also about who is saying it (Schmidt 2008, 306). This holds both for top-down communication (persuasion by policy makers, for instance) (Mandelkern and Shalev 2010), and for horizontal communication in informal or personal social networks (Druckman, Levendusky, and McLain 2018). The legitimacy of the discursive agent, in other words, ought to matter for the effectiveness of the message.

Existing scholarship partially addresses discourses by political actors, such as political parties and governments pursuing or opposing independence. Ironically, the business sector – the actor with a decisive say in levels of investment and employment, and thus the economic future of any secessionist region – remains completely ignored. The goal of this chapter is to provide a preliminary examination of both the way in which the business sector tries to influence the debates on independence and the manner in which those efforts are received by other political actors, particularly those who back secession. The interaction between these actors and the general public could be labelled 'strategic persuasion'.[3] The next section maps, in broad strokes, the manner in which regional big business seeks to influence debates on independence referenda.

HOW LARGE ENTERPRISES NAVIGATE SECESSIONIST CONTEXTS

Business organizations constitute an important part of the strategic playing field in secessionist regions. Scholars have recognized the political role business can play, both directly through lobbying and campaign contributions (Hillman, Keim, and Schuler 2004), and more broadly through their structural power, notably over investment decisions (Culpepper 2015).[4] The role of business as an actor influencing public debates has received much less attention, however. Yet where a referendum on secession is either probable or imminent, businesses find it necessary to participate in the shaping of public opinion. Enterprises can try to do this in more discrete ways, such as by promoting their own political agenda among their employees (Hertel-Fernandez 2016). Here, I focus on their participation in public debates in part because I believe such participation has potentially broader political impact than internal firm action. Moreover, while there have been some reported instances of companies trying to engage their employees on independence, my research suggests this is a rare occurrence.[5]

In this chapter, I focus on a specific segment of the business community – *big* business that is either based or has significant operational presence (a manufacturing facility, or a widespread network of branches for a bank, for instance) in secessionist regions. Defining the precise boundary that separates large from small- and medium-sized enterprises (SME) is not easy and would at any rate be fairly arbitrary. Instead of offering a precise definition based on revenues, market share, or employment, I use two proxies. I understand as big business those enterprises that are flagged by the relevant news sources as significant contributors to the regional economy. The press tends to underreport statements by SMEs, focusing instead on the large companies that are, by convention, thought of as important for regional economic performance. This is an adequate definition because it is precisely the attitudes of those businesses, of conventionally viewed as important, that matter in the model I develop here. Moreover, those trade organizations that are not explicitly dedicated to the representation of SMEs are considered to be representative of big business. Such organizations can include SMEs as well but are normally considered by the relevant political actors to speak on behalf of big business.

The pattern of business involvement in secessionist debates is shaped by three features. Big business has the incentive, the ability, and the legitimacy to challenge the economic feasibility of secessionist projects. This makes it unique and distinctive from individuals, or collective actors such as civil society organizations and political parties. Big business has a particularly compelling *incentive* to oppose secession. Together with revolutions and wars, secession ranks among the most politically destabilizing political phenomena, bringing uncertainty and unpredictability. Although instability can be profitable for some types of business,[6] most favour political stability (Aizenman and Marion 1999; Beazer 2012). Instability is associated with risk, and risk with a potential drop in future revenues and profitability. Even where secessionists offer a more competitive regulatory environment to corporate actors (far from a foregone conclusion, given the complexity of secession and the inability to even approximately forecast future institutional developments), the multiplication of regulatory regimes may present an unwelcome increase in transaction costs.[7]

At the same time, big business is an actor possessing unique political influence and power. Most importantly, it is more insulated from social and political pressures than are other actors, though this insulation is relative – as the later discussion will show. Businesses are key constituents for politicians, not only because they may be political donors but also because they directly influence macroeconomic aggregates such as economic growth, investment rates, and employment levels, and – indirectly, the fortunes of political incumbents (Duch and Stevenson 2008; Lenz 2012). They also confer a stamp of approval on a political party or government, with implications for how other investors will treat both that party and the region in the future. Corporate support is clearly important in case secessionists do obtain their majority and manage to secede. Yet if a secessionist bid is not successful, secessionist parties will need to compete in future elections, for which they will need business support. Businesses are thus more difficult to silence than everyday individuals who may be unwilling to speak out for fear of social sanctions.

As importantly, in the most extreme scenarios, businesses have recourse to an exit option that no other political actor has. They can either reduce investment or move shop altogether. While this is a costly decision, it is one that becomes increasingly attractive with greater uncertainty. One reason for this might be a spike in the cost of capital for companies (Tirtiroglu, Bhabra, and Lel 2004, 2240). Both Quebec and Catalonia have seen company headquarters move to other parts of their respective states, even though independence was not achieved. This option is not available either to most individuals or to political parties. A party losing electoral support because of opposition to independence cannot move to another jurisdiction. It will either shift its program to more closely approximate the shift in popular sentiment, languish or, in extreme cases, disappear.

Finally, business possesses unique *legitimacy* when it comes to evaluating economic risks of political change. Other opponents or sceptics can be delegitimized in at least two ways, paralleling discussions of candidate trustworthiness and competence in literature on voting behaviour (Bittner 2011; Kinder et al. 1980). First, they can be tarred as outsiders who do not have the best interests of the particular region at heart. This is most obviously the case with central governments and the political elites that draw their support from the majority population. But other 'outsiders', such as foreign journalists, academics, politicians, or representatives of international financial institutions, might be equally mistrusted. Second, even if dissenters are members of the community in question, their competence to speak on issues of economic risk may be questioned. Politicians and journalists, for example, may be subject to charges that, because they are not practitioners, they cannot speak on the possible economic costs with sufficient authority. Business owners and managers, on the other hand, are not only making actual decisions on investment and employment, but have a vested interest in profitability, thus potentially reducing the perception that they have a political, rather than a purely economic agenda. Naked self-interest, in other words, might confer legitimacy on business assessment of economic risk.

It is difficult to disentangle big business power from its legitimacy, since the two are tightly linked. Organizational and lobbying efforts, when successful, enhance the public standing of big business. This, in turn, can make it more difficult for politicians to exert pressure on the business community, enhancing the latter's political autonomy. Nevertheless, power and legitimacy are conceptually distinct categories. The former is a structural and organizational feature, based on the position of business in socioeconomic relations, and its organizational and financial capabilities. The latter belongs to the cultural-ideational domain. Moreover, there is no one-for-one relationship between the two – an actor's legitimacy among a segment of the population does not guarantee power nor does power guarantee legitimacy.[8]

How did these features translate into business strategies prior to the referenda in Quebec (1995), Scotland (2014), and Catalonia (2017)? First, it does appear that big business is indeed quite sceptical of secession. In all three cases, all major big business organizations, as well as chief executive officers (CEOs) of several large corporations, either openly opposed independence, or expressed scepticism at its prospects. This discursive activism inadvertently bolsters the counter-secessionist efforts of the central state to portray secessionism as politically and economically destabilizing, a strategy outlined by Muro and Griffiths in the introductory chapter.[9]

In Quebec, opposition was articulated by the largest business association, Conseil du Patronat du Québec, as well as the Federation of Quebec Chambers of Commerce, in addition to CEOs of several big businesses, such as Paul Desmarais of Power Corp. and Laurent Beaudoin of Bombardier (Hadekel 1995a). In Scotland, both the Confederation of British Industries (Scotland) and the Scottish Financial Enterprise, among them representing the largest companies in manufacturing and financial services, released statements or reports that indicated independence would bring economic uncertainty and would hamper future growth (Johnson 2013b; Riley-Smith 2014). In addition, towards the tail end of the campaign, Keith Cochrane, the CEO of Weir Group, one of largest Scotland-based manufacturers, was increasingly present in the news, enumerating the risks associated with independence (Carrell 2014). Finally, since the initiation of the so-called process of Catalonia's disassociation from Spain in late 2012, representative organizations of big business also expressed concerns about both independence and, since 2015, the increasing willingness of Catalan government to entertain a unilateral approach to achieving this goal. Foment de Treball, the representative organization of most Catalan business, and one to which the largest Catalan corporations belong, was the most vocal. The presidents of Cercle d'Economia, the business forum that brings together the representatives from the world of business, politics, and academia, were similarly active between 2012 and 2017 (Álvarez 2015). Presidents of Catalonia's largest financial institutions, La Caixa and Banco Sabadell, as well as several other key executives, played a similar role.

By contrast, big business support for secession was rare. In Quebec, the president of North America's largest credit union, Mouvement Desjardins, quickly retracted his support of independence after being criticized for not having consulted the membership on the issue (Hadekel 1994). In Scotland, the largest firm to express its backing to Scottish National Party's project was Aberdeen Asset Management, at the time Europe's second-largest listed fund manager (*The Guardian* 2014). In Catalonia, big business support for the independence referendum – though not for independence itself – came from the CEO of Grifols, a multinational manufacturer of plasma products (*La Vanguardia* 2014). However, it bears pointing out that not all businesses opposed independence. In Catalonia, in particular, but also in Scotland and Quebec, the smaller the business or the more its operations are tied to the seceding entity, the more likely it was to support independence. The few projects to research this issue systematically reproduce similar results. Brad MacKay's interviews with Scottish businesses tend to show greater concern among large, listed corporations, whereas smaller companies appear more willing to absorb the possible risks of secession and, indeed, emphasize opportunities related to independence (MacKay 2014). A rare survey of SMEs in Catalonia demonstrated a fairly high proportion of respondents (on an admittedly limited sample) supporting independence as well (Medina and Molins 2014). It is worth noting that the trend in Quebec was not as pronounced, with the majority of small enterprises supporting Quebec's continued association with Canada (Hadekel 1995b).

However, despite the strong incentives to oppose secession, and despite their apparent organizational and structural power, *individual businesses* are quite reluctant to speak openly on the matter of constitutional preferences, even if and when a constitutional breach seems afoot. There are several reasons for this. The first is a matter of custom and socialization. Business is accustomed to exercising its presence behind closed doors, in discrete contacts with individual politicians. The politics of secession is by definition a public affair, necessitating the kind of activity, including discursive action, that business is unaccustomed to and largely unprepared for. Perhaps more importantly, despite the structural power of business as a class, and instrumental power of larger business organizations,[10] individual businesses can be subject to market pressures as a consequence of their political participation. Any company that has a large consumer base in the secessionist territory may be target of a consumer boycott that would threaten its bottom line. This is more than conjecture, as this happened in Scotland with Asda (Johnson 2013a). In fact, those businesses that do tend to speak out fairly loudly tend to be those that are relatively insulated from local market pressures. The afore-mentioned Weir Group is an exporter dependent on global markets. Large banks such as La Caixa and Sabadell are also integral to local economies, and at any rate, banking is less substitutable than most other products.

Pooling of political risk is the main reason why big business lets the business associations handle the task of voicing scepticism towards independence. While individual businesses may be weary of being targeted, their associations are by definition not subject to the same kinds of pressures. Yet, regardless of the source of the message, both business associations and businesses themselves – when their representatives do speak out – normally deploy moderate discourse when addressing possible issues with secession. They tend to acknowledge the long-term economic viability of the region in question, but point to the balance of risks and benefits of independence. There are two likely reasons for this discursive approach. The first relates to the credibility of the message. Doomsday scenarios, such as the ones that are at times articulated by opponents of secession, are fairly easily portrayed as 'project fear' and painted as unrealistic. After all, such scenarios normally depend on the rump state engaging in intransigent action that would hurt its own economic prospects (e.g., attempting to economically isolate the seceding entity). Second, doomsday scenarios could damage the confidence (particularly of the financial markets and potential future investors) in the jurisdiction in question and even, potentially, the entire country. The business strategies for each of the cases are summarized in table 9.1.

Thus, the basic strategy of anti-secessionist business is to articulate relatively moderate positions and provide a critique of some aspects of

Table 9.1. Summary of Big Business Strategies

	Regional big business counter-secessionist strategies	
	Direct discursive action – enterprises	*Indirect discursive action – business organizations*
Quebec	Yes	Yes
	(e.g., Bombardier; Power Corp)	(Conseil du Patronat du Québec)
Scotland	Yes	Yes
	(e.g., Asda; Weir Group)	(CBI Scotland; Scottish Financial Enterprise)
Catalonia	Yes	Yes
	(e.g., La Caixa; Banco Sabadell; Grupo Planeta)	(Foment de Treball; Cercle d'Economia)

independence, rather than express outright opposition to it. Moreover, the position of the business community is normally voiced and defended by business associations and only relatively rarely by actual business representatives, who try to protect the economic position of their firms. Yet, this strategy is potentially damaging to the secessionist cause, which is why secessionist actors devise discursive countermeasures, a subject to which I turn next.

LEGITIMACY GAMES AND BUSINESS DILEMMAS

Secessionist actors have developed their own strategies to counter business scepticism about independence. Ideally, big business would endorse the goal of independence fully. However, given that this is an unlikely proposition for reasons laid out earlier, secessionist actors normally attempt to manage big business scepticism in the public domain in several interconnected ways. If such an important part of a regional community expresses serious misgivings about the project of independence, the legitimacy of secessionist project is put into question and could weaken public support for it. In secessionist referenda, this influence need not be particularly large. A five percentage point swing, or even less, might mean the difference between victory and defeat, as seen in all three cases.

Secessionist strategies of managing public scepticism by big business generally take two forms. First, secessionist actors, both governmental and nongovernmental ones, attempt to silence public big business opposition. Second, and given that silencing tactics generally tend not to be particularly effective, secessionists attempt to undermine the legitimacy of the anti-secessionist message. Attempts to quell business dissent were more prominent in Scotland and Catalonia, though in Quebec too there were pressures on sovereignty-sceptical business to tone down its opposition. In Scotland, First Minister Alex Salmond attempted to prevent the publication of a report on independence by the Scottish Financial Enterprise, in order to preclude open criticism by a business body that he manifestly considered important enough to risk both antagonizing large businesses and reputation should the intervention become public (Riley-Smith 2014). More diffuse pressure reached the signatories of a letter signed by over 100 business owners and executives from August 2014, with about half reporting threats and verbal abuse (Turner, Newell, and Watt 2014). In Catalonia, President Artur Mas asked businesses to join the efforts to achieve a referendum on independence and then noted that no business needed to openly support such a course, but that 'it would be sufficient not to oppose it' (Gisbert 2012).

As important is the possibility, actualized in very few cases precisely because so few companies participate in the debate openly, of consumer boycotts against those companies that dare to speak critically on the issue of independence. The most prominent examples were the call to boycott the supermarket chain Asda in Scotland, and the attempted boycott of the Catalan bank La Caixa. In the case of Asda (and several other supermarkets), at stake was the executives' statement that Scottish independence might cause an increase in the cost of supplies and that those costs would be passed on to Scottish consumers (Bennett 2013). In Catalonia, both La Caixa and Banco Sabadell noted, in the midst of the 2015 plebiscitary election called in place of an official independence referendum, that Catalonia's independence might prompt them to move their headquarters elsewhere. A similar online reaction followed (Iriarte 2015). While these are rare instances, they are prominent reminders of the potential costs of political involvement for companies with a significant consumer base in jurisdictions with independence movements. As mentioned in previous sections, this prompts businesses to channel their public engagement through business associations.

Attempts to silence business discourse about the costs and risks of secession are bound to be limited. They are both risky, since they threaten to antagonize very important constituents and send negative signals to the broader business community, and their effectiveness will be limited by the business community's resources (organizations, finance, and media presence) and exit options. This necessitates a subtler strategy – delegitimizing big business discourse. This is done in several ways. First, there is the attempt to undercut the legitimacy of the agents who claim to speak for the business community. Secessionist actors can plausibly question the legitimacy and representativeness of business associations, given these associations' often opaque decision-making processes and at times the leadership's autonomy relative to the membership. This gives rise to a dilemma – to the extent to which businesses leave associations as the sole spokespersons on the issue, they protect their individual market position, but undercut the legitimacy of the message. At the same time, if they were to bolster the legitimacy of the message, they would risk undermining their individual market position. Indeed, within Catalan associations and forums (both Foment de Treball and Cercle d'Economia), various pro-independence actors dissented from the message of risks to the region's economy. This fact alone leaves the impression that the business community does not speak with a single voice on the matter. In Scotland, secessionist actors were openly questioning the legitimacy and representativeness of CBI Scotland, for example (Johnson 2013b).

The second tactical move through which secessionist actors attempt to undermine the legitimacy of big business message is by forming pro-independence business associations or forums. Such organizations were present in all three cases. In Quebec, the organization in question was Regroupement Souveraineté Québec Inc., formed in 1992 (Martin 1995, 15). In the UK, the role was taken up by Business for Scotland. In Catalonia, the most explicit pro-independence platform was Cercle Català de Negocis. All three organizations were far from massive, being composed of small- and medium-sized businesses. In addition, pro-independence businesses often articulate their positions through existing organizations. This was done in Quebec through the Quebec Chamber of Commerce, whereas the Catalan associational landscape presented even more opportunities, with associations of small- and medium-sized businesses, PIMEC and CECOT, being especially active in the process between 2012 and 2017. The implicit role of these associations, and their discursive action, is to undermine the notion that the regional *business community as a whole* believes that the risks of independence outweigh the gains. We ought to remember that such statements could be made by politicians but the legitimacy of the agent articulating the message is obviously believed to be of decisive importance – thus, the participation of actual businesses and business associations in this endeavour. I offer a tabular summary of these patterns for all three cases in table 9.2.

Thus, both secessionists and counter-secessionists play the strategic game of legitimacy when it comes to the messages emanating from big business about the potential costs and risks associated with secession. Big business is an anti-secessionist actor (or, at the very least, secession-sceptical), though not without exceptions. As secessionist actors (both politicians and businesses or business associations) try to undercut the perception that business is uniformly opposed to secession, big business continues to act, both through business associations and, at times, through chief executives and owners. While the latter are reluctant to wade into open public debate, they nevertheless do so. They normally enter the public eye during or right before critical moments. Thus, the letter of 160 businesspeople warning of the possible risks of Scottish independence came only in August of 2014, a mere month prior to independence. Likewise, businesses and business associations in Catalonia

Table 9.2. Summary of Secessionist Counterstrategies

	Secessionist actor counterstrategies		
	Top-down silencing	Bottom-up silencing	Business counter-organization
Quebec	(Insufficient evidence)	(Insufficient evidence)	Regroupement Souveraineté Québec Inc.
Scotland	Yes (e.g., Alex Salmond)	Yes (e.g., Asda)	Business for Scotland
Catalonia	Yes (e.g., Artur Mas)	Yes (e.g., La Caixa)	Cercle Català de Negocis

spoke out openly in the fall of 2015, as it appeared that the process of pursuing independence was entering a qualitatively different, and from their perspective dangerous, phase.

WHERE TO NEXT?

The goal of this chapter was to outline the strategic field of action in debates on the costs and risks of independence, with particular attention paid to the role of business organizations in advanced economies. What is apparent is that both big business and secessionist actors (politicians and pro-independence business) engage in definable patterns of behaviour that could be termed *emergent strategies* of secession and counter-secession. Mintzberg and Waters define 'emergent strategies' as 'patterns or consistencies realized despite, or in the absence of, intentions' (Mintzberg and Waters 1985, 257). They juxtapose such strategies to deliberate ones, where the actors have a defined, systematic set of moves prior to commencing the strategic game. I was unable to detect any coordination on deliberate strategy among anti-secessionist business organizations in the three cases, and there is little reason to believe that such strategies were shared across these settings.[11] Rather, it would appear that the particular approaches developed in part as a consequence of the features of the strategic field (including the types of actors and the patterns of practice that pre-date secessionist referenda) and independently and as a consequence of learning-by-doing.

The strategic approach of big business opposed to independence normally takes the form of relatively subtle messages of scepticism, either by refusing to openly support secessionist initiatives or by issuing reports and statements pointing to the possible costs and risks associated with independence. These messages are normally tempered by statements about the economic viability of the jurisdiction in question and by dedication to the democratic process within the boundaries of existing legal frameworks. As individual large enterprises are subject to potential political pressures, they attempt to influence the public discourse through business associations that disperse the otherwise individualized risk. By entering the fray, business hopes to further legitimize messages of scepticism about secession that normally come from anti-secessionist politicians.

In turn, secessionist actors attempt to undermine the legitimacy of the message articulated by big business. They do so, less frequently, by attempting to silence such dissent, and more frequently by trying to demonstrate that business is divided over the issue and that a significant segment of business community does support the constitutional breach. Such division can then sow doubt about the credibility of the message – if not all businesses agree that independence might result in lower growth, higher interest rates, and less investment, perhaps such a scenario is not plausible after all. Such delegitimization is achieved in a number of ways, but three are the most prominent. The first is the questioning of the legitimacy of business associations (knowing individual big businesses are reluctant to state their preferences openly). The second tactic is the penetration of existing business organizations by secessionist business and then dissenting from the organizational line. This dissent can then be used to suggest that there is no agreement among businesses on key issues of the debate, lowering the certainty about risks and costs. The third tactic is to form pro-secession business associations, with much the same goal in mind – to demonstrate the heterogeneity of business preferences, despite the fact that one might doubt the representativeness of such organizations themselves.

Why study this issue? One reason is that it is possible that business dissent actually precludes the creation of secessionist hegemony and the spirals of silence that normally take place in contexts where emotional, identity-based issues start to play out (Kuran 1998; Noelle-Neumann 1974). We do not yet know whether or not this is the case, but both pro- and anti-secessionist actors in Scotland, Quebec, and Catalonia seem to believe that what big business has to say matters for the levels of support for independence.[12] In light of this belief, the logical next step would be to try to estimate whether or not the same message of scepticism towards the economic costs of secession is received differently by potential voters if it is articulated by a businessperson or a different type of actor (a politician, an academic, or a journalist). Another useful line of inquiry would be to see how costs of independence are framed in the absence of such actors – something that would require comparative studies turning to other sites of contestation over independence.

In addition to being a valuable contribution to the study of strategic politics of secession in its own right, this chapter also points to the importance of considering other actors that we normally do not think of when studying secessionist movements – thereby broadening our understanding of the strategic field and its components. Beyond businesses, such actors might be labour unions, pro-independence civil society organizations, and the media. In those cases where a referendum is not an option, one might expect a different set of players to have an important, and at times decisive, role, such as illicit networks or diasporas that might facilitate armed struggle.

NOTES

1. I portray a big business community as a unitary actor for the sake of brevity. I do not assume the entire business community speaks with a single voice – as seen in the rest of the chapter. Nevertheless, my research suggests that larger regional enterprises tend to share similar concerns with respect to the possible secession of a territory in which they are based.

2. The literature on framing is vast. For a sample of relevant sources, see Giuliano (2006); Gross (2008); Nelson, Oxley, and Clawson (1997); Snow and Benford (1988). For a conceptual discussion, see Druckman (2001).

3. Risse distinguishes between persuasion and bargaining, noting that the latter is strategic (Risse 2000). Yet persuasion, too, is strategic, particularly when one set of actors understands that there are counter-persuaders who might sway public opinion against their own preferences and ideas.

4. More recent scholarship has reconceptualized business as providers of public goods and as citizens that shape society through corporate social responsibility initiatives (Scherer, Palazzo, and Matten 2014).

5. One reason is that such companies could be easily outed and subject to the kinds of pressures they seek to avoid in these circumstances.

6. Although it is probably more accurate to note that businesses put up with instability (Frynas 1998).

7. Murphy's work on corporate regulatory preferences suggests that there are some businesses that welcome regulatory competition among jurisdictions. However, most enterprises, especially multinationals characterized by high asset specificity, prefer regulatory harmonization across borders to reduce transaction costs (Murphy 2004, 89).

8. The former can be seen in the willingness of the Catalan government to stage the 2017 referendum over vehement objections by the business community.

9. There is no room here to discuss in greater detail the extent of coordination between central government and regional big business. While I have found attempts by both big business and politicians outside of the secessionist regions to influence regional big business activism, such attempts were largely frustrated. It appears that regional big business has a different view of appropriate levels of involvement in anti-secessionist discursive action.

10. For the conceptual discussion of the difference between structural and instrumental power of business, see Lindblom (1977).

11. I am not referring to individual actions, such as the August letter written by a number of Scottish businesspeople – this is simply one particular instance. Strategy would refer to a class of agreed-upon approaches by both anti-secessionist and pro-independence business.

12. I base this conclusion in part on the amount of effort secessionist actors expend on countering big business scepticism about independence.

REFERENCES

Aizenman, Joshua, and Nancy Marion. 1999. 'Volatility and Investment: Interpreting Evidence from Developing Countries'. *Economica* 66(262): 157–179.

Álvarez, Dolors. 2015. 'El Cercle Alerta de Que Se Marchan Empresas y Pide Un Cambio Político'. *La Vanguardia*, 21 November 2015, 71.

Beazer, Quintin H. 2012. 'Bureaucratic Discretion, Business Investment, and Uncertainty'. *The Journal of Politics* 74(3): 637–652.

Bennett, Asa. 2013. 'Scottish Campaigners Threaten to Boycott Supermarkets'. *HuffPost UK*. 10 December 2013. http://www.huffingtonpost.co.uk/2013/12/10/supermarkets-scotland-independence_n_4417395.html.

Bittner, Amanda. 2011. *Platform or Personality? The Role of Party Leaders in Elections*. Oxford: Oxford University Press.

Carrell, Severin. 2014. 'Scottish Independence Will Bring "Guaranteed" Costs, Warns Weir Group'. *The Guardian*, 3 April 2014. https://www.theguardian.com/business/2014/apr/03/scottish-independence-guaranteed-costs-weir-group-scotland.

Collier, Paul, and Anke Hoeffler. 2006. 'The Political Economy of Secession'. In *Negotiating Self-Determination*, edited by Hurst Hannum and Eileen Babbitt. Lanham, MD: Lexington Books, pp. 37–59.

Culpepper, Pepper D. 2015. 'Structural Power and Political Science in the Post-Crisis Era'. *Business and Politics* 17(3): 391–409.

Druckman, James N. 2001. 'The Implications of Framing Effects for Citizen Competence'. *Political Behavior* 23(3): 225–256.

Druckman, James N., Matthew S. Levendusky, and Audrey McLain. 2018. 'No Need to Watch: How the Effects of Partisan Media Can Spread via Interpersonal Discussions'. *American Journal of Political Science* 62(1): 99–112.

Duch, Raymond M., and Randolph T. Stevenson. 2008. *The Economic Vote: How Political and Economic Institutions Condition Election Results*. New York: Cambridge University Press.

Frynas, Jedrzej George. 1998. 'Political Instability and Business: Focus on Shell in Nigeria'. *Third World Quarterly* 19(3): 457–478.

Gisbert, Josep. 2012. 'Mas Llama Al Mundo Económico a Hacer Piña Con El Proceso Soberanista'. *La Vanguardia*, 23 October 2012, 16.

Giuliano, Elise. 2006. 'Secessionism from the Bottom up: Democratization, Nationalism, and Local Accountability in the Russian Transition'. *World Politics* 58(2): 276–310.

Griffiths, Ryan. 2014. 'Secession and the Invisible Hand of the International System'. *Review of International Studies* 40(3): 559–581.

Gross, Kimberly. 2008. 'Framing Persuasive Appeals: Episodic and Thematic Framing, Emotional Response, and Policy Opinion'. *Political Psychology* 29(2): 169–192.

Hadekel, Peter. 1994. 'Business Leaders Must Take a Stand on Independence'. *Montreal Gazette*, 22 November 1994, C1.

Hadekel, Peter. 1995a. 'Yes-No Split Seen as Class Division'. *Montreal Gazette*, 7 October 1995, A1.

Hadekel, Peter. 1995b. 'Small Business Siding with No, Survey Shows; '80 Poll Showed More Yes Support'. *Montreal Gazette*, 19 October 1995, A11.

Hertel-Fernandez, Alexander. 2016. 'How Employers Recruit Their Workers into Politics – And Why Political Scientists Should Care'. *Perspectives on Politics* 14(2): 410–421.

Hillman, Amy J., Gerald D. Keim, and Douglas Schuler. 2004. 'Corporate Political Activity: A Review and Research Agenda'. *Journal of Management* 30(6): 837–857.

Horowitz, Donald L. 1985. *Ethnic Groups in Conflict*. Berkeley: University of California Press.

Iriarte, Marcos. 2015. 'Los independentistas responden a la banca en las redes: #BuidemLaCaixa (Vaciemos La Caixa)'. *El Mundo*. 18 September 2015. http://www.elmundo.es/economia/2015/09/18/55fc467246163f8f488b45b2.html.

Johnson, Simon. 2013a. 'Nationalist Anger at Supermarkets over Independence Food Price Warning'. *The Daily Telegraph*, 10 December 2013. https://www.telegraph.co.uk/news/politics/10506626/Nationalist-anger-at-supermarkets-over-independence-food-price-warning.html.

Johnson, Simon. 2013b. 'CBI Challenges Alex Salmond to Be "open" about Independence Risks'. *The Daily Telegraph*, 31 December 2013. https://www.telegraph.co.uk/news/politics/10542925/CBI-challenges-Alex-Salmond-to-be-open-about-independence-risks.html.

Kinder, Donald R., Mark D. Peters, Robert P. Abelson, and Susan T. Fiske. 1980. 'Presidential Prototypes'. *Political Behavior* 2(4): 315–337.

Kuran, Timur. 1998. 'Ethnic Norms and Their Transformation through Reputational Cascades'. *The Journal of Legal Studies* 27(S2): 623–659.

La Vanguardia. 2014. 'El Presidente de Grifols Pide Una Consulta Catalana Con "Dignidad"'. 17 June 2014. https://www.lavanguardia.com/politica/20140617/54410045042/presidente-grifols-pide-consulta-catalana-dignidad.html.

Lenz, Gabriel S. 2012. *Follow the Leader?: How Voters Respond to Politicians' Policies and Performance*. Chicago: University of Chicago Press.

Lindblom, Charles Edward. 1977. *Politics and Markets: The World's Political Economic Systems*. New York: Basic Books.

Liñeira, Robert, Ailsa Henderson, and Liam Delaney. 2017. 'Voters' Response to the Campaign'. In *Debating Scotland: Issues of Independence and Union in the 2014 Referendum*, edited by Michael Keating. New York: Oxford University Press, pp. 165–190.

MacKay, Brad. 2014. 'Business Decision-Making in Conditions of Constitutional and Political Uncertainty in the UK and Scotland: Evidence from Business Final Report'. Future of the UK and Scotland. University of Edinburgh Business School.

Mandelkern, Ronen, and Michael Shalev. 2010. 'Power and the Ascendance of New Economic Policy Ideas: Lessons from the 1980s Crisis in Israel'. *World Politics* 62(3): 459–495.

Martin, Pierre. 1995. 'When Nationalism Meets Continentalism: The Politics of Free Trade in Quebec'. *Regional & Federal Studies* 5(1): 1–27.

Medina, Iván, and Joaquim Molins. 2014. 'What Do Employers Think about a Possible Catalan Independence?' In *ECPR General Conference*. Glasgow. https://ecpr.eu/Filestore/PaperProposal/7ec6136f-e48a-4f88-abd8-f3d190552ea9.pdf.

Mendelsohn, Matthew. 2003. 'Rational Choice and Socio-Psychological Explanation for Opinion on Quebec Sovereignty'. *Canadian Journal of Political Science* 36(3): 511–537.

Mintzberg, Henry, and James A. Waters. 1985. 'Of Strategies, Deliberate and Emergent'. *Strategic Management Journal* 6(3): 257–272.

Muñoz, Jordi, and Raül Tormos. 2015. 'Economic Expectations and Support for Secession in Catalonia: Between Causality and Rationalization'. *European Political Science Review* 7(2): 315–341.

Muro, Diego, and Martijn C. Vlaskamp. 2016. 'How Do Prospects of EU Membership Influence Support for Secession? A Survey Experiment in Catalonia and Scotland'. *West European Politics* 39(6): 1115–1138.

Murphy, Dale D. 2004. *The Structure of Regulatory Competition: Corporations and Public Policies in a Global Economy*. Oxford: Oxford University Press.

Nadeau, Richard, Pierre Martin, and Andre Blais. 1999. 'Attitude towards Risk-Taking and Individual Choice in the Quebec Referendum on Sovereignty'. *British Journal of Political Science* 29(3): 523–539.

Nelson, Thomas E., Zoe M. Oxley, and Rosalee A. Clawson. 1997. 'Toward a Psychology of Framing Effects'. *Political Behavior* 19(3): 221–246.

Noelle-Neumann, Elisabeth. 1974. 'The Spiral of Silence A Theory of Public Opinion'. *Journal of Communication* 24(2): 43–51.

Riley-Smith, Ben. 2014. 'Alex Salmond "Personally Pressurised Financial Body to Drop Independence Report"'. *The Daily Telegraph*, 8 July 2014. https://www.telegraph.co.uk/news/uknews/scottish-independence/10952644/Alex-Salmond-personally-pressurised-financial-body-to-drop-independence-report.html.

Risse, Thomas. 2000. '"Let's Argue!": Communicative Action in World Politics'. *International Organization* 54(1): 1–39.

Sambanis, Nicholas, and Branko Milanovic. 2011. 'Explaining the Demand for Sovereignty: Policy Research Working Paper 5888'. Washington, D.C.: Development Research Group, World Bank.

Scherer, Andreas Georg, Guido Palazzo, and Dirk Matten. 2014. 'The Business Firm as a Political Actor: A New Theory of the Firm for a Globalized World'. *Business & Society* 53(2): 143–156.

Schmidt, Vivien A. 2008. 'Discursive Institutionalism: The Explanatory Power of Ideas and Discourse'. *Annual Review of Political Science* 11(1): 303–326.

Snow, David, and Robert Benford. 1988. 'Ideology, Frame Resonance, and Participant Mobilization'. *International Social Movement Research* 1: 197–217.

Sorens, Jason. 2005. 'The Cross-Sectional Determinants of Secessionism in Advanced Democracies'. *Comparative Political Studies* 38(3): 304–326.

The Guardian. 2014. 'Independent Scotland Would Be a Success, Says Investment Firm Boss'. 11 September 2014. https://www.theguardian.com/business/2014/sep/11/aberdeen-asset-management-boss-backs-independent-scotland.

Tirtiroglu, Dogan, Harjeet S Bhabra, and Ugur Lel. 2004. 'Political Uncertainty and Asset Valuation: Evidence from Business Relocations in Canada'. *Journal of Banking & Finance* 28(9): 2237–2258.

Turner, Camila, Claire Newell, and Holly Watt. 2014. 'Threats, Intimidation and Abuse: The Dark Side of the Yes Campaign Exposed'. *The Daily Telegraph*,

17 September 2014. http://www.telegraph.co.uk/news/uknews/scottish-indepen
dence/11102194/Threats-intimidation-and-abuse-the-dark-side-of-the-Yes-cam
paign-exposed.html.

Young, Robert A. 1994. 'The Political Economy of Secession: The Case of Quebec'.
Constitutional Political Economy 5(2): 221–245.

Chapter 10

Viability as a Strategy of Secession: Enshrining *De Facto* Statehood in Abkhazia and Somaliland

Giulia Prelz Oltramonti

INTRODUCTION

Even a *de facto* state has to keep the lights on and sustain its institutions, albeit on the cheap. This calls for some sort of economic viability, whether on the shoulders of patrons or of diasporas or on the revenues taken in through various forms of income-generating activities. Some *de facto* states might choose to keep their budget to the minimum; others might engage in some forms of positive sovereignty – either by building roads or by paying pensions.

In either case, a viability beyond the institutional one must be ensured in order to support the institutional viability that is the flagship of *de facto* states' claims for statehood. If a state cannot develop a certain level of viability, it is unlikely that it would succeed in its process of state-making, hence undermining the secessionists' strategy for enshrining their secession.

Can secessionist movements (having first managed to achieve territorial dominion over given areas and then gradually established themselves as *de facto* states) do that, namely keep the lights on in the territories that they control – or strive to control? Can they ensure the viability of the new state that they aim to create? They are invariably adamant that they can; home states usually argue that they cannot.[1] In fact, the latter often invest substantial resources in curtailing the viability of secessionist territories as selfstanding entities.

Secessionist actors have to hold on tight to the case that their coveted state is viable, as a partial justification of their aspiration for statehood. Hence, the search for viability is part of the strategies that secessionist movements and entities employ when seeking *de facto* and *de jure* statehood, legitimacy, and recognition by the international community (albeit not necessarily conjunctly). At the same time, numerous secessionist movements, having unilaterally established territorial independence from their home state, need to establish viability to secure the *de facto* secession and create *de facto* statehood.[2]

Viability is used as a strategy of secession both in the mid-term and in the long-term, as a tool to achieve, respectively, *de facto* statehood and *de jure* statehood (or international recognition). There are different interlocutors at play, both internal and external, and they are baited with viability to provide legitimacy and support. The chapter contributes to this volume – and the wider literature – with a comparative and cross-regional study of the strategies of secession. It looks at two geographically and historically removed cases of *de facto* states, namely Abkhazia and Somaliland. In these two cases, *de facto* independence has been established and secessionist entities are confronted with the issue of securing and managing it. This case selection avoids the often-trodden approach of comparing post-Soviet *de facto* states to one another and treating *de facto* statehood as an exclusively Eurasian strategy of secession. Such an approach, while informative regarding Eurasian cases, does not tell us whether the observations carried out transcend geographical borders or whether they are specific to the former Soviet Union. Looking at Abkhazia and Somaliland in unison tells us more about the strategies of secession of *de facto* states in general, if less about the post-Soviet region as a whole.

The chapter begins by differentiating between short-, mid-, and long-term strategies of secession and by explaining why viability is most relevant for the two latter ones. It shortly sketches out how Abkhazia and Somaliland ensured viability since their unilateral declarations of independence (UDIs) and then tackles how viability is used as a mid-term strategy (to secure *de facto* statehood) and, less successfully, as a long-term strategy (to secure *de jure* statehood). Finally, it underlines the links between viability and the search for legitimacy, whether internal or external.

SHORT-, MID-, AND LONG-TERM STRATEGIES OF SECESSION

By their very own definition, secessionist movements aim to create a new state on territory which previously pertained to a larger sovereign state (Griffiths and Muro 2019). The creation of a new state entails its recognition by the international community and its consecration of its membership in the club of states as one *inter pares*. To reach this goal, however, secessionist movements develop a range of short-, mid-, and long-term strategies that are meant to further their position in relation to their goals. This chapter is largely concerned with mid- and long-term strategies, as well as with uncoupling the two.

As pointed out in the introductory chapter of this volume, secessionist movements have two main avenues to gain international recognition as states: either through the acceptance of their home state or through the support of the international community. Movements that unilaterally declare independence and that achieve some level of territorial independence through violent means are very unlikely to be successful in their quest for support from the home state. Consequently, their main *long-term strategy* is to circumvent the home state and appeal to the international community on a number of grounds. This is notwithstanding the fact that, as long as the home state opposes independence, the international community would be wary to infringe upon the territorial integrity of one of its existing members.

However, while striving for inclusion in the international community and addressing its members as part of its long-term strategy to gain it, secessionist movements have additional short- and mid-term avenues for action. For the sake of clarity, it is useful to reiterate what the *short-term strategies* are, although viability does not play a role there. For *de facto* states, which are the result of UDIs, these are the strategies that allow them to territorially break away from home states. While this is often achieved through violent means, it is not exclusively so, as shown by the cases of Somaliland and, to a lesser extent, Transnistria.[3]

In the case of UDIs, after establishing (including through violent means) the existence of a self-standing entity, secessionist actors have to focus on their *mid-term strategies*, ensuring the existence of a *de facto* state, which might not be recognized as such, but which will be territorially independent from the home state. In other words, secessionist movements can unilaterally take control of a given territory (whether the whole or part of the territory concerned by secessionist claims) and then resist reintegration into a wider national realm. This is what a number of secessionist movements have done in the past, some less successfully, others more so. While the former have been reabsorbed into their home states (Chechnya, Tamil Eelam), many of latter have formed *de facto* states, as a result of implementing their mid-term strategies of securing *de facto* statehood but failing to achieve their long-terms goals (including Northern Cyprus, Transnistria, and Nagorno-Karabakh). But such *de facto* statehood, which is not consecrated by the international community, is a hazardous position to be in. First, *de facto* states are under constant threat of reabsorption into the home states from which they seceded. Second, they are hampered by their lack of recognition, which often prevents them from acting as members of the international community in a vast range of realms (diplomacy, trade, finance, etc.).

In order of priorities, therefore, the strategy of secessionist movements that opt for achieving independence through UDIs run from short-term (territorial independence) to mid-term (*de facto* statehood) and long-term (international recognition). They first have to achieve control of a given territory and establish their *de facto* independence from the home country, then ensure their *de facto* statehood throughout time, and finally achieve recognition in order to become full-fledged states, which in turn then will guarantee international protection. In parallel, secessionist movements strive to become authorities of *de facto* states (mid-term strategy), and eventually of internationally recognized states (long-term strategy). Viability is a factor that plays a role in the two latter ones. The following section looks at how viability is achieved in the two cases of Abkhazia and Somaliland, in order to illustrate the spectrum of factors that contribute to it.

HOW DO *DE FACTO* STATES ENSURE VIABILITY? BY LIMITING ISOLATION

For *de facto* authorities, viability is closely linked to breaking away from the isolation imposed by a lack of international recognition; secessionist entities need to become facilitators of relations with the outside (whether political or commercial) that would ensure a survival of the secessionist entities in a globalized world.

Abkhazia is a point in case. Abkhazia's history in its post-*de facto* independence era can be divided into three periods: isolation broadly characterized the 1993–1999 period; the 2000s witnessed a progressive easing of sanctions and opening of the *de facto* border with Russia; and after 2008, Russia's presence in Abkhazia became more open and dominant. The viability of the Abkhaz *de facto* state is to a large extent correlated.

In the 1990s, the Abkhaz *de facto* state, while broadly existent, had very limited viability. This was due to a combination of isolation, war damages, and botched post-Soviet transition. Sanctions banning trade, financial, transportation, communications, and other ties with Abkhazia at the state level were imposed on Abkhazia in January 1996 by the members of the Commonwealth of Independent States. In relations to the war in the north Caucasus, in December 1994, Russia closed its border to all men between the ages of sixteen and sixty (Le Huérou et al. 2014; Zverev 1996). In addition, Soviet passports gradually expired, leaving the residents of Abkhazia with no documents to travel. This period is widely seen in Abkhazia as the time of the 'Georgian embargo', irrespective of whether travel limitations on people were imposed by Russia.

People survived with no support from the state, and the secessionist authorities drew legitimacy from their military victory but not by providing support to its population, aside from guaranteeing security from Georgia. The very limited viability that existed rested largely on coping and depletive strategies.

Some of the coping strategies that were adopted in Abkhazia broadly resemble those observed in the rest of Georgia – and in most of the former Soviet Union – in the early 1990s: return to subsistence agriculture, depletive strategies, and migration. In Abkhazia, however, isolation and depopulation shaped those coping strategies in a unique way (Oltramonti 2017).

To fill up their coffers with a minimum of liquidity, the secessionist entities in Abkhazia exported scrap metal, its main export in the early 1990s (interview Bardon 2012). The *de facto* government relied on the income of the sale of dismantled factories and facilities, being unable to raise revenues through taxation (as productive activities had collapsed) or customs, due to its lack of control of its *de facto* borders (interview Gagulia 2012).[4] With these revenues, basic food imports from Russia and Turkey were paid for – providing, inter alia, a daily loaf of bread to state employees (interview Gagulia 2012).

In parallel, shuttle trade was a crucial survival strategy throughout the period of isolation and later. For this small-scale trade to continue as it did, notwithstanding the sanctions, an extensive network of corruption developed along the Psou border and at the checkpoints between Abkhazia and Russia, benefiting middlemen and Russian customs guards. Private initiative kept Abkhazia afloat, but the *de facto* authorities were largely unable to regulate or support it. On the contrary, *de facto* authorities benefitted from informality often on a personal basis (Oltramonti 2017).

The trickle of informal trade between Abkhazia and its neighbours is what allowed for a minimum amount of viability. This shows that viability is dependent on connections with the wider world, whether formally or informally. At the same time, however, showing the connections that Abkhazia maintained with its neighbours does not take away from the impact that severe isolation had on the region. It crucially curtailed access to credit and to aid for postwar rehabilitation of infrastructure, affecting Abkhazia's transition to a market economy and its reliance on distorted economic practices. Isolation, in fact, limited viability to a minimum.

The attempt to build greater viability into the Abkhaz *de facto* state started with the reinstatement of more stable and substantial links with the outer world (and Russia, in particular). Travel and trade restrictions were slowly eased starting in 1999 (Diasamidze 2003) and Russian passports became available in 2002.[5] Interestingly, citizens of Abkhazia may not hold dual citizenship; an exception was made for Russian citizenship, which provided a connection to the outside world. Russian and Turkish investments in transport, tourist infrastructure, and natural resources grew. This included investments in roads (International Crisis Group 2006a), railroad (Lynch 2006; Sepashvili 2004),[6] and tourist complexes on the coastline (Trier, Lohm, and Szakonyi 2010, 110). The opening of the border between Russia and

Abkhazia in 2000 entailed a jump in foreign trade of up to 90% in exports of natural resources and agricultural produce (Baratelia 2007).

While the partial easing of trade restrictions on the Russian side have meant that Abkhazia's viability has expanded, its overdependence on Russia, and still very limited access to the outer world aside from Russia, limits the scope of development and resilience that the Abkhaz's authorities can aim to (International Crisis Group 2008). This is why they are actively looking for other partners, although hindered in their search by the lack of recognition and the tensions between Russia, on one side, and Georgia and its backers, on the other, which Abkhazia is drawn into (interview Abkhaz *de facto* government officials 2015).

Since 2008, Abkhazia has been recognized by Russia and a handful of other countries.[7] While this would seem to entail a reduction of isolation, it is not so. While on paper diplomatic isolation decreased, this was done by establishing links with countries that are themselves either isolated or insignificant on the global stage. The outcome is that Abkhazia has been unable to establish links with the wider world (with the exception of Russia) and to diversify its relationships with international actors. At the same time, Russia has established a monopoly over Abkhazia's links to the outside and meticulously maintains its role of self-imposed intermediary. As a result, Russia is also functioning as an actor of isolation, a role that numerous patron states have adopted with the *de facto* states that they back (Armenia and Nagorno-Karabakh; Turkey and Turkish Republic of Norther Cyprus), albeit to various extents and in conjunction with a support role.

It is worth noting that Somaliland's case lacks both a patron state and a decisive home state but that the issue of limiting isolation has still been key to the *de facto* state's survival in Somalia, as Somaliland's home state has been unable to isolate the *de facto* state, aside from producing declarations condemning Somaliland's secession. Somalia's collapse and its lack of capacity to control southern Somalia and, during extensive periods, even its capital means that it cannot act as a legitimate and/or effective actor of national unity. Somalia is unable to control Somaliland's terrestrial, maritime, or aerial borders. At the same time, it also never managed to build consensus around trade or mobility restrictions implemented by third parties, which would limit transit of people and goods to and from Somaliland. Hargeisa's airport is fully functioning and connects Somaliland with regional centres and several hubs in the Arabian Peninsula. Also, Somaliland's port is one of its key infrastructures and is a matter of interest for Ethiopia, which could lessen its dependence of Djibouti as a transit country (Pegg and Walls 2018).

In fact, Somaliland is viable only because its home state is unable to limit its connections with the outside, on which it is extremely dependent. Remittances and exports of livestock account for almost the entirety of its gross domestic product. Viability rests largely on the shoulders of the diaspora who support residents of Somaliland with significant remittances, at an estimated US$500–900 million per year (World Bank 2016, 45). Remittances from the diaspora contributed to the creation of infrastructures such as schools and hospitals (Hansen 2004).[8]

The money transfer businesses that connect the diaspora to the Somalis living in Somaliland are the key element of transmission between in and out, notwithstanding the increasing hurdles to financial transfers towards Somalia that were developed since the 2000s as a result of the 9/11 attacks, increasing regulatory requirements in the United States and more stringent anti-money-laundering rules. While the money transfer businesses have been affected by increasing regulation at the source – in the countries of the remittances' origin and, in particular, in the United States – in Somaliland, the secessionist authorities have been largely unable to influence, control, or support them. After the leading transfer firm, Al-Barakat, was labelled as a terrorist entity after 9/11, a charge which was later dropped, it was replaced by a myriad of others, including the Dubai-based Dahabshiil, funded by a Somali originating from Somaliland. The funds transfer industry in Somaliland shows incredible resilience and only recently are secessionist authorities starting to play a regulatory role (Unknown Author 2018).

In addition to remittances, viability is provided by an additional connection with the outside, namely the export of livestock to the Arabian Peninsula (World Bank 2016, 12). This means that Somaliland's economy remains small and prone to setbacks due to the major impacts that droughts have on the agricultural sector, which is the segment of the economy that employs the vast majority of the population.

Clearly, in the case of Somaliland, *de facto* state authorities did not contend with private actors but largely relied on them. It is a clear case of state-making where private actors played the predominant role, with the state providing one precious element in the region: security. This does not mean that the state had the monopoly of legitimate violence as clans and individuals retained weapons and criminal affairs were and are dealt with at a clan level. But the secessionist authorities had co-opted such structures and could, with their support, guarantee the control of its territory and a level of security in which investments could be carried out.

Such security partly obviated the secessionist deficiencies in being able to invest in infrastructure or establish official relations with their counterparts abroad. Security allowed Somaliland to remain connected to its wider diaspora and ensured that, with the material support of the diaspora, residents of Somaliland did not have to migrate *en masse* out of its borders to access external resources.

MID-TERM STRATEGY: SECURING *DE FACTO* STATEHOOD

The first step of *de facto* states' secessions (securing territory) often occurs via violent means, but not necessarily. The Georgian-Abkhaz war (1992–1993) is a good point in case of the employment of violent means, and so are the wars in Nagorno-Karabakh, in Transnistria, and in Northern Cyprus, among other cases – although the level of violence employed varied sharply in terms of intensity and duration. In Somaliland's case, however, the establishment of a separate entity was partly a response to the violent process of state collapse taking place in Somalia and an attempt to curtail the violence spreading from the home state.

Also, this first step of acquiring territorial control may be drawn out in time and fuse into the secessionists' strategy to secure the perimeters of the territory that they control. In both Abkhazia and Somaliland, the first key step in the establishment of their *de facto* statehood (securing territory) was not complete until the second decade of *de facto* independence. In the 1990s, the Abkhaz government controlled the north and centre, but the Gali district, which straddles the ceasefire line with Georgia, remained a sort of Far West until 2008.

In Somaliland, the *de facto* government took the borders of the British Protectorate as its official borders. But this did not mean that it controlled the territory included in those borders in the early 1990s; in fact, the process of expanding its authority outwards from the central areas of Somaliland has been a very gradual one. It did not have the capacity in the early 1990s to extend its reach and could only claim control of its central and western territories after 1997 (Hoene 2015). Its eastern borderland has remained more problematic: Somaliland had to fight for its control with the neighbouring entity, Puntland, in the 2000s and with local militants since the mid-2000s. The process of extending Somaliland's actual control to its claimed colonial borders is still taking place. While Somaliland has certainly its area of control and the number of districts where it is unable to hold elections has gone down, parts of the eastern regions remain contested as seen in the summer 2018 fighting between Somaliland and Puntland (International Crisis Group 2018).

In addition to taking control over a given territory, secessionist actors need to maintain that control – without the protection of the international community – and manage the territory and the resident population or, in other words, establish *de facto* statehood. How do they do this? Partly by ensuring their viability or by keeping the lights on. Viability is a multidimensional concept better understood in terms of continuum. At one end, the lights are switched off, and secessionist entities are unable to sustain secessionist claims. At the other end, the lights are on and secessionist entities operate as fully functioning states, regardless of their juridical status in the international arena. This is dependent on economic and financial factors, as well as on the management of infrastructure, energy, and other aspects of public policy that allow for the provision of a minimum level of service in a given territory or to a given population.

It is worth pointing out here that ensuring viability serves numerous pillars that support the larger mid-term strategy of securing *de facto* secession. One the one hand, viability serves survival and goes hand in hand with statemaking processes; on the other hand, secessionist movements harness viability for internal legitimacy. This is in addition to the longer-term strategy of putting viability at the heart of their discourse about independence, recognition, and legitimacy on the international arena.

Secessionist actors' ultimate goal is to create a new state. However, the issue of statehood is dependent, in addition to international recognition, on governance, involving state capacity and institutionalization.[9] Secessionist actors in control of given territorial areas strive to develop both, with various results. Just as varied is how observers rate the results of these attempts.

For example, the field was quite evenly split in its pre-2008 evaluation of Abkhazia's strengths and weaknesses. If Pegg (1998), Kolossov and O'Loughlin (1998), and King (2001) underlined its robustness, Lynch (2002), Fairbanks (2002), and Kolstø (2006) argued that Abkhazia was deficient, if not in their institutional structure, then definitely in their governmental capacity. However, conflicting assessments on the strength of *de facto* states concern not only Abkhazia and the other cases in the Caucasus but also Somaliland and Trandnistria (Kolstø 2006).

This is due to a few elements. First, the development of the institutional capacity of a *de facto* state should be examined in its regional context. In the cases of Abkhazia and Somaliland, for example, this means taking into consideration the institutional collapse that affected the former Soviet Union and Somalia, respectively. Second, institutional capacity varies throughout time and, in Abkhazia's and Somaliland's cases, it has varied considerably throughout the 1990s and 2000s. But conflicting assessments are also due to the predicament of establishing what states' weaknesses and strengths are, spanning from the definition of a weak state as one that 'meets minimum Weberian definitions of institutions of rule and is able to carry out some basic functions but is far from performing according to domestic and international expectations of a "normal state"' (Young 2002, 446), while the strong ones are 'states that are capable of carrying out functions that they themselves claim and that they are reasonably expected by their populations to carry out' (Nodia 2002, 415).

Notwithstanding the difficulty that scholars encounter in computing the success and failures of secessionist movements in establishing their *de facto* states, secessionist movements are often busy in building institutions characteristic of independent states. While there is no scope here for detailing the various developments of the two cases examined in this chapter throughout a time span of twenty-five years, it can be asserted that Abkhazia and Somaliland have been undergoing – nonlinear and certainly not unidirectional – processes of state-making in the years since their declaration of secession.

However, it is useful here to qualify two different aspects of state-making, along the lines of Lonsdale's distinction between state-building and state formation. If the former refers to the conscious process to create a state apparatus, which Lonsdale saw in terms of an apparatus of control, state formation designates the unintended result of interactions of individuals and groups who struggle for the establishment of their own position in the process of state-making (Berman and Lonsdale 1992). The literature on informality shows that this coexistence of state institution and private actors is present even after the process of state-making is consolidated (Ledeneva 2018). A symbiosis between the two exists to the point that they can be seen as the two ends of a formality/ informality continuum.

This double-faced understanding of state-making carries a few implications. On the one hand, state-making is only partly the result of the policies designed and implemented by state actors, in line with goals of state-building; the result of processes of state-making must therefore be seen as a concomitance of institutional and non-institutional factors. On the other hand, the state-building strategies of state actors do not exist in a void and must contend with a series of other actors, interests, and processes. What is more, they do not only contend with private actors, but they also largely rely on them. I have previously shown how Abkhaz authorities relied, especially in the 1990s, on informal practices (Oltramonti 2017); even more widely known is the reliance of the *de facto* state of Somaliland on the diaspora and remittances. At the same time, informal practices have sometimes been institutionalized: Somaliland has also incorporated traditional clan elders into its modern state as the Guurti (or upper house of parliament). Whether this *modus operandi* is effective or not is up to debate;[10] in any case, it is worth pointing out its existence.

If there is a symbiosis between authorities and private actors in the process of state-making, there must be benefits for both sides to nurture this interdependence. Secessionist authorities – either openly or tacitly – rely on private actors and on the informal sector for a range of purposes; at the same time, however, they must also provide support to their counterpart. They can do so by providing environments that are supportive enough of their counterpart that their counterpart feels compelled to remain in this relationship – and not actively undermine the state.

In other words, secessionist authorities need to create and nurture stakeholders of independence. They can do that by showing that the project of independence is a viable one and that such stakeholders are better off by opting in than by calling themselves out.

This concerns also the residents of *de facto* states – secessionist actors need to turn a sizeable portion of them into stakeholders of secession. Patriotism and nationalism are the tools of choice; however, economic opportunities also factor in. In fact, secessionist movements sometimes spring up and gain momentum in regions that are more prosperous – or have more generous social security systems – than the rest of the home state. This was the case of Abkhazia in the late Soviet period but has also been the case in places where secessionism has led to less violent outcomes (e.g., Catalonia).

Secessionist authorities argue that residents are better off in a newly independent state than as part of a larger polity. To back this claim they need, if not in the short-term than definitely in the mid-term, to turn into service providers. In order to do so, however, they must develop an adequate level of state capacity that would sustain the provision of all sorts of services. In the process of establishing the new state – whether *de facto* or *de jure* – secessionist entities try to expand their positive sovereignty, that is, their capacity to support their residents, in tandem with their coercive power.[11] This is especially true in situations, such as those faced by *de facto* states, where their statehood is unrecognized and where authorities lack the legitimacy of international recognition.

In the mid-term, then, viability is therefore harnessed for internal legitimacy in a process of state consolidation and in the production of stakeholders' constituencies. But viability is also used to sustain a longer-term strategy of secession, namely the search for independence, recognition, and legitimacy in the international arena.

LONG-TERM STRATEGY: SECURING *DE JURE* STATEHOOD

Securing *de facto* statehood is not enough for secessionist entities, as lack of recognition threatens both their security and their ability to develop internal viability. The long-term goal remains international recognition as states or, in other words, full membership of the international community. Granted, Abkhazia has received some degree of recognition after 2008, but this can in no way be seen as 'international' recognition. It was recognized by its patron state and a handful of its allies and so turning it into a pariah on the international arena instead of making it a member of the international community. Whatever security guarantee Abkhazia draws from Russia, it does not come from recognition but by Russia's successful attempt to push its own security border South (Oltramonti 2016).

As mentioned earlier, as a long-term strategy, secessionist movements opt to engage with the international community and circumvent the home state, especially in cases of UDIs. To achieve their goal, they exploit a number of channels, including para-diplomacy and membership of bodies such as the Unrepresented Nations and Peoples Organization or the Confederation of Independent Football Associations, as well as informal links provided by the diaspora. The arguments that they put forward in favour of their claim for international recognition are just as varied, some of which have received considerable attention in the literature on secessionist movements, such as remedial rights theories (Caspersen 2009).

One of the tactics for appealing to the international community is that of mobilizing the argument of democracy and showcasing democratic achievements, sometimes in the context of less democratic home states. The elites of Abkhazia and Somaliland strove to build institutions characteristic of independent democratic states, both as a strategy of state consolidation and as a tool for claiming international recognition. Repeatedly staged elections in Abkhazia led to a change of leadership in 2004. While no external monitors were present, the loss by the incumbents shows that the electoral results were far from predetermined. In Somaliland, the institutional makeup of the *de facto* state was formed in 1993, with the establishment of a two-chamber parliament, as well as distinct executive, legislative, and judiciary branches of government. The first local, presidential, and parliamentary elections took place in 2002, 2003, and 2005, respectively, and were deemed free by international observers (Terlinden and Ibrahim 2008).

As an argument in favour of recognition, viability is less prominent but nonetheless present. This argument can be traced back to the decolonization period, when sovereignty in international relation was largely attributed on the basis of what was then considered as viability and stability – largely in line with colonial institutions. This is one of the reasons why the colonial borders and administrations were maintained and supported in their postcolonial transitions (Barkin and Cronin 1994, 112). Seen from today's perspective, it might appear that, post-1945, the international society forsook viability as a criterion for statehood. According to Jackson (1990), to be a state today you need only have been a former colony yesterday. It is worth noting, however, that a former colony yesterday was perceived, in the international arena, as a bedrock of the international order – and hence the only guarantee of stability and the only envisaged territorial expression of viability. It is precisely as a consequence of decolonization that a shift from empirical to juridical statehood occurred. While the results of this shift clearly surfaced during the processes that led to the dissolution of the Soviet Union and Yugoslavia, *de facto* states are still playing yesterday's game (empirical statehood) in violation of today's rules (juridical statehood).

As statehood is largely understood in its normative dimension (a population; a territory; a government; and relations with other states), sovereignty follows suit, entailing the need to assess the ability of the state to control or develop those attributes. In fact, when the link between viability and institutional makeup has been made, it has entered the discourse on sovereignty (Hobsbawm 1990, 31–32). Viability is associated with sovereignty in function of a state being able to act as an enforcer – which is able to control its territory, its population, and protect its borders: 'State sovereignty emphasizes the integrity of borders based on historical possession, national frontiers, and viability. If we follow this logic, the viability of a state is based on the ability of established institutions to exercise authority over the population. This control is best assured by stable, effective states with strong institutions rather than by newly defined nations that may lack administrative competence and social stability' (Barkin and Cronin 1994, 112).

It is important to note that many cases of secession took place in the framework of declining stability and viability of the home states. When looking at Abkhazia and Somaliland, for example, it is worth keeping in mind the regional contexts of institutional collapse after the end of the Soviet Union and Somalia, respectively. The end of the Soviet Union engendered a process of institutional collapse, which was observable to various degrees throughout the newly independent states. Institutions in charge of maintaining internal and defence securities had to be reorganized around a new centre and that would no longer be Moscow. This was a lengthy process and, in the meanwhile, levels of violence rose exponentially. It could hardly be argued that states such as Georgia had the monopoly over organized violence. For most of the 1990s, Georgia could also not claim to be in control of its territory, even leaving aside the separatist territories. The process of consolidation of institutional control over its borders and territory is a process that took more than a decade, starting from less than zero in the early 1990s, when Russian troops manned the border with Turkey.[12] This was the case not only for the provision of security but also of services.

Similarly, the emergence of the *de facto* state of Somaliland is linked to Somalia's demise. Not only a total process of state collapse took place with the end of Siad Barre's regime, but this collapse turned out to be extended in time. Notwithstanding the intervention of foreign troops on Somali's territory to stabilize the situation and support of the international community to various kinds of transitional governments, especially since 2000, the Somali National Government still controls limited areas of some urban centres, in addition to Mogadishu, and is threatened by local strongmen and Islamists (International Crisis Group 2014).

As shown above, secessionist authorities target various audiences with the concept of viability, which represent different strategies that *de facto* authorities develop to enshrine secession. In fact, viability can be harnessed to produce both internal and external legitimacies, which, in turn, can support *de facto* states' mid- and long-term strategies.

VIABILITY AS A SOURCE OF INTERNAL AND EXTERNAL LEGITIMACIES

Viability is harnessed by secessionist movements as a source of legitimacy, in addition to keeping the lights on, and as such it plays, once again, into both mid- and long-term strategies. The audiences to which viability is presented as a justification for secession – and for the secessionist movements to be in charge of guaranteeing secession – differ, as legitimacy can be sought after both internally and externally. The two cases of Abkhazia and Somaliland exemplify this dynamic clearly: in the former, internal support is gathered through viability, in the latter viability is used as an argument for external recognition.

In Abkhazia, isolation imposed from the outside was a key factor in limiting its viability; but there was also an endogenous factor that severely limited its ability to keep the lights on. This is *de facto* authorities' management of transition and their role, in the 1990s, as actors – or obstacles – to the economic development of Abkhazia.

Abkhaz *de facto* authorities had very little tradition of state management before 1991 and were not qualified for devising and implementing the necessary reforms, for transitioning away from a centrally planned Soviet economy. Few programmes aimed at kick-starting privatization and supporting the development of businesses and were designed to maximize political returns, showing little concern for their economic impacts. Privatization of large businesses reinforced a system of clientele which centred on the two successive *de facto* presidents, while the Fund for Support of Enterprises operated as a dispenser of cash in return for political support and not as a tool for encouraging business.

A state rhetoric on trade sanctions masked an absolute stasis with regard to establishing the foundations of a new, and more viable, Abkhaz economy, and this resulted in a decline of key industries, which came to terms with the change in market conditions for Abkhaz produce and services (tea and tobacco production, tourism). Across the former Soviet Union, governments struggled with the modalities of transition; in Abkhazia the issue of transition was mostly sidelined, while creating opportunities for a few strategically positioned members of the elites. To sum up, two factors made Abkhazia in the 1990s largely unviable/or very limitedly viable: first, isolation, over which *de facto* authorities had little control and, second, lack of reform, which was swept under the carpet and left unacknowledged. This was possible thanks to the depletive strategies put in place by the residents and the legitimacy that the political elites drew from the war victory.

This sort of legitimacy started waning in the late 1990s. As early as 1996–1997 a switch occurred in how the residents of Abkhazia attributed legitimacy to the government – from drawing legitimacy from winning the war to seeing the government as a provider of governance, services, and security, both external and internal (interview Inal-Ipa 2012). The shift became apparent in 1999, when the first serious opposition movement, 'Vozrojdenie' (Rebirth), was registered and started questioning the government and advocating for services. Previously, as the post-ceasefire society was based on an idea of unity and on Ardzinba as a hero-like figure, it had been largely unacceptable to express criticisms towards the government (interview Inal-Ipa 2012). However, the corruption and the mismanagement of resources, which had initially been accepted as a matter of fact, led to a change of power in 2004–2005.[13] The role of the government as a guarantor of viability for Abkhazia became a central issue of the political debate.

For Somaliland, viability is an argument presented to the international community in favour of recognition. To show its viability, Somaliland relies on two strategies: first, acquiring the symbols of a viable state and, second, contrasting its viability with Somalia's lack of it.

Numerous developments stand to indicate an acquired viability: the founding of Radio Hargeysa as early as 1991, as well as newspapers, and the development of school curricula. A national currency is established in 1994; monetary policy, developed in view of stabilizing the shilling in its exchange rate to the U.S. dollar is implemented and as of late (2018) with the intent of phasing out the U.S. dollar as a functional currency in the local economy. The airport and a number of roads are functional, and the vast majority of Somaliland is secure. This is leaving aside the gradual institutionalization of political power and the electoral cycles mentioned in the first part of the chapter.

At the same time, Somaliland has underlined its own viability as a state as opposed to its home state. It eschewed associations with terrorism and piracy, linked to the state failure of Somalia, and promoted itself as a heaven of stability in the region. In this light, it has cooperated with international efforts to repatriate up to 200,000 refugees from Ethiopia and Djibouti in 2006, as much of Somalia was controlled by hard-line Islamists, and accepts repatriations from EU member states of asylum seekers (International Crisis Group 2006b).

Viability is an argument in the quest for recognition, because, to a large extent, that is what recognized states have. A viable state can legitimately claim recognition from the international community and support from its own population. As discussed earlier in the chapter, this was true during the decolonization period, when sovereignty in international relation was largely attributed on the basis of viability and stability (or, at least, the viability and stability embodied by colonial institutions), and secessionist movements hope that it will eventually be true also for them. According to their strategy, if the authorities of a *de facto* state can keep the lights on, and in some cases also operate as services and welfare providers, they would prove the legitimacy of their claim to recognition and secure *de jure* secession.

CONCLUSION

Viability is clearly much more successful as a mid-term strategy of secession (establishment of *de facto* statehood) than a long-term one (international recognition). In fact, it is so successful as the former, that it has sustained the existence of Abkhazia and Somaliland (together with an array of other factors, including the weakness of the home state and external support, whether from a patron or from the diaspora) as distinct territorial entities from their home states for more than twenty-five years despite the lack of recognition and the security that such recognition would have provided them.

This chapter has not delved into the intentionality of the search for viability as such and, in function of the finalities outlined earlier, and this aspect remains open to future research. However, it is worth noting that, in both cases analysed in this chapter, the strategies to shore up the gains of the initial short-term strategies (territorial independence) consisted in managing such territories through *de facto* state-like entities and to establish a viability of such entities – whether relying more on state intervention, such as in Abkhazia, or depending extensively on the process of state formation and its actors, such as in Somaliland. In both cases, *de facto* authorities kept the lights on, at least at a relatively tolerant level for most residents. It seems safe, therefore, to argue that this was indeed intentional, as it granted support towards the perpetuation of the secessionist project and legitimacy towards those steering such a project forward.

NOTES

1. 'Home state' is the terminology used in the Introduction chapter of this volume to designate the states from which secessionist movements aimed to break away; alternatively, the appellation 'parent state' is also used in the literature.

2. The appellation 'de facto state' is, therefore, understood as a state-like entity that lacks international recognition (Pegg 1998; Lynch 2004). There is no absolute

consensus on the characterization of these political entities. They are alternatively called 'unrecognized quasi-states' (Kolstø 2006; Baev 1998), 'unrecognised states' (King 2001), 'pseudo-states' (Kolossov and O'Loughlin 1998), and 'contested states' (Geldenhuys 2009; Ker-Lindsay 2015). While at times the denominations are used interchangeably, for some authors they point towards important differences in the level of institutionalization that these regions have established; however, as Pegg (2017) points out, the terminological proliferation creates a fundamental weakness of this literature.

3. Broers (2013) highlights how comparatively low the level of violence was in Transnistria versus how much higher it was in Abkhazia and Nagorno-Karabakh.

4. Note that the official version, as of 2012, is that, 'Budget revenues in the first post-war years derived from customs duties and taxes. By the late 90s, internal taxation began to exceed customs revenues' (interview Stranichkin 2012).

5. As of 2002, granting Russian passports to Abkhaz residents became possible thanks to the passing of a new law on citizenship by the Russian State Duma (Russian Federation 2002) and so allowing Abkhaz residents to seek employment and claim pensions. As of 2003, a majority of retirees started receiving Russian pensions, estimates of annual disbursements to Abkhazia by the Pensions Fund of the Russian Federation being calculated at more than $20 million per year (interview Baratelia 2012).

6. An additional segment of the line (between Sukhumi and Ochamchira) was restored from May to August 2008 by Russian engineering troops. The Georgian government claimed that the refurbishment had military purposes in the build-up to the 2008 war (Trier et al. 2010, 108).

7. After the Russo-Georgian war in 2008, Abkhazia's and South Ossetia's independences were recognized by the Russian Federation, Venezuela, Nicaragua, Nauru, and, intermittently, Vanuatu and Tuvalu.

8. However, both of these major sources are viewed as inherently fragile. There are concerns that younger generations of expatriates will not be nearly as well connected to Somaliland, and hence their remittances will diminish; as for livestock, climate change and recurrent droughts, as well as Saudi bans on imports from Somaliland, threaten the sustainability of this industry.

9. While it cannot be developed here, for a matter of length, an argument has successfully been made that there is a strong relationship between state-building, security provision, and war. In parallel with keeping the lights on, a (contested) state also needs to find resources to fund its security arrangements; at the same time, its security needs lead to an expansion of state capacity and institution-building.

10. Walls and Kibble (2010) is a good example of the previously prevailing positive views on this, while Hoehne (2013) is perhaps the most forceful critique that neither part of this system (modern or traditional) is working well.

11. It is worth noting that many *de facto* states devote a disproportionate share of their very limited revenues to security/military forces, partly as a consequence of the lack of security guarantees from the international community and partly because of the very limited resources that they can count on to begin with. This share diminished when a patron state (such as Russia) guarantees a *de facto* state security through its own military apparatus.

12. Shevardnadze relied on bilateral agreements signed in 1992 for protecting the borders and providing border guards for the following two years (Serrano 2007).

13. For a review of the electoral system in Abkhazia and an assessment of its dynamism, see Ó Beacháin (2012).

REFERENCES

Baev, P. 1998. 'Peacekeeping and Conflict Management in Eurasia'. In *Security Dilemmas in Russia and Eurasia*, edited by A. Allison and C. Bluth. London: Royal Institute of International Affairs, pp. 209–225.

Baratelia, B. 2007. 'Macroeconomic Aspects of Abkhazia's Development at the Modern Stage', Paper presented at the Zatulin Conference. [*Макроэкономические аспекты развития Абхазии на современном этапе, Доклад к конференции Затулина*] Unpublished document.

Barkin, J. Samuel, and Bruce Cronin. 1994. 'The State and the Nation: Changing Norms and the Rules of Sovereignty in International'. *International Organization* 48(1) (winter) pp. 107–130.

Berman, B., and J. Lonsdale. 1992. *Unhappy Valley*. London: James Currey

Broers, L., 2013. 'Recognising Politics in Unrecognised States: 20 Years of Enquiry into the *De Facto* States of the South Caucasus'. *Caucasus Survey* 1(1): 59–74.

Caspersen, N. 2009. 'Playing the Recognition Game: External Actors and *De Facto* States'. *The International Spectator: Italian Journal of International Affairs* 44(4): 47–60.

Diasamidze, T. (ed.) 2003. *Regional Conflicts in Georgia – the Autonomous Oblast of South Ossetia, the Autonomous SSR of Abkhazia, 1989–2002: the Collection of Political-Legal Acts*. Tbilisi: Regionalism Research Centre.

Fairbanks, C. 2002. 'Weak States and Private Armies'. In *Beyond State Crisis?: Post-Colonial Africa and Post-Soviet Eurasia in Comparative Perspective*, edited by Beissinger, M. and Young, C. Washington, DC: Woodrow Wilson Center Press, pp. 129–159.

Geldenhuys, D. 2009. *Contested States in World Politics*. London: Palgrave Macmillan.

Griffiths, Ryan D. and Diego Muro. 2019. 'Introduction'. In Strategies of Secession and Counter-secession, edited by Griffiths, Ryan D. and Diego Muro. London: ECPR Press, pp. 1–11.

Hansen, Peter. 2004. 'Migrant Remittances as a Development Tool: The Case of Somaliland', Danish Institute for Development Studies (DIIS), Working Papers Series No.3 – June 2004.

Hobsbawm. 1990. *Nations and Nationalism since 1780: Programme, Myth, Reality*. Cambridge: Cambridge University Press.

Hoehne, M. V. 2013. 'Limits of Hybrid Political Orders: The Case of Somaliland'. *Journal of Eastern African Studies* 7(2): 199–217.

Hoene, M. H. 2015. *Between Somaliland and Puntland. Marginalisation, Militarisation and Conflicting Political Visions*. London: Rift Valley Institute.

International Crisis Group. 2006a. *Abkhazia Today*. Europe Report N°175. Brussels.

International Crisis Group. 2006b. *Somaliland: Time for African Union Leadership*. Report 110. Brussels.

International Crisis Group. 2008. *Abkhazia and South Ossetia: Time to Talk Trade*, Report 249. Brussels.

International Crisis Group. 2014. *Somalia: AL-Shabaab – It Will Be a Long War*. Africa Briefing 99. Brussels.

International Crisis Group. 2018. *Averting War in Northern Somalia*. Africa Briefing 141. Brussels.

Jackson, Robert H. 1990. *Quasi-States: Sovereignty, International Relations, and the Third World*. Cambridge: Cambridge University Press.

Ker-Lindsay, James. 2015. 'Engagement without Recognition: The Limits of Diplomatic Interaction with Contested States'. *International Affairs* 91(2): 1–16.

King, C. 2001. 'The Benefits of Ethnic War: Understanding Eurasia's Unrecognized States'. *World Politics* 53(04): 524–552.

Kolossov, V., and O'Loughlin, J. 1998. 'Pseudo-States as Harbingers of a New Geopolitics: The Example of the Trans-Dniester Moldovan Republic (TMR)'. *Geopolitics* 3(1): 151–176.

Kolstø, P. 2006. 'The Sustainability and Future of Unrecognized Quasi-States'. *Journal of Peace Research* 43(6): 723–740.

Ledeneva, Alena (ed.) 2018. *The Global Encyclopaedia of Informality*, Volume 2. London: UCL Press.

Le Huérou, Anne, Aude Merlin, Amandine Regamey, Elisabeth Sieca-Kozlowski (eds.) 2014. *Chechnya at War and Beyond*. London: Routledge.

Lynch, D. 2002. 'Separatist States and Post-Soviet Conflicts'. *International Affairs* 78(4).

Lynch, D. 2004. *Engaging Eurasia's Separatist States: Unresolved Conflicts and De Facto States*. Washington, DC: US Institute of Peace Press.

Lynch, D. 2006. *Why Georgia Matters*. Paris: Institute for Security Studies.

Nodia, G. 2002. 'Putting the State Back Together in Post-Soviet Georgia'. In *Beyond State Crisis?: Post-Colonial Africa and Post-Soviet Eurasia in Comparative Perspective*, edited by Beissinger, M. and Young, C. Washington, DC: Woodrow Wilson Center Press, pp. 413–443.

Ó Beacháin, D. 2012. 'The Dynamics of Electoral Politics in Abkhazia'. *Communist and Post-Communist Studies* 45(1–2): 165–174.

Pegg, S. 1998. *International Society and the De Facto State*. Aldershot, UK: Ashgate.

Pegg, Scott. 2017. 'Twenty Years of De Facto State Studies: Progress, Problems, and Prospects'. In *Oxford Encyclopedia of Politics*. Oxford: Oxford University Press.

Pegg, Scott, and Michael Walls. 2018. 'Back on Track? Somaliland after Its 2017 Presidential Election'. *African Affairs* 117(467): 326–337.

Prelz Oltramonti, Giulia. 2017. 'Southbound Russia: Processes of Bordering and De-Bordering between 1993 and 2013'. *Connexe 2*: 103–124.

Prelz Oltramonti, Giulia. 2017. 'Conflict Protraction and the Illegality/Informality Divide'. *Caucasus Survey* 4(3): 85–101.

Russian Federation. 2002. 'Federal Law on Citizenship of the Russian Federation, N 62-FZ', Adopted by the State Duma on 19 April 2002. Accessed 13 June 2013. http://www.refworld.org/pdfid/50768e422.pdf.

Sepashvili, G. 17 September 2004. 'CIS Summit Reveals Rift in Russian/Georgian Relations'. *Civil Georgia Report*. Accessed 27 July 2009. http://www.civil.ge/eng/article.php?id=7852.

Serrano, S. 2007. *Géorgie : Sortie D'empire*. Paris: CNRS.

Terlinden, U., and Ibrahim, M. H. 2008. 'Somaliland: A Success Story of Peace-Making, State-Building and Democratisation?' In *Hot SpotHorn of Africa Revisited*, edited by E. M. Bruchhaus and M. M. Sommer. Hamburg: Lit Verlag, pp. 68–85.

Trier, T., H. Lohm, and D. Szakonyi. 2010. *Under Siege: Inter-Ethnic Relations in Abkhazia*. New York, Columbia University Press.

Unknown Author. 14 March 2018. 'eDahab Complies with Somaliland Govt Regulations on Money Transfer', *Capital Business*. Accessed 25 September 2018. https://www.capitalfm.co.ke/business/2018/03/edahab-complies-somaliland-govt-regulations-money-transfer/.

Walls, Michael, and Steve Kibble. 2010. 'Beyond Polarity: Negotiating a Hybrid State in Somaliland'. *Africa Spectrum* 45(1): 31–56.

World Bank. 2016. *Somaliland's Private Sector at a Crossroads: Political Economy and Policy Choices for Prosperity and Job Creation*. Washington, DC: World Bank.

Young, C. 2002. 'After the Fall: State Rehabilitation in Uganda'. In *Beyond State Crisis?: Post-Colonial Africa and Post-Soviet Eurasia in Comparative Perspective*, edited by M. Beissinger and C. Young. Washington, DC: Woodrow Wilson Center Press, pp. 445–463.

Zverev, A. 1996. 'Ethnic Conflicts in the Caucasus 1988–1994'. In *Contested Borders in the Caucasus*, edited by Coppieters, B. Brussels: VUB Brussels University Press.

List of Interviewees

Abkhaz *de facto* government officials, September 2015, Sukhumi.

Baratelia, Beslan (dean of the Economics Department at Sukhumi's Abkhaz State University), November 2012, Sukhumi.

Bardon, Antoine (president of the Chambre de commerce et d'industrie Française en Géorgie), November 2012, Tbilisi.

Gagulia, Gennady (head of the Chamber of Commerce and Industry; previously: former *de facto* prime minister of Abkhazia 1995–1997, and 2002–2003), November 2012, Sukhumi.

Inal-Ipa, Arda (member of the Centre for Humanitarian Programmes), October 2012, Sukhumi.

Stranichkin, Alexandr (*de facto* vice prime minister of Abkhazia), October 2012, Sukhumi.

Chapter 11

Patterns of Strategic Interaction in Self-Determination Disputes: A Comparative Analysis of East Timor, Aceh, and West Papua

Livia Rohrbach

Southeast Asia experienced a wave of democratization in the late 1990s, serving as a catalyst for many of the self-determination disputes in the region. The growing acceptance of the idea that providing a certain degree of self-rule to groups would help reduce social fragmentation, as well as growing secessionist tendencies, created a unique moment for positive change.[*] Most notably, a general shift of government strategy from military towards institutional solutions took place. This trend was also evident in Indonesia, where the government had faced secessionist challenges in different regions since its independence in 1949, most prominently in East Timor, Aceh, and Papua. All three of these self-determination disputes gained new momentum after the collapse of the authoritarian regime of President Suharto in 1998 with the democratization process opening a window of opportunity for the renegotiation of the *status quo*.

The aim of this chapter is to investigate the strategic interaction in the bargaining over self-determination between the Government of Indonesia and the separatist groups in East Timor, Aceh, and Papua. The strategies and tactics deployed vary greatly not only between the different key actors but also over time. In addition, the outcomes of the bargaining process could hardly be any more different. In the case of East Timor, the campaign for independence succeeded. The former Portuguese colony was annexed by Indonesia in 1975, but a long clandestine struggle and the backing of the international community finally secured a referendum leading to independent statehood in 2002. In the other two cases, the government offered special autonomy in an attempt to diffuse secessionist demands. In the case of Aceh, the region was granted wide-ranging autonomy as the outcome of a negotiated and internationally

---

[*] My research received financial support from the Swiss National Science Foundation (project number 166228).

mediated peace deal after an escalation of the dispute into full-scale civil war in the 2000s. In Papua, where the self-determination movement abandoned low-level insurgency in favour of nonviolent resistance, the government too granted special autonomy. In this case, however, the autonomy law can be considered a failure, not least because it failed to address the deep-rooted grievances, and the implementation of the provision can be considered flawed at best. The dispute is far from being settled, as demonstrated by the recent upsurge of violence and political tensions.

What explains these different outcomes? I argue that it is one often-neglected factor in particular that has a large impact on the bargaining process, both in terms of government's and group's strategy, and ultimately its outcome – the position of the international community. In cases where the government is open for (or has been coerced into) renegotiating the *status quo*, bargaining remains a strictly domestic matter. However, as soon as the government takes on an uncompromising stance and is willing to forcibly supress demands for greater self-determination or independence, access to and support of the international community becomes crucial. The government will try to restrict the group's access to the international arena and undermine attempts at lending credibility to its self-determination claim. The group, on the other hand, will try to bypass the uncompromising government and make a normative appeal to the international community with the aim of raising both domestic and international supports.

With this in mind, this chapter attempts to explain the variation in bargaining outcomes in East Timor, Aceh, and West Papua and illuminate the role of the international community in these particular cases. A specific focus is given to the use of and shift in strategies of tactics of the key actors involved. The ultimate goal of the comparative analysis is to provide an empirical example of self-determination disputes that take place on a strategic playing field linking the domestic and international levels and further illustrate the crucial role of the international community in such disputes. The main takeaway point from the comparison is that it is the position of the international community that not only ultimately determines the outcome of self-determination disputes but also influences the strategies and tactics employed by key actors – particularly in cases where the government is uncompromising. As will be demonstrated in the following section, all three of the separatist groups used international norms surrounding democracy and human rights that are explicitly linked to self-determination to promote their demands and seek legitimacy and support in both the domestic as well as the international spheres precisely because of the uncompromising position of the government. Despite trying to concede as little as possible, the Indonesian government is receptive to international pressure when reaching a certain tipping point, thus indicating a need for a better understanding of the impact of international regimes on self-determination disputes.

SELF-DETERMINATION DISPUTES – WHO GETS WHAT, WHEN, AND HOW?

Several general observations with regard to self-determination disputes are puzzling; first, even though governments do have incentives to make concessions, we often observe violent crackdown and the eruption of conflict. In the context of self-determination disputes, where less costly alternatives exist, the willingness of governments to pay the high price for prosecuting a civil war is particularly surprising (Walter 2009, 247). Second, the same state does sometimes behave differently towards different (or even the same!) groups (Grigoryan 2015, 171). There is a clear variation in accommodation, regarding both outcome and strategies, or in other words, what exactly groups get and how they get it.

One argument for why a state is reluctant to let a separatist group secede (or grant increased autonomy rights) is that a larger country may contain multiple internal nations and many potential secessionist regions. This argument is directly related to the reputational theory of conflict, which states that governments weigh their immediate interests and capabilities when assessing whether to grant certain concessions while at the same time carefully assessing the effects such a decision may have on future challenges and losses (Walter 2006). However, recent research has shown that specific scope conditions determine whether such 'ethnic dominoes' fall. For instance, concessions granted after fighting are more likely to trigger additional conflict, and groups with grievances against the state are more likely to turn to violent means (Bormann and Savun 2018). In general, recent findings point towards the context and issue sensitivities of state behaviour in self-determination disputes (Sambanis, Germann, and Schädel 2018). Another prominent argument is that internal diversity of self-determination groups is vital for understanding when and to what extent accommodation takes place and its consequences for conflict and mobilization. On the one hand, internal division creates uncertainty over what the population actually wants and, on the other hand, making credible commitments on the group's behalf becomes difficult (Cunningham 2014).

Regarding group strategies, separatist groups can employ a variety of tactics ranging from conventional politics to nonviolent tactics or, ultimately, to violence. They carefully weigh the costs of such approaches in anticipation of achieving success through them, which is in turn affected by structural features of the state and group (Cunningham 2013). Both violent and nonviolent tactics can be used to impose costs on the government; the key difference is that they require different types of mobilization. Whereas nonviolent tactics such as protests and boycotts require large numbers of people to participate in order to be effective, violent tactics such as suicide bombings can inflict large costs on the government without requiring a great number of participants (Chenoweth and Stephan 2011).

The Strategic Playing Field and the Role of the International Community

Self-determination disputes can be understood as a series of strategic interactions between the central government and a group demanding a change in the *status quo* (Cederman, Hug, and Wucherpfennig 2015). The strategic playing field consists of two levels – it links the domestic with the international level, where the ultimate decision regarding independent statehood is made. The process is dynamic in nature and both actors, the government and the group alike, attempt to secure the most favourable outcome. The government, thus, attempts to minimize the costs that an ongoing self-determination dispute puts on the state while at the same time conceding as little as possible. For the group, the main aim is to gain concessions related to self-determination, which can vary from protection of their identity (i.e., cultural rights) to outright independence (i.e., secession). If a group's aim is outright independence, the central government is very unlikely to let it secede. The reasons for this are manifold – the territory inhabited by the separatist group is in most cases of a certain value to the centre. It can be an economic asset, of political and symbolic value, or, indeed, both (Siroky, Mueller, and Hechter 2016). The group will try to coerce the government into negotiations, often using violent and nonviolent approaches in tandem. The home state, if entering negotiations, has a set of options, and one of them is offering autonomy concessions to the separatist group. Even though falling short of full independence, most groups will be willing to settle for an autonomy arrangement if their demands are addressed sufficiently (Sorens 2012).

If, however, the government is not willing to enter into negotiations, and the group is unable to coerce it, the role of the international community becomes crucial. The government will try to restrict the group's access to the international arena and undermine attempts at lending credibility to its self-determination claim. The group, on the other hand, will try to bypass the uncompromising government and make a normative appeal to the international community with the aim of raising both domestic and international supports. This chapter, thus, argues that in such situations, not only group's and government's strategy are interdependent, but strategies and tactics are also further tailored to regulate the access to the international arena and gaining international support. We are, thus, likely to experience no change in the *status quo* when a government successfully blocks a group's access to the international level and manages to delegitimize its cause, thus making it a purely domestic matter. If, however, the group manages to gain the support of the international community by making a credible claim for its right to self-determination, a change to the *status quo* becomes more likely.

Subnational Comparison – an Illustrative Empirical Example

To illustrate the use of different strategies and tactics in self-determination disputes and related outcomes, this chapter analyses the three most salient self-determination disputes in Indonesia over the period 1967 to 2018.[1] The period after Indonesia's independence up to 1967 was excluded since both Papua and East Timor only became part of Indonesia afterwards. In all three cases, the development of secessionist movements was a direct reaction to 'the way in which the New Order state under Suharto attempted to realise the nation-building goals of Indonesian nationalism [and were] fuelled by brutal and indiscriminate state violence' (Aspinall and Berger 2001, 1004). The cases of East Timor, Aceh, and Papua are thus utilized to conduct a sub-national within-nation comparison (Snyder 2001). The cases are well suited for the aim of this study for several reasons. First, although the three groups operate within the same state and thus interact with the same central governments, the strategies and tactics in the self-determination disputes differ between the three cases and through time, which makes it possible to shed light on the use of and shifts in strategy and tactics and their link to certain outcomes in detail. Second, the importance of the two-level playing field can be illustrated – access to and support of the international community varied greatly throughout time and between cases. Although not claiming generaliz-ability, the dynamics identified in these three cases are highly relevant for many other self-determination disputes.

SELF-DETERMINATION DISPUTES BETWEEN THE INDONESIAN GOVERNMENT AND GROUPS IN EAST TIMOR, ACEH, AND WEST PAPUA

In moments of transition, there may be a 'sudden reduction in the potential costs of secession, either through the weakening of central government authority or external support for the seceding community, [which] can generate secession attempts' (Bartkus 1999, 217). The democratization process following the resignation of President Suharto in 1998 led to a highly fragmented political landscape and served as a catalyst for the three self-determination disputes analysed in this section. The opening of the political space created opportunities for renegotiating the *status quo* in all three cases. However, the approaches and related outcomes varied greatly, and so did the role of the international community. The following subsections analyse the strategic interaction between the government and the three separatist groups in detail, giving special attention to the role of the international community.

East Timor

The island of Timor was partly a Portuguese (East) and Dutch (West) colony since the sixteenth century. As the Portuguese withdrew from East Timor in 1974, the Revolutionary Front for an Independent East Timor (Frente Revolucionária de Timor-Leste Independente [FRETILIN]) made a unilateral declaration of independence (UDI) in November 1975 and after only nine days the Indonesian military invaded East Timor, marking the beginning of the more than two-decade-long occupation (ICIET 2000, §5). In response to the invasion, the General Assembly of the United Nations (UN) deplored the unlawful integration of East Timor into Indonesia. In a General Assembly resolution (GA/RES/ 3485) from December 1975, it considered the military intervention to be a violation of Portuguese Timor's territorial integrity and recommended the Security Council to take urgent action to protect the inalienable right of the people of East Timor to self-determination and independence. Two Security Council resolutions (S/RES/389 [1976] and S/RES/384 [1975]) were issued shortly after with a similar wording and the additional appointment of a Special Representative, however, ending with the decision to 'remain seized of the situation'. Serious criticism has been raised regarding the support of Indonesia's occupation by Western countries and human rights abuses carried out by the Indonesian occupation forces. In particular, the United States and United Kingdom are believed to have supported the invasion by selling arms and providing military training to Indonesian government troops (SIPRI 2017). By the end of 1976, the regime had deployed around 35,000 soldiers to East Timor – the number of troops remained in that range during the whole period of Indonesian occupation (Ramos-Horta 1987, 107–108). In December 1978, the Indonesian military admitted to having interned around 60% of Timorese people. The internment of civilians and the dire conditions in the camps led to famine that was described being 'as bad as Biafra and potentially as dramatic as Cambodia' by the International Committee of the Red Cross (Defert 1992, 121). At the beginning of the occupation, FRETILIN was able to assemble 15,000 fighters, but by the end of 1980, only some 700 remained, operating as a guerilla force in the mountains (ISCITL 2006, 17).

In the early 1980s, FRETILIN began to regroup and reorganize. The restructuring and tactical change – the establishment of guerrilla units supported by a clandestine front – was to prove crucial for the group's survival and its ability to sustain its resistance to the Indonesian security forces, which continued to launch military offensives against FRETILIN, but were unable to eliminate it (Soares 2012, 78). What began as the formalization of the system of clandestine resistance networks (NUEP) was reorganized into political resistance under the banner of the National Council of Timorese Resistance (CNRT) in the late 1980s (Durand 2011). The movement received a massive boost in domestic and international popularity as a result of the gross human rights violations conducted by the Indonesian military in the early 1990s. The massacre at the Santa Cruz cemetery in 1991 focused world attention on the Timorese struggle for independence and pressure for a resolution of the East Timor question increased. For the regime, the East Timor issue continued to put a strain on its international relations and standing on human rights.

Several thousand Timorese gathered for the funeral of a young separatist and marched through the streets of Dili on 12 November 1991, waving flags on their way to the cemetery. The Indonesian army fired on the crowd, filmed by a journalist and later broadcasted on Western TV, provoking outrage and protest. This incident sparked a new wave of international support. When President Suharto resigned in 1998, Vice President Habibie took over the presidency and entered negotiations with the international community, in particular Portugal, as the legally administering authority of East Timor, and the UN, over a possible solution to the East Timor crisis. Habibie announced a popular consultation where the East Timorese get to choose between greater autonomy within Indonesia and a transition to independent statehood, leading to the establishment of the UN Mission in East Timor (UNAMET), which administered the referendum held in August 1999. The officials in Jakarta and important figures in the military were initially sceptical of the decision; however, they firmly believed that should the referendum take place, the people would vote in favour of special autonomy (Soares 2012, 80). However, East Timorese instead voted convincingly in favour of independence as opposed to special autonomy within Indonesia (78.5% voted against remaining a part of Indonesia). The referendum was followed by immediate acts of violence, wide-scale and gross human rights violations, and a scorched-earth campaign, leading to the destruction of 70% to 80% of the territory's infrastructure.[2] Indonesia, facing several secessionist challenges at that time, was mainly concerned with contagion and further disintegration. Thus, the motive behind the campaign was not simply revenge for the independence vote but was rather simultaneously meant to deter other self-determination movements from pressing for independence (IISS 1999, 1). An Australian-led multinational force was deployed shortly after to calm the situation and establish law and order, followed by the UN Transition Administration in East Timor (UNTAET), which held the legislative and executive powers until East Timor's independence in 2002. The UN intervention had a strong focus on transitional justice.[3]

Table 11.1 shows an overview of the differing strategies and tactics of the actors involved in the self-determination dispute and role of the international

Table 11.1. Strategies and Tactics in East Timor

				Example
International community	**Non-supportive**	US arms trade	X	United States and United Kingdom hold biggest share of Indonesia's arms imports in the 1980s/1990s
	Supportive	GA/RES/3485 (1975); S/RES/384 (1975); S/RES/389 (1976)	X	Condemnation of the violation of the territorial integration of East Timor and reassurance of the right to self-determination and independence. Deployment of Special Representative
		Portugal's international lobbying		Portugal's persistent lobbying attempts
		Australian policy shift		'Howard letter' – major shift in Australian policy, recommendation of independence referendum
		UNAMET, UNTAET, UNMISET, UNOTIL		UNAMET administered referendum, UNTAET Transition Administration 1999–2002, Mission of Support (UNMISET), and UN Office in Timor-Leste (UNOTIL)

				Example
Government strategy	**Discursive engagement**			
	Executive and legal instruments	Forceful repression	X	Reacts to UDI with invasion and forceful repression during occupation (1975–1999)
		Referendum	X	International pressure facilitates the popular consultation (1999) which leads to independence

				Example
Group strategy	**Coercion**	Conventional politics	X	East Timor popular consultation 1999 (78.50% voted against the remaining part of Indonesia)
		Nonviolent	X	Political resistance under the banner of the National Council of Timorese Resistance (CNRT)
		Violent	X	FRETILIN insurgency, decreasing over time (reorganization from relatively well-trained troops in the 1970s to a clandestine network in the 1980s)
	Normative appeal	Decolonization	X	UDI in 1975 after former colonial power Portugal withdraws, followed by (internationally never recognized) Indonesian occupation
		Human rights	X	Gross human rights abuses and extremely high death toll
		Earned sovereignty Freedom to choose		

community in East Timor. During the first years of Indonesian occupation, the group pursued primarily violent tactics. FRETILIN managed to sustain a strong resistance and established parallel governance structures through a clandestine network; however, it did not possess the military capacity to expel Indonesia from its territory. Weakened by the successful counterinsurgency strategies of the Tentara Nasional Indonesia (TNI), it shifted tactics and started to coordinate political actions under the banner of the CNRT. It appealed normatively to the international and domestic audiences based on arguments of a remedial right to secession (mainly referring to the gross human rights violations[4] and the unlawful annexation) in an attempt to lend its cause the necessary legitimacy on the international stage. Portugal's lobbying activities, which started bearing fruits in the late 1990s, as well as the outrage caused by the gross human rights violations committed by the regime (the Santa Cruz massacre being a turning point) increased international pressure for finding a solution to the East Timor question. A further important factor was a major shift in Australian policy (previously the Australian government held close relations with Jakarta) in late 1998 when the then Prime Minister John Howard drafted a letter (later to be known as the 'Howard Letter') supporting the idea of autonomy up to an independence referendum (Connery 2010, 20).

Aceh

Aceh has a long history of rebellion against the central government in Jakarta. The first rebellion after Indonesia's independence occurred in 1953, when a violent conflict between the movement called Darul Islam and government forces erupted (ICG 2001b, 3). The outcome was that Aceh was granted the status of a special region with fairly broad self-governance provisions, especially regarding religion and education. The promise of special autonomy, however, turned out to be an empty one. The launch of the separatist movement Gerakan Aceh Merdeka (GAM, Free Aceh Movement), its UDI, and first separatist insurgency in 1976 can be seen as a direct reaction to the failure of the regime to honour the Darul Islam agreement and the relentless centralization efforts and cultural assimilation project, which rendered Aceh's special status meaningless over time. Undoubtedly, the economic exploitation further fuelled grievances in the Acehnese population – Aceh is the site of lucrative national oil and gas assets, yet most of the profits were channelled out of Aceh towards the elites in Jakarta.

From 1986 onward, GAM recruited mainly in rural areas and sent recruits to Libya for paramilitary training. With the return of the Libyan-trained fighters, GAM expanded its territorial control, and estimates of active members reached 200–750 (Ross 2005, 36), and launched its second insurgency in 1989. The regime reacted to the separatist challenge by deploying large numbers of security forces (ICG 2001b, 3), launching counterinsurgency campaigns and transforming the region into a military operations area (Daerah Operasi Militer, DOM) for the decade to come. The number of troops is estimated at around 12,000 after the declaration of DOM (Sukma 2004, 8), twice as many as previously. Accompanied by massive human rights violations, this period fuelled anger in the Acehnese community and alienated them further from the Indonesian government (Miller 2012, 36–39).

In 1999, the conflict escalated once again. Aceh was promised a referendum similar to the one in East Timor; when this was not delivered, it served as a powerful catalyst for the outbreak of the most intense phase of the conflict. When the authoritarian regime collapsed and the special military operations area was lifted in 1999, GAM gained unprecedented strength and transformed into a popular movement with broad support, not least because of the gross human rights violations conducted in the previous decade by the TNI and its militias. It increased its active membership numbers to approximately 15,000–27,000 (Ross 2005, 36) and controlled about 80% of the territory (ICG 2001b, 5). It even managed to establish parallel government structures (Schulze 2007, 81). Additionally, huge rallies calling for an independence referendum took place, mobilizing up to 1 million people (Aspinall 2009, 131). International focus shifted and the pressure to end the conflict increased as the war intensified. The government at the time was the first to ever initiate peace talks with GAM, mediated by the Henry Dunant Centre, a Swiss nongovernmental organization, which culminated in a ceasefire agreement in 2000.

The first post-Suharto concessions came in the form of the Law No. 44/1999, which formally recognized the 'Special Status of the Special Province of Aceh' in the areas of religion, education, and customary law. After came the Law No. 18/2001, which changed Aceh's name officially into Nanggroe Aceh Darussalam (NAD) and included significant political, economic, and legal concessions, inter alia the return of most of its natural resource wealth, the right to hold direct democratic local elections, and the establishment of new institutions to further the expansion of Islamic law (Miller 2012, 40–50). Under President Megawati (2001–2004), however, maintaining national unity was announced to be the top priority (Miller 2008, 105) and the government's position shifted from accommodative to non-accommodative, rendering the autonomy provisions meaningless. The breakdown of the ceasefire agreement soon after it was reached in 2002 led the government to declare martial law in Aceh and exit peace talks. By mid-2002, the total number of security forces present in Aceh was 34,000 – consisting of 21,000 TNI and 12,000 police personnel – and by mid-2003, the number had grown to 50,000 (Ross 2005, 50). The military operations severely weakened

GAM over time and by the end of 2002 their numbers had already dropped by half (Sukma 2004, 16), and they admitted to having lost up to 30% to 40% of the territory previously under their control (ICG 2002, 2).

After Yudhoyono became president in 2004, the government's strategy shifted once again – he emphasized a non-military approach to Aceh (Aspinall and Crouch 2003). International pressure to find a negotiated solution to the conflict was still high, and the internationally mediated peace talks finally led to the signing of the Helsinki peace agreement of 2005. The resulting Law No. 11 of 2006 on the Governing of Aceh conferred unprecedented powers of self-governance to Aceh and granted far more autonomy than what Indonesia's other provinces enjoy. Most importantly, direct democratic local elections were introduced, independent candidates were allowed to run for office, and Aceh-based political parties were permitted to form. Further, most revenues from resources were returned to the region (Miller 2012, 40–50). Reaching an agreement was only possible because both sides made major concessions, one of them being that GAM ultimately dropped its claim for independence.

Table 11.2 shows an overview of the strategies and tactics of the actors involved in the self-determination dispute and the role of international actors in Aceh. The government's double standards (granting autonomy while at the same time increasing centralization and assimilation efforts) created strong feelings of resentment within the Acehnese community and ultimately triggered violent insurgencies. The government strategy after the fall of the authoritarian regime shifted between accommodation and repression, parallel with changes in the administration in the turbulent early phase of democratic transition (Fujikawa 2017). The government entered internationally mediated negotiations with the group at several points and offered autonomy concessions. However, the reason why no final settlement was reached before 2005 can be traced back to major credibility problems. According to a report by the International Crisis Group, the problem with the concessions was that 'the credibility of the central government in Aceh is close to zero, amongst all sections of the population. Given a history of promises made and broken since the 1950s, even the minority of Acehnese who see autonomy as the best solution have little trust in Jakarta's good faith' (ICG 2001a, 19). The heavy military pressure on the province and the failure to prosecute the human rights abuses carried out by the TNI further hurt the credibility of the government (Aspinall and Crouch 2003). Despite having a long history of violent resistance to Indonesian rule, GAM also made use of nonviolent tactics as well as normative appeals to the domestic as well as the international community. The appeal was based on references to remedial rights, especially relating to the gross human rights violations during and after the authoritarian regime and systematic violations of agreements of self-government. As a direct consequence, popular support increased, which facilitated the expansion of tactics from the battlefield to the political (and international) sphere.

Table 11.2. Strategies and Tactics in Aceh

				Example
International community	Non-supportive	No support for independence	X	International community reaffirms Indonesia's right to territorial integrity and no support for independence claim
	Supportive	Mediation/ dialogue	X	Finding solution to conflict through internationally mediated dialogue

				Example
Government strategy	Discursive engagement	Territorial integrity and stability	X	Unity of the unitary Republic of Indonesia as top priority
	Executive and legal instruments	Special autonomy	X	Law 18/2001 on Special Autonomy for NAD; Law No. 6/2006 on the Governing of Aceh
		Forceful repression	X	Counterinsurgency campaigns and military operations area (martial law)

				Example
Group strategy	Coercion	Conventional politics		
		Nonviolent	X	Transformation into popular movement in transition period, huge rallies for independence
		Violent	X	GAM insurgencies
	Normative appeal	Decolonization Human rights	X	Cultural assimilation and gross human rights violations
		Earned sovereignty	X	Control 80% of territory, parallel government structures

GAM had to come to realize, after all, that independence was not a viable option. Since the movement's leaders went into exile in 1979, they had lobbied the international community to pressure Indonesia into letting Aceh secede. This strategy remained unsuccessful, which became obvious with the collapse of the ceasefire agreement in 2002 when not a single state supported GAM's independence claim. There was no international support for Acehnese independence; quite to the contrary, state governments reaffirmed Indonesia's right to protect its unity and territorial integrity. After the international community effectively abandoned GAM, its leaders shifted strategy. They were now keen on 'going political' and reformulated their demands, effectively demanding self-government. It was in the aftermath of the devastating tsunami when talks resumed – after a crucial shift in paradigm because of GAM's essentially complete military defeat and absence of international support for independence. They were now willing to consider what Indonesia had to offer rather than hoping for international backing of independence (Schulze 2007, 94–95).

West Papua

The New York Agreement of 1963 sealed West Papua's integration into the Indonesian Republic after being under Dutch colonial rule. The agreement stipulated that a plebiscite should be held to determine whether West Papua wanted to remain with Indonesia or establish an independent state. In the end, the people of West Papua voted unanimously in favour of integration with Indonesia in the highly contested Act of Free Choice, held in 1969. Critics argue that the outcome was heavily influenced by months of military intimidation and repression prior to the plebiscite, where approximately 1,000 handpicked West Papuan leaders cast votes. Unsurprisingly, many question the legitimacy of the act, including international observers present at the time (ICG 2006, 3). A UDI followed in 1971, in which the Republic of West Papua was proclaimed and the later banned Morning Star Flag was made the national symbol. Similar to Aceh and East Timor, the security approach dominated the government's strategy towards the separatist group in West Papua ever since its integration into Indonesia (Singh 2012, 59). There was consistent resistance to Indonesian rule, but a strong, armed movement never emerged. The group named Organisasi Papua Merdeka (OPM, Free Papua Organization) was founded in 1965 and mounted sporadic attacks on soldiers and government properties (ICG 2006, 4). Further hindering the transformation into a strong movement was internal factionalism – the group was divided among different scattered factions. Despite its relative weakness, it was a symbol of consistent resistance to Indonesian rule and thus a threat to the project of national unity (Bertrand 2014, 180). This led the government to initiate disproportionate and indiscriminate military operations to weed out and eliminate the OPM.

In the wake of the transition towards democracy and the promises of a referendum in East Timor, the people of West Papua began to mobilize too. West Papuan leaders have adopted nonviolence as their main political strategy and the moderates among the group seized the opportunity and sought to negotiate a compromise on autonomy (Bertrand 2014, 181). Mobilization remained mostly peaceful and brought about new representative institutions beyond the state – two large congresses were organized, a list of demands formulated, and representatives elected in the form of the Presidium Dewan Papua (Papuan Congress). These efforts were backed by broad popular support; however, international support remained absent. Similar to Aceh, a law on Special Autonomy for Papua (Law no. 21, 2001) was introduced. The government anticipated that granting special autonomy to West Papua would prevent it from becoming the next East Timor or spiralling out of control like the then-failing peace process in Aceh. The law provided wide-ranging autonomy and created a special assembly, the Papuan People's Assembly (Majelis Rayak Papua, MRP), to represent indigenous peoples in West Papua and include members of all sectors of society. Besides promoting and protecting the rights and customs of indigenous Papuan peoples, the MRP powers were limited to consultation, since the legislative powers resided with the provincial legislature (Dewan Perwakilan Daerah Papua) (Bertrand 2014, 179–182).

Most of the provisions of the special autonomy law for West Papua were not implemented. A lack of consensus within the Indonesian government and the fear that any concession would strengthen the demand for independence are part of the reason for the protracted implementation. The divide-and-rule strategy adopted by this administration – West Papua was divided into three provinces without prior consultation – severely weakened the group, and at the same time international pressure to find a solution to the West Papua question remained virtually absent (Bertrand 2014). The Indonesian military still had a very influential role to play in West Papua, where it effectively ran a parallel governance system to the civilian administration (Mietzner 2013, 108) and still applied highly repressive measures (Bertrand 2014, 183).

Resistance to Indonesian rule in West Papua was an intricate interplay of political opportunity and capacity to mobilized and the extent of state repression. The transition away from violent resistance was anything but linear, but as MacLeod (2015, 46) puts it: 'The ideology, strategy and tactics of violent resistance are being displaced by other theories of change that favour civil resistance, diplomacy, civilian-based media activism and transnational advocacy'. Examples are the Papua Peace Network (Jaringan Damai Papua), a network of representatives from different groups who support political dialogue between Jakarta and West Papua, and The International Parliamentarians for West Papua, founded by independence leader Benny Wenda.

The situation in West Papua remains unchanged to date – the provisions of the special autonomy law are poorly implemented and the continued Indonesian transmigration programme,[5] Jakarta's policy to reduce the overcrowding population in Java and to populate remote islands fuels local conflicts between the native population and immigrants. In recent years, calls for independence have gained new momentum. In September 2017, the United Liberation Movement for West Papua collected 1.8 million signatures throughout the two provinces in Papua for an independence petition and delivered it to the UN, where it was rebuffed. The recent upsurge of violence and political tensions is a clear indication that the dispute in West Papua is far from being resolved.[6]

Table 11.3 shows an overview of the strategies and tactics of the actors involved in the self-determination dispute and the role of international actors

Table 11.3. Strategies and Tactics in West Papua

				Example
International community	Non-supportive	UN Special Committee on Decolonization	X	UN Special Committee on Decolonization refuses to accept petition, arguing West Papua's cause was outside its mandate
	Supportive			

				Example
Government strategy	Discursive engagement	Territorial integrity and stability	X	Unity of the unitary Republic of Indonesia as top priority
	Executive and legal instruments	Forceful repression	X	Repression and closing off from outside scrutiny
		Modernization	X	Promoting large-scale development projects and transmigration
		Special autonomy	X	Law 21/2001 on Special Autonomy for the Papua Province

				Example
Group strategy	Coercion	Conventional politics		
		Nonviolent	X	Nonviolence as main tactic (Papuan Congress, Papua Peace Network)
		Violent	X	OPM low-level insurgency (during authoritarian period and recent upsurge of violence)
	Normative appeal	Decolonization	X	Review of Act of Free Choice 1969 and independence petition handed over to UN Special Committee on Decolonization and UN High Commissioner for Human Rights
		Human rights	X	Gross human rights violations, high civilian death toll, cultural assimilation
		Earned sovereignty		

in West Papua. The government's strategies since 1963 consist of three main components: repression, including the widespread use of targeted or indiscriminate torture; international isolation by closing West Papua off from the outside world and public scrutiny; and the transmigration programme under the banner of modernization accompanied by large-scale development projects that did in effect not benefit ordinary Papuans (MacLeod 2015, 50). The granting of special autonomy, which was effectively aimed at diffusing the demands for independence, ultimately backfired: fuelled by the discontent over the protracted implementation process (autonomy was never fully implemented), West Papuan mobilization gained new momentum.

Most notable is the transition of the self-determination movement in West Papua from violent to predominately nonviolent resistance. A factor complicating the coordinated action of the movement is its divide among different scattered factions inside and outside West Papua. Its organizational capacity is further weakened by the government's efforts at closing it off from the outside world. The separatist movement relies on normative arguments, predominantly centred around attempts to lobby foreign countries and international organizations into reviewing the Act of Free Choice from 1969, which it has always perceived as a historic wrong. In 2017, Papuan activists handed over a petition to the UN, demanding an investigation into human rights abuses and an internationally supervised vote on the question of independence. The UN Special Committee on Decolonization refused to accept the petition, arguing that West Papua's cause was outside the committee's mandate, which extends only to seventeen states identified by the UN as 'non-self-governing territories', and it reaffirmed Indonesia's sovereignty over West Papua.[7] In a new attempt, the petition was delivered to the UN High Commissioner for Human Rights, Michelle Bachelet, in January 2019.[8]

CONCLUSION

This chapter has focused on the dynamics of the strategic interaction between the government of Indonesia and three separatist groups in East Timor, Aceh, and West Papua. The ultimate aim was to broaden our understanding of the underlying logic of pursuing, combining, and shifting both strategies and tactics in self-determination disputes. The analysis suggested that domestic determinants only partly explain the strategies and tactics deployed by key actors involved in self-determination disputes. A focus on both domestic and international determinants is needed in order to not just understand the choice of strategy but also ultimately understand the outcome of self-determination disputes.

Table 11.4 provides an overview of the strategies and tactics deployed in the three cases. The comparative analysis revealed that the common government

Table 11.4. Strategies and Tactics in East Timor, Aceh, and West Papua

			East Timor	Aceh	West Papua
International community	Non-supportive	Arms trade	X		
		Non-recognition of independence claim		X	
		UN Special Committee on Decolonization			X
	Supportive	International lobbying	X		
		UN intervention	X		
		Mediation		X	
Government strategy	Discursive engagement	Territorial integrity and stability		X	X
	Executive and legal instruments	Forceful repression	X	X	X
		Autonomy (failure)			X
		Autonomy (success)		X	
		Independence referendum	X		
Group strategy	Coercion	Conventional politics	X		
		Nonviolent	X	X	X
		Violent	X	X	X
	Normative appeal	Decolonization	X		X
		Human rights	X	X	X
		Earned sovereignty		X	X

strategy during the authoritarian period towards all three separatist movements was characterized by heavy repression, counterinsurgency operations, and gross human rights abuses. The government took an uncompromising stance throughout, and the groups lacked the capabilities to coerce it into negotiations. In the wake of the democratic transition, however, the successive governments have tried a wide range of approaches including repression, offers of autonomy, peace talks, and a combination of these. It also engaged discursively with the separatist challenges, mainly by referring to its right to territorial integrity and strongly defending its national unity. Critical was the loss of East Timor, which at the same time heightened fears of disintegration and fuelled nationalist mobilization in Aceh and West Papua. Hoping to appease these two provinces and diffuse calls for independence, the government issued autonomy laws, which given the circumstances appeared entirely irrelevant to the separatist.

In all three cases, the separatist movements made use of various coercive tactics, both violent and nonviolent, and normative appeals to legitimize their cause. Ultimately, the position of the international community has proven vital for understanding the different outcomes. In the case of East Timor, the group was most efficient at securing international support, which ultimately paved the way for independence. The right of East Timor to self-determination under international law was relatively undisputed. The legal right of secession – even in situations of gross human rights abuses – remains highly contentious, except in the colonial context, where there exists a sufficient level of international consensus on the rules governing the exercise of self-determination (Drew 2001, 656–657). This raises the question of how much of the outcome was simply determined by colonial history. It certainly played an important role; however, the choice of strategies mattered too. The movement was more successful at relating its cause to the norms of international society around democracy and human rights, linked explicitly to the right to self-determination. International support arose in response to the brutal repression of the East Timorese and the growing common understanding of democratic sovereignty as a more legitimate source of authority. The case of Aceh is qualitatively different – Aceh, which was a Dutch colony like the rest of Indonesia, had a more difficult stance convincing the international community of the legality of its claim (Stanton 2016, 150) – the movement predominantly referred to the protection of religious rights and an Acehnese territorial identity. Here, the international community played a major role in reaching an agreement for a protracted and long-term conflict, but at no point supported the group's fundamental independence claim. In the case of West Papua, self-determination demands have been suppressed and only limited concessions have been made. The resistance to Indonesian rule has been predominantly nonviolent in West Papua – the OPM never constituted an armed threat to the state as opposed to GAM in Aceh. The ubiquitous presence of the Indonesian security apparatus and the government's successful attempt at closing it off from international scrutiny has kept the violence and exploitation largely hidden from the outside world. Disunity in the movement further hampered progress towards self-rule – the factionalism among various resistance organizations have undoubtedly hindered successful mobilization (cf. Cunningham 2014). Taken together, these factors help explain how West Papuan activists failed at securing the support of the international community, exemplified by the non-acceptance of the petition by the UN Special Committee on Decolonization.

Self-determination disputes are complex and have many layers, and the strategic behaviour of the actors involved as well as the contextual and historical contingencies of individual cases will continue to challenge scholars and practitioners in search for explanations and best practices. The findings presented here contribute to a better understanding of dynamics of such processes and demonstrate how a focus solely on domestic determinants is insufficient when attempting to explain the outcome of such disputes. Ultimately, self-determination disputes are carried out on a strategic playing field linking the domestic with the international sphere.

NOTES

1. Secessionist tendencies, to varying degrees, can be found in Central and South Sulawesi, Riau, across the three provinces of Kalimantan, in North and South Maluku, throughout Nusa Tenggara, and even in Java.

2. For a detailed report on the events in the aftermath of the referendum, see KPP-HAM (2000).

3. Commission for Reception, Truth and Reconciliation (CAVR); East Timor trials at the Indonesian ad hoc Human Rights Court in Jakarta, Joint Commission for Truth and Friendship.

4. The Commission for Reception, Truth and Reconciliation in East Timor estimated the total number of conflict-related deaths to lie between approximately 100,000 and 200,000 (CAVR 2005).

5. See McGibbon (2004), for a thorough analysis of the transmigration programme and its impacts.

6. See Kingsbury (2019).

7. See Doherty and Lamb (2017).

8. See Miles and Da Costa (2019).

REFERENCES

Aspinall, Edward. 2009. *Islam and Nation: Separatist Rebellion in Aceh, Indonesia*. Stanford: Stanford University Press.

Aspinall, Edward, and Harold A. Crouch. 2003. *The Acehnese Peace Process: Why It Failed*. Washington, DC: East-West Center.

Aspinall, Edward, and Mark T. Berger. 2001. 'The Break-Up of Indonesia? Nationalisms after Decolonisation and the Limits of the Nation-State in Post-Cold War Southeast Asia'. *Third World Quarterly* 22(6): 1003–1024.

Bartkus, Viva O. 1999. *The Dynamics of Secession*. Cambridge: Cambridge University Press.

Bertrand, Jacques. 2014. 'Autonomy and Stability: The Perils of Implementation and "Divide-and-Rule" Tactics in Papua, Indonesia'. *Nationalism and Ethnic Politics* 20(2): 174–199.

Bormann, Nils C., and Burcu Savun. 2018. 'Reputation, Concessions, and Territorial Civil War: Do Ethnic Dominoes Fall, or Don't They?' *Journal of Peace Research* 55(5): 671–686.

CAVR (Commission for Reception Truth and Reconciliation in Timor-Leste). 2005. 'Chega! (Enough!): The Report of the Commission for Reception, Truth and Reconciliation Timor-Leste'. Dili: CAVR.

Cederman, Lars-Erik, Simon Hug, and Julian Wucherpfennig. 2015. *Autonomy, Secession and Conflict: A Strategic Model*. Barcelona: ENCoReConference.

Chenoweth, Erica, and Maria J. Stephan. 2011. *Why Civil Resistance Works: The Strategic Logic of Nonviolent Conflict*. New York: Columbia University Press.

Connery, David. 2010. *Crisis Policymaking: Australia and the East Timor Crisis of 1999*. Canberra: ANU E Press.

Cunningham, Kathleen G. 2013. 'Understanding Strategic Choice: The Determinants of Civil War and Nonviolent Campaign in Self-Determination Disputes'. *Journal of Peace Research* 50(3): 291–304.

Cunningham, Kathleen G. 2014. *Inside the Politics of Self-Determination*. New York: Oxford University Press.

Defert, Gabriel. 1992. *Timor-Est, Le Génocide Oublié: Droit d'un Peuple et Raisons d'Etats*. Paris: L'Harmattan.

Doherty, Ben, and Kate Lamb. 30 September 2017. 'West Papua Independence Petition Is Rebuffed at UN'. *The Guardian*. https://www.theguardian.com/world/2017/sep/30/west-papua-independence-petition-is-rebuffed-at-un.

Drew, Catriona. 2001. 'The East Timor Story: International Law on Trial'. *European Journal of International Law* 12(4): 651–684.

Durand, Frédéric. 2011. 'Three Centuries of Violence and Struggle in East Timor (1726–2008)'. In *Online Encyclopedia of Mass Violence*. Paris: SciencesPo.

Fujikawa, Kentaro. 2017. 'Drifting between Accommodation and Repression: Explaining Indonesia's Policies toward Its Separatists'. *Pacific Review* 30(5): 655–673.

Grigoryan, Arman. 2015. 'Concessions or Coercion? How Governments Respond to Restive Ethnic Minorities'. *International Security* 39(4): 170–207.

ICG (International Crisis Group). 2001a. *Aceh: Can Autonomy Stem the Conflict?* Jakarta/Brussels: International Crisis Group.

ICG. 2001b. *Aceh: Why Military Force Won't Bring Lasting Peace*. Jakarta/Brussels: International Crisis Group.

ICG. 2002. *Aceh: A Slim Chance for Peace*. Jakarta/Brussels: International Crisis Group.

ICG. 2006. *Papua: Answers to Frequently Asked Questions*. Jakarta/Brussels: International Crisis Group.

ICIET (International Commission of Inquiry on East Timor). 2000. 'Report of the International Commission of Inquiry on East Timor to the Secretary-General'. New York: ICIET.

IISS (The International Institute for Strategic Studies). 1999. 'The East Timor Crisis: A Disaster for Indonesia'. *Strategic Comments* 5(8): 1–2.

ISCITL (Independent Special Commission of Inquiry for Timor-Leste). 2006. 'Report of the United Nations Independent Special Commission of Inquiry for Timor-Leste'. Geneva: ISCITL.

Kingsbury, Damien. 2019. 'War "declared" in West Papua'. Accessed 5 April 2019. https://blogs.deakin.edu.au/deakin-speaking/2019/02/03/war-declared-in-west-papua/.

KPP-HAM (National Commission of Inquiry on Human Rights Violations in East Timor). 2000. 'KPP-HAM Executive Summary Report on the Investigation of Human Rights Violations in East Timor'. Jakarta: KPP-HAM.

MacLeod, Jason. 2015. 'From the Mountains and Jungles to the Villages and Streets: Transition from Violent to Nonviolent Resistance in West Papua'. In *Civil Resistance and Conflict Transformation: Transitions from Armed to Nonviolent Struggle*, edited by Véronique Dudouet. London: Routledge, pp. 45–76.

McGibbon, Rodd. 2004. *Plural Society in Peril: Migration, Economic Change, and the Papua Conflict*. Washington, DC: East-West Center.

Mietzner, Marcus. 2013. 'Veto Player No More? The Declining Political Influence of the Military in Postauthoritarian Indonesia'. In *Democracy and Islam in Indonesia*, edited by Mirjam Künkler and Alfred C. Stepan. New York: Columbia University Press, pp. 89–108.

Miles, Tom, and Augustinus Beo Da Costa. 27 January 2019. 'West Papuan Separatist Hand Petition to U.N. Human Rights Chief'. *Reuters*. https://www.reuters.com/article/us-indonesia-papua-un/west-papuan-separatists-hand-petition-to-u-n-human-rights-chief-idUSKCN1PL0K7.

Miller, Michelle Ann. 2008. *Rebellion and Reform in Indonesia, Jakarta's Security and Autonomy Policies in Aceh*. Abingdon: Routledge.

Miller, Michelle Ann.2012. 'Self-Governance as a Framework for Conflict Resolution in Aceh'. In *Autonomy and Armed Separatism in South and Southeast Asia*, edited by Michelle Ann Miller. Singapore: Institute of Southeast Asian Studies, pp. 36–58.

Ramos-Horta, Jose. 1987. *Funu: The Unfinished Saga of East Timor*. Trenton, NJ: Red Sea Press.

Ross, Michael L. 2005. 'Resources and Rebellion in Aceh, Indonesia'. In *Understanding Civil War: Evidence and Analysis*, edited by Paul Collier and Nicholas Sambanis. Washington, DC: World Bank, pp. 35–58.

Sambanis, Nicholas, Micha Germann, and Andreas Schädel. 2018. 'SDM: A New Data Set on Self-Determination Movements with an Application to the Reputational Theory of Conflict'. *Journal of Conflict Resolution* 62(3): 656–686.

Schulze, Kirsten E. 2007. 'From the Battlefield to the Negotiating Table: GAM and the Indonesian Government 1999–2005'. *Asian Security* 3(2): 80–98.

Singh, Bilveer. 2012. 'Autonomy and Armed Separatism in Papua: Why the Cendrawasih Continues to Fear the Garuda'. In *Autonomy and Armed Separatism in South and Southeast Asia*, edited by Michelle Ann Miller. Singapore: Institute of Southeast Asian Studies, pp. 59–76.

SIPRI (Stockholm International Peace Research Institute). 2017. 'SIPRI Arms Transfers Database'. Accessed 31 January 2019. https://www.sipri.org/databases/armstransfers.

Siroky, David S., Sean Mueller, and Michael Hechter. 2016. 'Center-Periphery Bargaining in the Age of Democracy'. *Swiss Political Science Review* 22(4): 439–453.

Snyder, Richard. 2001. 'Scaling Down: The Subnational Comparative Method'. *Studies in Comparative International Development* 36(1): 93–110.

Soares, Adérito de Jesus. 2012. 'The Parallels and the Paradox of Timor-Leste and Western Sahara'. In *Autonomy and Armed Separatism in South and Southeast Asia*, edited by Michelle Ann Miller. Singapore: Institute of Southeast Asian Studies, pp. 77–92.

Sorens, Jason. 2012. *Secessionism: Identity, Interest, and Strategy*. Montreal: McGill-Queen's University Press.

Stanton, Jessica. 2016. *Violence and Restraint in Civil War: Civilian Targeting in the Shadow of International Law*. Cambridge: Cambridge University Press.

Sukma, Rizal. 2004. 'Security Operations in Aceh: Goals, Consequences and Lessons'. Washington, DC: East-West Center.

Walter, Barbara F. 2006. 'Building Reputation: Why Governments Fight Some Separatists but Not Others'. *American Journal of Political Science* 50(2): 313–330.

Walter, Barbara F.2009. 'Bargaining Failures and Civil War'. *Annual Review of Political Science* 12(1): 243–261.

Conclusion

Ryan D. Griffiths and Diego Muro

The strategic interaction between secessionist movements and sovereign states is an important object of study. Even in the best of circumstances, the breaking of states creates turmoil. Social polarization follows and populations are sundered when new borders are established. In most instances the population of the breakaway region is divided on the matter of secession, and in some cases the resulting tensions lead to violence if not full-blown civil war. There are over sixty contemporary independence movements and many more potential movements. It is vital that we obtain a clearer understanding of both their strategies and the counterstrategies of the states that oppose them.

The goal of this volume was to break new ground in the study of secession and counter-secession. We began by outlining the strategic playing field between these actors, and describing the process by which aspiring nations become recognized sovereign states. A set of specialists then provided a unique perspective on these dynamics in the chapters that followed. Part I provided a set of high-level conceptual/theoretical studies. Aleksandar Pavković examined the normative language used in declarations of independence, and, in a related manner, Argyro Kartsonaki investigated the utility of using remedial language in unilateral declarations of independence (UDIs). Next, a set of authors explored the counter-secession strategies of states; Eiki Berg and Scott Pegg looked at how home states attempt to block the independence bids of internal, *de facto* states; Ahsan Butt researched the reasons why governments will allow tensions to escalate into violence; and Rivka Weill considered the ways in which democracies use the legal, constitutional structure of the state to thwart secessionist efforts.

Part II zoomed in for a closer inspection of a set of secessionist movements and issues. Faruk Aksoy and Melike Ayşe Kocacık-Şenol scrutinized the effects of democratic institutions on secessionist methods and outcomes.

Bart Maddens et al. probed the effects of the European Union (EU) on the discourse of secessionist parties. André Lecours tracked the secessionist methods of the Parti Québécois during its two independence referenda in the final decades of the twentieth century. Karlo Basta evaluated the important role of business elites in the dynamics of secession. Giulia Prelz Oltramonti appraised the efficaciousness of the viability argument for winning international support. Finally, Livia Rohrbach provided a more controlled multicase comparison in the context of Indonesia and its internal movements. All of these chapters presented important and original contributions on the topic.

Our goal is this concluding chapter is to bring these individual studies together and draw out the broader themes. A good place to start is by recognizing the diversity of settings in which secessionism plays out, and, laterally, the diversity in the resulting research. Broadly speaking, the research on secessionism can be broken up into three subareas. These include the work on *de facto* states, the research on secessionist political parties, and the study of secessionist civil war. In their own way, chapters 3–5 are examples of these subareas. In each case, the authors analyze what states do to counter secession, but the methods vary considerably. For Berg and Pegg, home states counter *de facto*, breakaway states by trying to isolate and suffocate them. For Weill, democratic governments use legal/constitutional methods to block secessionist parties. For Butt, states faced with external security concerns may resort to violence. Each of these chapters represents a perspective on what states do to counter secession given their circumstances. In general terms, they are talking about the same phenomena; it is in the details regarding tactics and methods that they differ. In other words, Georgia, Spain, and India (all countries under observation by these authors) are united by the fact that they face formidable secessionist movements that aspire to join the United Nations (UN) as a full member, even if their settings encourage different counter-secession strategies.

The remaining chapters fall within and cut across these subareas. The chapters by both Lecours and Maddens et al. are focused on the strategies of secessionist political parties in advanced democracies. Likewise, Oltramonti is focused on secessionist methods of *de facto* states. But the remaining chapters transcend these divides. Aksoy and Kocacık-Şenol provided a relatively transversal analysis by showing how secessionist methods—be they institutional, extra-institutional, or violent—are related to the democratic structure of the state. Their larger point is that institutions shape the strategic playing field. Similarly, the remaining chapters contribute to the broader literature and demonstrate the ways in which the research on secession can work across these subareas.

We contend that there is much to be gained by integrating these different literatures. *De facto* states are just secessionist movements that have successfully (usually with outside help) split off from the larger state. They are examples of one path for secessionist movements where freedom has been gained but sovereign recognition remains elusive. The study of these entities is related to the work on secessionist civil war, because they are almost always born from conflict. However, as the case of Tamil Eelam demonstrated, they sometimes end in conflict. Further research should study the two subareas—civil war and *de facto* states—as a continuous process. How do the strategies of secessionists and states vary in accordance with the level of connectedness? What is at stake in winning *de facto* independence if it is not recognized, given that such cases can endure for long periods? The relationship between the work on secessionist political parties and civil war is perhaps even more continuous. As Rohrbach showed, weak democracies like Indonesia can oscillate between institutional and military options when responding to internal movements. Likewise, as Basta discussed, business elites can shape outcomes in different types of regimes. In sum, there is much that can be learned by bringing together the diversity of secession scholarship.

A recurrent feature in many of the chapters was the observation that strategies of both secession and counter-secession often do not work. In her analysis, Kartsonaki found that the use of remedial rights language in UDIs did not correlate positively with successful secession. Similarly, but more tentatively, Pavković questioned whether the appeal to human rights or the listing of grievances in UDIs had any impact on the likelihood of outside recognition. Berg and Pegg distinguished four different strategies used by home states to resolve conflicts with breakaway regions and concluded that they were not effective in the cases under observation. Lecours carefully traced the methods of the Quebecois through two referenda, but, of course, that movement ultimately failed. Oltramonti examined the so-called viability strategy in the cases of Abkhazia and Somaliland, but neither region has come any closer to obtaining international recognition. Are all of these secessionist and counter-secession efforts a waste of time?

There are at least two ways to answer this question. First, there is a simple counterfactual problem. We do not know how these secessionist cases would have played out in the absence of these strategic efforts. Perhaps some of the *de facto* states under observation would have already earned international recognition in the absence of the blocking efforts of their parent states. Conversely, perhaps the viability strategy has won Abkhazia and Somaliland smaller gains that are difficult to detect without a controlled comparison. Quebec came quite close to winning their 1995 referendum; what would the results have been had the secessionists not deployed the strategies outlined by Lecours? One way to address the counterfactual problem is to compare successful with unsuccessful cases. A different way is to vary the dependent variable to look at other outcomes besides successful secession. Are smaller gains being made, either for or against the secessionist movement? It is important to consider that the efforts on both sides have important political, social, and economic consequences. Understanding the methods as outcomes in and of themselves has value.

Second, there may be a fair amount of error in these strategies. In the Introduction chapter, we outlined the strategic playing field where secession is concerned. Secessionist movements have incentives to become independent states, just as states have reasons for limiting secession. Both sides are knowledgeable about the game and are able to direct resources toward achieving their end. However, this is not a perfectly understood and bounded game like chess, where the rules are fixed and the moves are finely delimited. The game played between secessionists and states is a bit more like poker, given the element of bluffing, but even there the rules are clear and unchanging. In contrast, in the secession game the rules are fuzzy and protean. That vagueness has a number of consequences. For example, it can lead to poor choices and misaligned tactics. Perhaps Kartsonaki's findings are correct about the invocation of remedial rights language in UDIs; they do not work, but many secessionists think they do. Further research might explore the relationship between what is expected to work and what actually does work. A related subject for study focuses on the causes of bad tactics. Is it simply a matter of poor information and imperfect knowledge of the game? What is the role of wishful thinking? Finally, these secessionist and state actors are not uniform. Butt showed how there are often external factors that motivate the behavior of states. Similarly, as Basta demonstrated, there are multiple players in the dynamics of secession that belie the simple model of states versus secessionists.

There are a number of other questions and themes that can be drawn out of these chapters. One question that lurked in the background of every chapter pertains to the international community: Who is the international community and does it vary depending on circumstances? In figure I.1, we described this "third" actor as monolithic for stylistic purposes, but it does encompass a heterogeneous set of actors. It includes the UN Security Council, particularly the P-5, because that body controls admission into the UN General Assembly. However, as Maddens et al. discussed, it includes powerful regional actors like the EU. How does the importance of regional gatekeepers like the EU and African Union vary across the globe? Similarly, business elites appear to have conditioning effects on secession and counter-secession strategies, as Basta showed. In some regions neighboring states can act as additional veto players, as the Iraqi Kurds know. In others, as Butt demonstrated, neighboring states can be enablers. Overall, a richer analysis of the role of the international community is needed.

Where secessionist strategy is concerned, what is the relationship between coercive methods and tactics of normative appeal? Does the appeal to norms even work, and, if so, when? Pavković and Kartsonaki offered rather sober conclusions about the limited utility of normative arguments. Yet, as Rohrbach discussed in the case of East Timor, normative arguments can gradually persuade key actors. Must normative arguments always be coupled with coercive methods to be successful? What is the role of violence, and does it pay to use it selectively?

Although we have attempted to offer a balanced examination of the strategy of both secession and counter-secession, we think it is the first subject in this dyad that has received more scholarly attention. To some extent this makes sense because secessionists are the ones seeking change. They are the rebels and the apparent cause of the conversation. Moreover, they are perhaps easier to study, given that they have a clear purpose and are usually keen to showcase their cause. States, in contrast, have many purposes and counter-secession is rarely the most important. They typically do not have departments of counter-secession, at least not overtly, and they may have good reason to not discuss a secessionist movement if international attention is unwanted. In some ways it is harder to study counter-secession strategy because it is less visible. This is why the best work on counter-secession comes from the scholars who study *de facto* states; in those cases, the situation has become more internationalized and the home state must engage diplomatically to prevent the recognition of the breakaway region. The study of counter-secession is an area ripe for research, and the chapters in this volume provided vital contributions to it.

Finally, what can be done to improve the dynamics of secession and make them less conflictual? The chapters in this volume point in two directions. The first pertains to domestic institutional arrangements. One of Weill's central claims is that militant democracy can push frustrated secessionists into using extra-institutional, even violent, methods. This trade-off between political access and extra-institutional forms of contestation was demonstrated empirically in the chapters by Aksoy and Kocacık-Şenol and Rohrbach. In sum, the turmoil of secessionism can be reduced when states respond in a prudential, but institutionally grounded, manner that provides political voice without a high risk of exit or violence. The second direction points to the international system. Although the methods and tactics of any independence movement are shaped by their setting, all movements are playing on the same strategic playing field. There is only one UN, one club of sovereign states that they aim to join. Kartsonaki found that the appeal to remedial rights language did not correlate with successful independence, and other authors questioned the appeal to other normative arguments like functional viability. Are the rules and practices of international recognition too vague and would clearer guidelines improve clarity and reduce conflict? Future studies should bring the politics of international recognition into the analysis to find ways to mitigate the turbulence of secession.

Index

227

Notes on Contributors

Faruk Aksoy is a PhD candidate in the Political Science Department at Sabanci University. His primary research area focuses on political psychology, voting behavior, and the nexus between political regimes and political violence.

Karlo Basta is an associate professor of comparative politics at Memorial University of Newfoundland, Canada. He writes about identity politics in multinational states, symbolic aspects of political institutions, and the politics of events and temporality. His work has been published in *Comparative Political Studies*, *Publius: The Journal of Federalism*, *Nations and Nationalism*, and other scholarly journals.

Eiki Berg is a professor of international relations at the University of Tartu. He has published widely in leading peer-reviewed journals on bordering practices, identity politics, and *de facto* states. He is co-editor of *Routing Borders between Territories, Discourses and Practices* (Ashgate 2003), *Identity and Foreign Policy: Baltic-Russian Relations and European Integration* (Ashgate 2009), and *The Politics of International Interaction with de facto States: Conceptualising Engagement without Recognition* (Routledge 2018). During the years 2003–2004, he served as an MP in Estonian Parliament and observer to the European Parliament, EPP-ED faction, Committee on Foreign Affairs, Human Rights, Common Security, and Defence Policy. In 2012, he received National Science Award in the field of Social Sciences for the research in "Identities, Conflicting Self-Determination and *De Facto* States."

Ahsan I. Butt is an associate professor at the Schar School of Policy and Government at George Mason University and a nonresident fellow at the

Stimson Center. His research focuses on nationalism, security, international order, and South Asia. His book *Secession and Security: Explaining State Strategy against Separatists* (Cornell University Press, 2017) won the 2019 Best Book Award by the International Security Studies Section of the International Studies Association, and he has published articles in journals such as *International Organization*, *Politics and Religion*, and *Security Studies*, among others.

Ryan D. Griffiths is an associate professor at the Maxwell School of Citizenship and Public Affairs at Syracuse University. His primary research area focuses on the dynamics of secession with a particular emphasis on the international and domestic causes of secessionist conflict over time. He is the author of *Age of Secession: The International and Domestic Determinants of State Birth* (Cambridge University Press, 2016), and he has published related articles in *International Studies Review, Review of International Studies, Nations and Nationalism*, and *International Organization*, among others.

Argyro Kartsonaki is a research fellow in the School of Government and Society at the University of Birmingham. Her research interests include nationalism and ethnic conflict with a focus on separatist demands. She is the author of *Breaking Away: Kosovo's Unilateral Secession* (Lexington Books, 2018). The research for this contribution has been funded by the ESRC project *Understanding and Managing Intra-State Territorial Contestation: Iraq's Disputed Territories in Comparative Perspective* [ES/M009211/1].

Melike Ayşe Kocacık-Şenol is a PhD candidate in political science at Sabanci University. She received her BA degree in economics and MA degree in political science at Sabanci University. Her primary research of interest is civil conflict onset, nonviolent and violent protests, along with the third-party attitudes toward civil conflict and nonviolent protests.

André Lecours is a professor in the School of Political Studies at the University of Ottawa. His main research interests are Canadian politics, European politics, nationalism (with a focus on Quebec, Scotland, Flanders, Catalonia, and the Basque country), and federalism. He is the editor of *New Institutionalism. Theory and Analysis* published by the University of Toronto Press in 2005; the author of *Basque Nationalism and the Spanish State* (University of Nevada Press, 2007); the co-author (with Daniel Béland) of *Nationalism and Social Policy. The Politics of Territorial Solidarity* (Oxford University Press, 2008); and the co-author (with Daniel Béland, Gregory Marchildon, Haizhen Mou, and Rose Olfert) of *Fiscal Federalism and Equalization Policy in Canada. Political and Economic Dimensions* (University of Toronto Press, 2017).

Bart Maddens is full professor of political science at the KU Leuven, Belgium. He obtained a PhD in political science at this university with a dissertation about voting behavior and party strategy. His research focuses mainly on party and campaign finance, elections, political careers, and the reform of the state in Belgium. He regularly contributes to the debate on Belgian politics and separatism in the media. His research has been published in *Election Studies*, *West European Politics, Party Politics*, *European Journal of Political Research*, *Political Psychology*, and *Politics and Gender*.

Diego Muro is a senior lecturer in the School of International Relations at the University of St Andrews. His research interests include political violence, nationalism, and ethnic conflict, with a regional focus on Europe. His work has been published in peer-reviewed journals such as *Ethnic and Racial Studies, Ethnicities, Mediterranean Politics, Nations and Nationalism, Studies in Conflict and Terrorism, South European Society & Politics*, and *West European Politics*. His latest book is *When Does Terrorism Work?* (Routledge, 2019).

Gertjan Muyters is a junior researcher at the Public Governance Institute of the KU Leuven where he prepares a PhD on a project of the Flemish Research Foundation on candidate turnover in list-proportional elections systems, both at the national and the European levels. He studied political science, policy economics, and statistics and has conducted research on European and economic policy, as well as on higher education governance.

Giulia Prelz Oltramonti is an assistant professor at the European School of Political and Social Sciences at the Université Catholique de Lille. Her research focuses on violent and nonviolent processes of bordering in the Caucasus and the Sahara-Sahel, on political economies of violent conflicts, and on secession and *de facto* states.

Aleksandar Pavković teaches political theory and comparative politics at Macquarie University, Sydney. His interests are in comparative secessionism and declarations of independence. He is the author of *The Fragmentation of Yugoslavia* (London, 2000), *Creating New States: Theory and Practice of Secession* (with Peter Radan, 2007), and *Anthems and the Making of Nation States: Identity and Nationalism in the Balkans* (with Kit Kelen, 2016). He is also an editor of *On the Way to Statehood: Secession and Globalisation* (2008), *Ashgate Research Companion on Secession* (with Peter Radan, 2011), and *Separatism and Secessionism in Europe and Asia: To Have a State of One's Own* (2013).

Scott Pegg is professor in the Department of Political Science at Indiana University Purdue University Indianapolis. He is the author of *International Society and the* De Facto *State* and the co-editor of *Transnational Corporations and Human Rights*. He has published articles in such journals as *African Affairs, Community Development Journal, Foreign Policy Analysis, Geoforum, International Studies Perspectives, Journal of Modern African Studies, Resources Policy*, and *Security Dialogue*. His current research interests focus on Somaliland, *de facto* states, and the resource curse.

Livia Rohrbach is a PhD fellow in the Department of Political Science at the University of Copenhagen. Her primary research focus is on territorial self-governance in multiethnic states and its potential for mitigating conflict. More specifically, she analyzes the strategies and tactics groups use to achieve greater self-determination, how governments accommodate such demands, as well as how specific institutional designs relate to violent conflict. She has conducted substantial field research in East Africa, with particular focus on Ethiopia.

Steven Van Hecke is an associate professor in comparative and EU politics at the Social Sciences Faculty of the KU Leuven. His research focuses on European political parties, the European Union institutions, and European integration history. His work has been published in peer-reviewed journals like *European Politics and Society, Politics and Governance, Acta Politica, Journal of Common Market Studies, Journal of Contemporary European Research, International Journal of Iberian Studies*, and *Journal of European Public Policy*. He also co-edited *Readjusting the Council Presidency. Belgian Leadership in the EU* (Academic and Scientific Publishers, 2011).

Rivka Weill is a professor of law (tenured) at the Radzyner Law School, Interdisciplinary Center (IDC). In recent years, she was a visiting law professor at Yale Law School, University of Chicago Law School, and Cardozo Law School. Her work focuses on constitutional law as well as administrative law with a focus on theoretical and comparative dimensions.

Wouter Wolfs is a researcher at the Public Governance Institute of the University of Leuven (Belgium). His research interests include the organization and finance of political parties, legislative studies, EU politics, and Euroscepticism.

www.ingramcontent.com/pod-product-compliance
Lightning Source LLC
Chambersburg PA
CBHW022354280326
41935CB00007B/182